JEWISH PARENTS

a teacher's guide

Strategies for Developing Active Partnerships

Between the Classroom and the Home

JOEL LURIE GRISHAVER

WITH DR. RON WOLFSON

ISBN# 0-933873-10-7

Copyright © 1997 Joel Lurie Grishaver

Published by Torah Aura Productions. All rights reserved.

No part of this publication may be reproduced or transmitted in any form or by any means graphic, electronic or mechanical, including photocopying, recording or by any information storage and retrieval system, without permission in writing from the publisher.

TORAH AURA PRODUCTIONS • 4423 FRUITLAND AVENUE, LOS ANGELES, CA 90058

(800) BE-TORAH • (213) 585-7312 • FAX (213) 585–0327 • E-MAIL <MISRAD@TORAHAURA.COM>

MANUFACTURED IN THE UNITED STATES OF AMERICA

To educate a child without educating and involving the parents and the entire family can be compared to heating a house while leaving the window open.

MORDECAI KAPLAN

TABLE OF CONTENTS

NOT "SHABBAT-IN-A-SACK": THANK YOU

This book was built through workshops given around the world. Not only were the stories and the ideas honed through trying to teach them over and over, but, more importantly, most of the good ideas came from the teachers and educators who participated. It started out as a research paper and wound up as something practical. That is always nice.

Jewish Parents: A Teacher's Guide started out because we at the Shirley and Arthur Whizin Institute for Jewish Family Life were interested in the actual practices of family education being manifest in the field. We knew that at our Institute and among our colleagues, we were busy pushing the envelope of what could be done with the tools, insights, assumptions, and practices we call "family education." But, we were interested in the diffusion of those ideas in the "outback" to the actual "line workers." In other words, we were interested in how the "state-of-the practice" contrasted with the "state-of-the art." So, Joel went into a lot of communities and taught *Jewish Parents: A Teacher's Guide* workshops and also used Torah Aura's electronic communications network to ask teachers, center folks, educators, etc. to share with us the best of their work. Ron, meanwhile, kept his eyes and his contacts open. We did what is called a snowball sample. We asked not only "Tell us your good stuff" but also, "Tell us who else is doing good stuff." Then we called them and asked the same questions. We did three years of such looking.

We found two things: (1) There is a lot of "Shabbat-in-a-Sack," and (2) there is all the other stuff we crammed into this book.

"Shabbat-in-a-Sack" is one of a bunch of names for the most basic of family education practices. It is one or more variations of a program where a bag, basket, box of Friday night paraphernalia and instructions are sent home to each family in the class in rotation (sort of like taking the class hamster for the weekend). The good news is, "each family is invited to make Shabbat." (Then they return Shabbat so the next family can have it.) The bad news is the meta-message that Shabbat is a once-a-year experience. We've debated Shabbat-in-a-Sack a lot. Basically, the two schools in our discussion were [1] "it is bad for the Jews" because it doesn't really root Shabbat in the home and [2] "at least it is a beginning" from which Shabbat can grow. None of us was happy that this was the single most predominant program out there. The good news, however, is all the wonderfully creative NOT Shabbat-in-a-Sack stuff we have found and put in this book.

BUT—if you are a Shabbat-in-a-Sack lover or practitioner, we've even included one really creative variation (just to prove there is always a good way to do things). Take a look at Nachama Skolnik Moskowitz's Note on her account about the "Story Bears."

We would like to thank Atlanta where we held the first *Jewish Parents: A Teacher's Guide Workshop*. We would also like to thank the groups of teachers we have worked with literally from Oxford, England to Seattle, Washington—from Alaska to Hawaii, too. And, everywhere, from every group of teachers we worked with—thanks for the inspiration of your creativity and tenacity, dedication and persistence. Everywhere we went, even when the ideas were not the most adaptable—we encountered a wonderful spirit of experimentation and exploration. The ongoing experience of the energy Jewish teachers invest in succeeding and making a difference was our reward from this process.

We would like to thank the following:

The Members of the Whizin Team: Janice Alper, Harlene Appelman, Adrianne Bank, Risa Gruberger, Vicky Kelman, Jo Kay, Joan Kaye, Esther Netter, Rachel Sisk, Sally Weber, Bruce Whizin, Shelley Whizin.

The Members of the Torah Aura Team: Deborah Greenbaum, Debi Rowe, Deena Bloomstone, Jane Golub.

Contributors: Carol Starin, Susie Wolfson, Sharon Halper, Terry Kalet, Ettie Davis, Donna Gordon Blankinship, Rabbi Cherie Koller-Fox, Treasure Cohen, Shirley Barish, Irene Bolton, Andy German, Susan Fish, Ellen Brosbe, Elise Cohen, Sharon Lerner, Steffi Aronson Karp, Laura Harari, Elaine Rubinstein, Ziva Green-Kredow, Ralph Moses, Dorit Lehavy, Orna Levinson, Sima Cohen, Rosanne and Allan Arnet, Claudia Shaifo, Vic Levinson, Hariet Hunter, Reilly Coleman, The Kindergarten of the Heschel Day School, Patti Kroll, Joan Carr, Jessie Kerr-Whitt, Cantor Sheldon Levin, Lisa Goldstein, Harriet Rossetto, Daniel Nussbaum II, Flor Kupferman, David Parker, Linda Forest, Michelle Stansbury, Shelley Siegel, Jeremy Wilgus, Nachama Skolnik Moskowitz, Sandy McDermet, Sandy Rosenfield, Lisa Slobodow, Sally Ann Wollace, Jeffrey S. Hersh, Lisa J. Goldstein, David Barany, The Jacksonville Jewish Center, Eileen Ettinger.

And thank you—and we are sorry—to anyone who helped and whose name we excluded by mistake.

And I would like to thank my editor and co-author Ron Wolfson who helped tune this work and merge his energy and vision into this project. No one understands how to work with families as well as Ron does. His help was invaluable.

Joel Lurie Grishaver
Erev Shavuot, 5756

A GLIMPSE OF THE MESSIAH

[An Opening Fantasy] A teacher gets a message in her box to call the parent of a difficult student with whom there have been a number of escalating incidents—and then a real behavior crisis. The note asks the teacher to call the parent. She holds her breath and dials the number. When the phone is answered, you can see her flinch a little bit. After less than a minute of small talk, the parent gets down to business. The teacher braces herself—if you watch, you can see the defense lining up.

The parent surprises her and says, "Here is what I would like to do. We've been hearing some interesting things at the dinner table. I'd like to tell you what we've heard, then listen while you tell me what you know. Then I'd like to put our heads together—and see what we can figure out to do from here."

Forget all that nonsense about the Messiah sitting in the gates of Rome working with a band aid box. Ignore the fantasy of the Messiah as Shabbat inspector looking for the second time. Here is our truth: "When five parents with kids in Jewish schools work with teachers in that way, the Messiah will be here."

This book is all about making that possible.

Chapter 1
PARENTS ARE NOT THE ENEMY

"The Farmers and the Cowboys can be Friends"

[Joel's Opening Rap]: If someday, somehow, someone makes a movie out of my Hebrew School Comedy script it will contain a great "case of mistaken identity" sequence. The script is Hebrew School as a mystery-action-adventure-comedy thriller (anything but a monster movie). It is no Hebrew School horror show. This is the important sequence:

Junior walks into class late, without books, and tells the teacher he is there today because there was nothing else important for him to do, but for the next two weeks his parents are taking him elsewhere because they know that is more important. (The teacher mutters something nasty about parents and soccer practice under her breath.) What then follows is the rest of a really good lesson about Jewish insights into ending homelessness.

After class, Junior gets into the car and in grunted responses to his parents' questions, tells his folks that it was: "Boring!" "Holidays—again!" "Still picking on me!" The father mutters, "Just like when I went to Hebrew school."

In a series of cross-dissolves—scenes of class—scenes of carpools which fade into each other—Junior's restatements of the truth (as he sees it) manage to drive a wedge between parents and teacher. In his descriptions, the Hebrew school classroom is run by graduates of the Marquis de Sade Institute for Jewish Teaching. According to his accounts, his parents have been taking Jewish motivational classes with Torquemada.

Meanwhile, the teacher, who also has a real life on the side, one other than Hebrew School hag, shows up a couple of times a week (between driving her own kids' carpools) to share her love for things Jewish with the next generation. The teacher is getting more and more frustrated—and is seriously thinking about quitting. She teaches lots of Juniors and often says, "Who needs this?"

Meanwhile, the parents, who may not be Satmar Hasidim, but who are legitimately committed to transmitting their positive sense of Jewishness to their children, are thinking about pulling them out of Hebrew School because the negative experiences there are destroying their children's love of being Jewish (which was so strong when they were little).

Meanwhile, Junior is figuring that soon he will be able to sleep late on Sunday mornings and hang out with the guys more afternoons a week.

In my comedy, the teacher and the parents are trapped in an elevator together and share their problems (the parents not knowing that *this* teacher is Junior's teacher, and the teacher not knowing that *these* parents are Junior's parents). It is an encounter rich in support, understanding, and growth for each of them. They do an "if only you were Junior's teacher"—"if only you were the parents of the kids I teach" farewell. The sequence ends with Junior getting his come-uppance at Family Education Day the following Sunday.

This little mental movie is not intended to state that all the problems Jewish teachers have with the parents of their students are exclusively the result of the children's fabrications. Nor is it to say (as we all have to admit) that all complaints about Jewish schools are exclusively the kids' fantasies. While there is room for some legitimate concern on each side, the "Truth-of-Truths" about Jewish Parents and Jewish Teachers is that they need to be allies. They have a common agenda which can only be actualized through communication and active partnership.

Let us understand this: No one who teaches in a Jewish school does not want to transmit deep knowledge of and affection for the Jewish tradition—to the best of their abilities—to their students. We all know that the pay is so low and the frustration level so high that no one goes into Jewish teaching for the money. Jewish teaching is all about love and commitment, even if it is seldom perceived that way.

Understand this, too: In a day and an age where more than half of Jewish families provide their children with no Jewish education, paying the money, driving the carpools, having the "yes, you have to go" fights is an act of positive and significant commitment, too. This is profoundly true, even though this is not always the side of parents that teachers seem to meet.

You may not be Mr. Chips, the world's most beloved teacher. They may not be Tevye and Golda, quintessential authentic parents, oozing Judaism with every step. But, you need each other. This book is a guide to finding that cooperation and understanding.

Louie's Grocery

[Ron's Opening Rap]: My grandfather Louis Paperny (everyone called him "Louie"—I called him "Zaydie") taught me one of the most important lessons I ever learned about teaching.

Zaydie was a businessman. He had immigrated from Russia to Omaha, Nebraska, in 1905 and to make a living, began selling fruit from a roadside stand. Over the years, the business grew until he was able to build one of the first modern supermarkets in the Midwest. Its name was Louis Market, but everyone called it "Louie's."

It seemed as if everyone in Omaha knew Louie. One of his favorite things to do was take the "*gantze mishpoche*" (big family) out to dinner. The restaurateurs loved him. We all were big eaters and Louie was a big tipper. So, whenever he walked into a restaurant, Louie was warmly greeted and we got the best table. More amazingly, a steady stream of people would come up to Louie to shake his hand, to say hello... My Zaydie was a real celebrity. As a kid, I never understood why he was so popular.

Today, I know why.

When you shopped at Louis Market, you traded with Louie. Just inside the front door of the store was a place called the "courtesy counter." It was the first stop for most patrons. You could cash a payroll check. You could return pop bottles. And, you could say "Hi" to Louie. Because that's where he spent most of his day—at the front of the store, greeting his customers.

Louie knew most of them by first names. He knew their stories—where they worked and where they lived. He knew their families—the names of spouses and children. And they knew Louie. They knew his four daughters and his four sons-in-law, all equal partners in the business. They saw the grandchildren growing up in the store. They knew of his generosity—how he contributed food to the orphanage, how he donated the tallest Christmas tree to the Catholic archdiocese, how he would let you buy groceries on credit if you were between jobs or had a run of bad luck. In a time long before celebrity CEO's, Louie's portrait was painted on the wall above the produce section. If you ever visit Omaha, you can still see it today, even though Louie died twenty years ago.

I once asked him for the secret to his success. In his broken English, he said: "*Tataleh*, I treat each customer who comes into the store as if it's the last customer I'll ever have. I treat them like gold...and they come back." He loved them, and they loved him.

The lesson is about greeting and welcoming. It is about extending a hand, opening doors, inviting in. It is about *relationship* as the foundation for teaching.

Zaydie taught me well. When I first started teaching in an afternoon religious school, I quickly learned that "class" needed to begin well before the bell rang. I never waited in my room for the students. I would hang out in the lobby, on the ball field, in the hallway, schmoozing with the kids. To this day I begin every class, every parent workshop, every seminar, every lecture by standing just outside the entrance to the room, greeting my students with a warm welcome. I introduce myself by name ("Hi, I'm Ron!") and ask for the student's name. If there is time, I will begin some sort of conversation. I will not remember everyone's name, but that brief moment of contact establishes the fact that there is a real person behind the teacher, a person who genuinely desires to establish a connection between teacher and student. Without that, how can I possibly teach anything?

The Reason for *Jewish Parents: A Teacher's Guide*

[Ron & Joel]: This book has one simple central purpose and that is to share the insights gained in the last ten or so years which inform the way that Jewish teachers can expand and improve their communication and relationships with their students' parents. We have learned from the family education movement that there are both **concrete strategies** and **attitudes** which can make a difference. And we have learned that if a stronger connection—a classroom-home partnership—can be built, the cause of Torah is advanced. This happens because:

- Students have a much greater context, motivation and incentive for taking Jewish learning seriously. *When parents are accessible, teachers have direct access to the help they need.*

- Parents grow their own Jewish knowledge and commitment by continuing their own Jewish learning both for themselves and to assure their child(ren)'s success. *When we reach parents, we double the impact of each lesson.*

- Jewish teachers feel more successful by feeling more rooted in the greater school community, more understood, more supported, by experiencing a greatly enhanced awareness that their work is being done "in a context" which allows them to make a difference. *It is very nice when you are appreciated.*

- Such partnerships create a much greater confluence between that which a Jewish school teaches and that which its families (students included) actualize as part of their lives. *In other words, Judaism has a much greater possibility of becoming not "just a school," but a way of life.*

The new wisdom gained from the family education movement is that when teachers realize that not just the child, but the entire family system are our "clients," the impact of our work is increased *me'ah she'arim*, a hundred fold.

By transforming our classrooms to not only teach children, but also to reach past them to include parents and even the whole family—sometimes even bringing the family into the classroom and always trying to send the classroom home—we feel renewed as Jewish teachers and our teaching has greater impact.

The Problem = The Door

Here is a secret. Most of us become Jewish teachers because our classrooms have doors.

We all know that Jewish teachers are not well paid. We all know that we are not publicly treated as a "community treasure" the way the Talmud suggests. The truth is, there is little that is rewarding about the job, other than the job itself. And, a "door" has usually defined the job we do.

Here is what I mean. As I teacher, I can walk into "my" room, shut the door, and be with "my" class, in "my" classroom. Behind the door is where I am in control. It is where I am responsible, where I can create and actualize, and where I get to be the hero—without a cavalry. Behind the door is where I can make a difference. When my classroom door is opened by another adult, I, as a teacher, fear that intruder will have a clipboard in his hand or in her heart.

- If it is my principal—I worry about my job. Very few of us are secure enough to think of our supervisors as our coaches (rather than as judge and jury).

- When a parent walks into our room—usually our hearts begin to palpitate. We tend to ask ourselves: "What have I done wrong now?"

While some teachers will deny it, and while some of us get past it, it is a "teacher truth" that we like to be alone in our classrooms, with our classes, working our magic.

Here, however, is that sword's second edge. The very door which creates the unique space in which we work our magic, also creates the loneliness and under-appreciation most teachers (Jewish or secular) feel. Our work is never seen. No one really understands what we do. Only our kids are available to give us feedback—and they usually have other agendas. At the end of the period, when the door is opened and the room empties, we are left alone with our memories. Sometimes they are good enough to sustain us—sometimes not.

Now hear this: There are times and ways those doors can be opened, others can join the conversation, and our classrooms will still remain our classrooms.

The Trauma of Change

Let's be honest, this book is about change; and change is never easy and never comfortable. In this case:

- It means we have to open our classroom doors and let other adults see what we do there. *This is difficult for any teacher to do, because our sense of control and privacy is one of the things which led many of us to be teachers. It also means (for good and bad) that the number of times our work is "evaluated" will dramatically increase.*

- It means more preparation and more work. *We wish we could tell you that working with parents, too, takes no extra time. But it does. Communication takes time. Relationships take time. New friendships and partnerships take time. Rethinking your process takes time. Being inclusive takes time. And, the need to compound a growing success is a great time-eating challenge.*

- It means rethinking many of our assumptions. *It means we have to begin to think of a teacher's domain as much larger than the classroom. We can no longer view the "outside" world as something which either helps or impedes our classroom work. Rather, we have to see our efforts spilling out of the classroom and actively (not just symbolically) changing those whom they touch.*

This change in "attitude" is the toughest part of the whole process. Whether you as teacher are making the decision to "expand" the focus of your teaching, or whether a principal or committee "has helped you" with this decision—the first step is the longest. It takes a deep breath to think about interfacing more with the most difficult parent of your most problematic student. Now you can let the breath out. It is like the first leap off the high board at the pool (if you've ever been brave enough to make that leap). Really scary—but very exhilarating. It is a *Nahshon* moment. He is the Jewish hero (according to the midrash) who had to leap into the Red Sea before it would divide. Sometimes you have to jump. You can do it! If you can deal with kids—parents are a cinch.

For me, family education is Torah as *oobleck*, Torah oozing and fitting in everywhere. [For those of you who know Dr. Seuss. If not, find and enjoy *Bartholomew and the Oobleck*, by Dr. Seuss. Think of it as a midrash on Torah.]

The bottom line is this: Involving parents means changing our practices and our attitudes. It means more work—but it also means a greater potential for a much deeper and richer success. It provides much greater assurances of a positive Jewish future.

A Final Truth: To feel comfortable with parents involved in your class, you have to feel comfortable with yourself as a teacher. You need to get past the need to "hide" your work—because it will not hold up. [Every classroom teacher—Jewish, non-Jewish, brand-new, or veteran—has his or her own version of "stage-fright."] **Once you've linked your classroom to the home, and enlarged your learning community, you will feel better about yourself as a teacher. It is good to have students. It is even better to have friends and partners.** You can do this!

Jo Kay's Tips Regarding Teachers & Teacher Training

Staffing is crucial in planning and developing Family Education Programs. What should you be looking for in a teacher/coordinator, etc.? Here are some thoughts gleaned from research begun on the PACE Family Education Program.

- Not all excellent teachers of children will be excellent teachers of adult groups (the reverse is also true).

- Therefore, when working with groups of combined ages, it is helpful to have someone who:

    1. Is a good group facilitator (knows group dynamics)

    2. Can be non-judgmental

    3. Is truly interested in working with the whole family

    4. Is willing and able to be a Jewish role model

    5. Is willing to share personal Jewish experiences

    6. Is willing to share personal parenting experiences

    7. Can listen and respond to student needs

    8. Cares about the families

    9. Doesn't request that the families do anything they are not prepared to do

    10. Has a stake in the success of the program

Most Jewish Parents Still Have Pimples on Their Souls

Or—how am I supposed to work with my students' parents when I am scared of—or angry at—them?

[Ron's Comment]: Joel, there is an overriding assumption here that all (most) parents hated Hebrew School and all (most) kids think Hebrew school is torture. Can't we tone it down just a bit? You've overdone it. We don't want to turn them off.

[Joel's Comment]: Ron, you're right that there are good and positive parents. You're right that there are kids who love their Jewish education. This needs to be stated—and restated. Yet, the story of "I hated it and I had to go"—"You'll hate it and have to go, too."—is so ubiquitous that it needs to be dealt with.

[Jo Kay's Comments]: Whenever I begin to work with teachers who will be working with family or with parents, and they express some apprehension about the job, which is normal, I usually share my own experiences with them. I have been able to overcome my fears of working with adults by beginning with the disclaimer "I am not an expert on this subject. But, I love to study and to learn. I will search for resources and we will study together." This helps me feel comfortable and just be myself.

When it comes to their Jewishness, most Jewish adults are still teenagers—and just barely teenagers at that. Here is the deal.

Most Jews stop their Jewish education right after their Bar/Bat Mitzvah celebrations. Even though they are grown and are sending their own children to Jewish schools, when they look in the "Jewish" mirror, they still see a Jewish kid in need of *Clearasil®*. In most ways, their Jewish part is only a hair's breadth past twelve. When they look at you, their kid's Jewish teacher, they still see their own Jewish teacher. (If, for whichever reason, they never had a Jewish teacher, their ambivalence is even more complex!) In their hearts, they still believe they are Hebrew School failures, Jewish impostors rather than legitimate adult Jews—and *davka* they have been kept after school because of their behavior. We, as the symbolic Every-Teacher, sometimes make them feel stupid, bad, and bored—all at the same time.

Most Jewish parents have to deal with three things when they face us:

• Their own ambivalent or even bad memories of Jewish schooling. *In St. Paul, (and probably a lot of other cities) graduates of the Talmud Torah, the community Hebrew school, refer to it as "Talmud Terror." Each time they do, they suggest, often without kidding, that their Jewish education was a horrific experience.*

- Their own sense of Jewish inadequacy.

- Their embarrassment over their children's forthcoming Hebrew School failure (for which they feel ultimately responsible.)

When we choose to do the full job of Jewish teacher today—and that job involves working with parents, too—one of our first responsibilities is to help many of them get over the past—and see us as who we are (rather than as who they remember us to be.)

So let's talk about parents.

A simple question: "Why do parents today send their kids to Hebrew/Sunday/Day School—especially when most of them don't seem to act in ways that support a Jewish school?"

The answer: "Most of them don't."

Today, depending on whose figures you are reading, less than 50% of Jewish kids receive any substantive Jewish education. (Though for me, Steven M. Cohen argues effectively that something close to 90% have at least one contact point with organized Jewish life at least once in their childhood.)

So let us re-ask: **"Why are the kids we teach being sent to Jewish schools?"** Why would a generation of Jewish kids who hated Hebrew School and who swore that when they grew up they would never subject their children to the same kind of "torture," become the parents of the kids who now claim to be suffering in our classrooms? To answer this question—we need to look at **"The Parent Part"** and **"The Jewish Parent Part."**

The Parent Part: The Marble Maze of Child Rearing

It is hard to be a parent today. Our friend Sam Joseph tells the story of one of his friends who keeps an empty peanut butter jar on the bookcase in the living room. Every time he loses control and "yells" at his toddler, he puts ten dollars in the jar and says "This is for your psychiatrist when you're sixteen."

It is hard to be a parent today: AIDS. Cults. Drugs. Gangs. Being a parent today is terrifying. It is like one of those wooden marble-mazes, where by turning the two knobs on the side, you try to guide the marble from start to finish, but there are all these holes which want to suck your marble in and take it out of the game. There is teenage pregnancy, teenage alcoholism, teenage suicide, autoerotic asphyxia, anorexia, drunk drivers, Satanism, child abuse, drive-by shootings and more. Every day Oprah, Sally Jessy and Geraldo chronicle the ever-shrinking odds that any parent can ever successfully bring a child to full-term adulthood. Everything in the world today seems to be addictive, dangerous, toxic or full of the bad kind of cholesterol. We now know enough to fear every teacher, to panic over what's in the apple juice, to tremble at the dangers of television and computers and especially video games—the air, the water, and the times are all poisoned.

What compounds and further frustrates the whole thing is that just about every parent feels—but can't admit, often, even to themselves—that they (just like their parents) are inadequate. They all know that a real parent, a good parent, could succeed. But, in this age, all of us "know" we are just the dysfunctional inheritors of a dysfunctional family heritage. We do the best we can. We have our moments. And we live with the deep hidden fear that we don't have what it takes—that it won't be enough. **It is hard to be a parent today.**

The fact that most parents do pretty good jobs—and the truth that raising kids has a lot of tolerance for errors—doesn't often impact on parental feelings. Many parents I know are shocked at watching themselves become a second-rate impersonation of their own parents. They feel like kids still dressing up in their parents' clothes and attitudes. They confess: "I never thought you'd ever hear me say that." They remind themselves that they had promised "to remember what it was like" when they got to be parents, that they had "promised to be different." The problem today is the word "no." In the days of *Donna Reed* and *Father Knows Best*, parents got to use words like "disappointed" and give advice. Today, parents are stuck saying "no" a lot, or not saying "no" and thinking they should have—or even more often, looking for permission to say the "no" they think they should say, but don't want to or are afraid to. In a time where parenting requires great authority, the inner security needed to make and enforce judgments is in short supply. This is the age of *No One* (except the Religious Right) *Knows Best*, and *Mother Does the Best She Can.*

Yet, today, it is much harder for a parent to "Just Say No." Once there seemed to be a secret coven of parents who met at midnight in the glen and decided the things to which all of them would say "No." They even seemed to decide which things they would forbid, which things they would forbid but let their kids get away with, and which things they would forbid and make sure that no kid could ever successfully experience. Today, everything seems to be permitted by some parents. Some kids seem to get away with everything. Each parent often feels as if he or she is the last one on the block who is trying the hold off the Vandals, the Goths, and the Visigoths. In an age which needs much more "No," despite the preponderance of DARE T-shirts, "No" is much harder to say, mean, enforce and explain when you have to say: "Pass the latch-key please!"

No wonder parents are so confused! Parenting is very hard.

The Jewish Parent Part: Studies in Ambivalence

Here is the truth every teacher knows. There are two kinds of Jewish parents. One kind (a grand total of seven parents according to one recent survey) are authentic Jewish parents, the other kind of Jewish parent (all the rest) give far too much credibility to soccer practice. You already know about the seven—let's talk about the others.

So here is the question (again): *Why would a generation of Jewish kids who hated Hebrew School and who swore that when they grew up they would never subject their own children to the same kind of torture, become the parents of the kids who now claim to be suffering in our classrooms?*

The answer in one word: "ambivalence." Ambivalence does *not* mean not caring. Ambivalence means feeling two different ways. Contrary to the most frequent teacher complaints (including those frequently voiced by the two teachers who wrote this book) that parents don't care enough about what we do, the truth is that most of the parents we work with do care a lot, but they care in different ways than we want. To understand that, we need to understand two general truths.

- **Extended Adolescence.** For many of them their own Hebrew School experience was not particularly successful, and their 13-year-old exit from the Jewish community has not been resolved. In retrospect, they feel they didn't learn a lot. They feel that what they did manage to learn isn't particularly valuable to them now, and what they now want to know about Judaism either wasn't taught or wasn't learned. They feel inadequate as Jews. They are embarrassed about not knowing the essentials.

- **The Marble Maze of Child Rearing.** For many of them parenting is terrifying. In the crazed world: AIDS, Cults, Drugs, Gangs—their kids need some source of stable and wholesome values—and despite their own negative image and memory of Hebrew School— the synagogue is the only place they know they can turn to, to teach their child not to kill themselves, kill others, or in other ways waste their lives. Like the aforementioned marble mazes, the world is full of holes which are ready to suck their children down and quickly end the game. Still, like everyone else, they want the "gain" without the "pain." They are looking for the stability and sense of "belonging" Judaism offers without the discipline and the time commitment.

When you put these two tendencies together, you understand why so many kids have returned to receive a Jewish education, despite parental ambivalence. These parents (the skeptical ones) come back to Hebrew School because their kids need it, and they don't know where else to turn. For them, Judaism is a form of "protection," a way of inoculating their children with survival values. When you listen to them, parents will tell you:

a. **Parents want their children to have a sense of Jewish history, culture, and ethics.** This means that they want them to have a sense of who they are in the world, and being a Jew is one piece of that identity. *We (the Jewish school) usually interpret this (in our own way) and equate "history and culture" with "rituals" and "spirituality." That is sometimes what parents mean, but not always.*

b. **Then they will tell you in the next sentence—always the second sentence, if it wasn't the first—that they want their child to feel good about being Jewish.** This means to them that a *Good Time* (must be) *Had By All* every time the experience is Jewish. It must be a GTHBA experience all the time. To feel good about being a Jew, in a world where no one is making them a Jew, a *Good Time* must always be *Had By All*. *If you dare point out that it is hard to always have fun when you are acquiring language, history, or culture—they will tell you, "Find a way to make it fun." It's not that they are against you—it is just that they are more afraid of having another "No" they have to say in their lives. Our friend Barbara Zeidman's favorite chorus these days is: "There are only so many fights you can fight..."*

c. **Parents want their child "anointed" as an authentic Jew so he or she can call on Judaism at those moments when she or he needs or wants it.** Usually we translate this one as "Have a nice bar/bat mitzvah." We and they name the "event." But to understand the importance of the "Affair" we have to assign the meaning assigned to it. *For some of them, bar/bat mitzvah is a public Jewish authentication, it is a conversion ceremony which, once achieved, grants the child permanent Jewish status. They don't see Judaism as a lifestyle. They don't see it as a mitzvah system. They think of it as an identity, a privilege which grants access—not a set of obligations. They feel worried, lost and lonely—not commanded.*

If you listen very closely, you will all hear the two things parents don't want...

d. **Parents don't want to have to force their kids to be Jewish.** They've learned that if you force them it probably won't work. Their parents forced them, and it almost didn't work.

e. **And they don't want to be embarrassed about their own Jewish inadequacies.** This is the big one. *We are the ones who will know it if they mess up the Torah blessings—at the bar/bat mitzvah.*

And here are the three things which make most parents "children who don't know how to ask." They don't know how to tell you, or even often themselves, that:

f.   **They want their own Jewish past healed.** They want a way to feel good about themselves as Jews.

g.   **They want a shared bond, a family process—a RITUAL—which against all the odds, can hold their family together and give their children the stability needed to build a good life.**

h.   **They want to belong.** They want a place to admit that life is scary. That raising children is difficult. That the future is too uncertain and too unknown. They want support. They want a community which is there when they need one.

All this is for us to understand and use, empathize and provide. Even though there may be gaps between our goals and theirs, we have enough in common to begin the work.

> **[Cherie Koller-Fox's Comment]:** Parents and grandparents are the main transmitters of Judaism, not rabbis and teachers. They can transmit love of Judaism and they can transmit their ambivalence. I think every teacher understands the futility of teaching children about something they do not do in their own home, or worse, something their parents undermine. Today, we are blessed with a generation of parents who want to raise Jewish children, but were all too often not given sufficient background to do so in the way they would like. It is the responsibility of the rabbis and educators to support these parents in their efforts and empower them.
>
> The classroom teacher has a role to play in this process, to be sure; however, in my opinion, all of family education cannot be based in the classroom because it is to a great extent adult education. Parent participation (which describes a lot of what is discussed in this book) is a key role for the classroom. Making the parents active partners in the learning process, communicating with them regularly, and involving them wherever appropriate are the keys to success in this area. But, in my view, there are clear boundaries here for the expectations that we have for the classroom.
>
> Adults' spiritual lives do not often change in their child's classrooms. That cathartic change that causes an adult to change their behavior happens most often around life cycle events. It is a big deal for an adult to suddenly start lighting candles or keeping kosher. When's the last time you made a major change in your behavior? Someone told me once she'd begun exercising and dieting. I commended her and asked her why she had made that change. "Because" she said, "the doctor told me if I didn't, I would die." It takes something major to change behavior and that is not likely to happen when participating with your child in a classroom event.
>
> The classroom can become a partner in this larger process. The teacher needs to be seen as an important part of the team involving the rabbi, cantor, educator and lay leadership of the congre-

gation. The positive educational experiences the children and parents have in the classroom can add to the experiences provided by the whole team and by the whole experience of being part of a synagogue community.

One of the limitations of classrooms is that they do not contain all the members of the family. Family education is most effective when it involves the whole family. I would hope however, that we are not at the place where we would consider replacing the classroom learning experience. Children need knowledge taught in an orderly fashion. They need to become literate in the texts and traditions of our people. That is a central role for the classroom, supported by a community that values the learning and creates a context for it.

Danger: Minefield Ahead! Special Cases

This section of this chapter is the "disclaimer." We've asked you to try this at school and at home—so this is where we tell you to be careful.

"Family" is not as simple a reality as it once seemed to be. We use terms like "parents" and "families" far too easily. We imply the universe of 2.2. We have spoken as if all Jewish families are made up of two Jewish parents, a pet, and 2.2 Jewish children. The truth which you already know from your classrooms, is that we are more likely to find more innovative and transformed families than a "normal 2 + 2.2 family." Today the so-called "normal" family is a minority. Included in the admixture are: single parents, blended (re-married families), same sex parents, grandparents raising grandchildren, parents who are Jews-by-choice, custodial parents of Jewish children who are not Jewish, latch-key families—and don't forget the miracle of shared custody.

> **[Vicky Kelman's Comment]:** You shouldn't even use the word "normal" in teaching that there are no "normal" families.

> **[Sharon Halper's Comment]:** "Normal" is to be regarded as a four-letter word.

Whenever you go into a home, there are suddenly a lot of closets to open. That is what makes a home different from a classroom. The closets add fear. And, the closets provide powerful stories, which give learning a reality not found in the Lysol soaked hallways of institutions. As Jewish teachers, when we start dealing with families and not just students, we have to learn to walk softly and carefully, but we also increase incrementally the power of the interaction. Here are just a few basic guidelines to help.

- Always think of a "family" in terms of the way it functions, not in terms of its closeness to a Norman Rockwell Painting. A "family is" as a "family does." All kinds of living and caring arrangements can successfully be the "family place" in someone's life.

- Don't make assumptions about who will be part of a family. When you talk to or about families, when you assign projects to be done with or about families—be inclusive. Don't ask questions which assume "a traditional family." We are long past the day when you can assign an essay about "What my father does for a living!!" Phrase such questions and activities in such ways that everyone will be able to answer them without feeling like an exception.

Ten years ago, doing a family tree was the most popular of "family activities." It gave, we thought, everyone a chance to talk about or talk to Bubbie and Zaydie. Since then, we've learned that some student in the class will have her Grandpa Jesus from El Salvador, and another child will ask if he should put his birth father, his former step-father, or his mother's new friend on the chart. These things get more complicated and have to be thought through in advance.

> **[Ron's Comment]:** A worksheet of "family" with a mommy and daddy—all set to color in—suggesting that two parents families are the norm—can be just as problematic.

- Be ready to hear and talk about home concerns that you may find surprising (or even sometimes shocking) but also, unless you are dealing with solving a specific crisis, always leave space for people *not* to share such things. When we work with people, we always have to make it safe to talk; working with families, today, means we have to work very hard to make things very safe.

Please do not panic. You are already an expert in such matters. Even if you have never done these things as a teacher, you are a person, too. You may even be a parent, too. The subtle skills of listening and responding, of knowing when asking is an *invitation* and when it is a *confrontation*, is something you already deal with all the time. You can get better at it. We can work on it, but you have already mastered the basics.

> **[Sharon Halper's Comment]:** We need to be careful with the language we use in our classrooms. During family education programs I use "adult" not "parent."

> **[Nachama Skolnik Moskowitz's Comment]:** I am very depressed after reading this chapter. Where is the uplifting moment?

> **[Joel's Response]:** You're Right! These four stories are for you, Nachama. We do need to talk more about the rewards of working with families.

Family Rewards (An Addition for Nachama)

STORY ONE: One day Barbara Zeidman called me on the phone and said, "Wednesday I am going to come into your class and cook latkes with your seventh grade." I wasn't planning a Hanukkah party. I would never have done hot oil and seventh-graders. And, if I wanted a party, I probably wouldn't have thought to ask. Barbara volunteered and created one of the best moments in the year. She did hot oil and grating. I did games, stories and the rest. A Good Time Was Had By All. It was a great classroom moment. A parent created it on her own and added it to my class. (It was a "pay-back" for the moments I had created for her son and her family.)

STORY TWO: It was the first family camp I had ever done. It was early in the 1970s and no one knew much about family education. I was young, twenty-two. I was scared. The parents of my kids felt almost as old as my parents. I was deep into anxiety. I was overplanning and going crazy. Maynard Louis was one of the parents. Maynard is great. Maynard is cynical. Maynard complains and points out weakness. Maynard is always in your face. In those days he scared me. I was doing chicken with my head cut off. Trying to get the litany of programs together. Maynard sat me down and asked, "What's wrong?" I gave him the "Yet to do" list. He said, "No problem. I'll do Saturday night." He put together an evening of human Jewish sculptures (organized by his daughters), a Jewish sundae sculpture program (organized by his wife Judy), and a tag-team ping pong game with 20 people on each team. You hit the ball and passed the paddle. It was a great evening. It took a big load off. And, it turned a fearsome parent into a good friend. The educational program was good, but the sundaes made the weekend (after we cleaned up all the whipped cream).

STORY THREE: I didn't know Dalia; I knew her son Oren (fake names to protect some wonderful people). He was eleven, ADHD, and angry. Oren and I had a fragile relationship. I let him play *Prince of Persia* on my laptop. He occasionally talked to me. He was angry at everyone—and I wasn't too convinced that his parents "understood" him. That made sense—Dahlia was a therapist. But on this weekend I was doing mainly adult teaching. On the next-to-last night of the retreat, I wound up being cornered by a suicidal 30-year-old who was literally just out of a mental hospital and who had signed up for this conference. He was way out of my league. I didn't know if he was seriously "crazy" and at risk, or if I was just "freaked" by the whole thing. I was talking about it with another staff member, forgetting that Oren was hidden in a corner playing with my laptop. He didn't say a word. I was worried about the next day when I would have to go round two with this guy. At breakfast, Dalia said, "Let's talk." She told me what she had heard, and offered to walk me through it. She coached me through the next encounter and offered to back me up. It turned out that the situation was "less scary" and I was "more spooked" but I got through it only because of Dalia. She too became a good friend.

STORY FOUR: You'll hear a Brett story much later in this book. He was a behavior problem (chronic immaturity) who took a lot of work. In the process of doing the "work" his parents became good friends. They helped with a lot of programs. Here is the punch line. Six years later, knowing I am single, the family still calls to make sure I have a place to go for Hanukkah.

Parents can be really cool, too.

The Day School Coda

Day Schools are different from Hebrew Schools. For a lot of reasons, we have constructed this book primarily from the vantage point of Sunday School and afternoon Hebrew School teachers, but we want to be inclusive. Therefore, (1) where things are essentially identical, we will not bother to clarify, but we will strive to also use Day School examples. (2) Where things are somewhat different, or very different, we will address separate sections to the universe of the Day School. Here are some of the generalized truths we know in advance.

- Day Schools tend to be better at communicating with parents, involving parents in support roles, etc., but nowhere near as good at involving parents as co-learners with their children.

- When you work in a Day School, even if you are in the Jewish studies side, communication with parents often has a sharper edge, and can be more confrontational, because parents feel that (1) "grades count," and (2) "real" education is at stake. Ironically, this heightened sense of reality doesn't always benefit the Jewish studies program.

- Day Schools also have a unique way of unintentionally intimidating their parents. Parents of Day School kids often feel very inadequate about their own Jewish background because they contrast it with what their kids are learning. It is the *"I can't help my daughter with her Humash homework"* syndrome.

- Because you work in a Day School, and because statistically most Jewish mothers work outside the home, it is much harder to have access to families. Doing family education means asking the whole family to carve out a time and attend an "extra" event which isn't part of the normative school day.

• Many Day Schools, but not all, are independent community entities, not directly connected to one synagogue. (In Los Angeles, we have the opposite experience.) This means that easy flow from the classroom into the larger community of practice (read: Holiday Celebration), which Hebrew Schools can easily accomplish, is a harder connection to make. It is not as easy to have the 5th grade Shabbat, or let the Senior class lead the first *Hakafah* on *Simhat Torah*, etc.

Day Schools have an opportunity to share many Jewish daily life experiences. However, many of these experiences are not continued after hours. Think of the typical scene of a child running out of the classroom as he grabs the *kippah* off his head and stuffs it in his notebook for tomorrow.

> **[Cherie Koller-Fox's Comment]:** It is critical for Day Schools today to involve parents because, in many cases, a Day School education makes a child better educated Jewishly than their parents. I respect parents that want their children to know more, but I suspect that these parents are expressing in part their own desire to learn more. Day schools should seize the opportunity by offering constant encouragement and multiple opportunities for adults to learn. Parents should be given the tools to be the teachers of their own children. Most people are in the Day School system for over a decade (given the seven, nine, or more years of schooling and multiple children). Wouldn't it be wonderful if they themselves left the system enriched with a decade of deepening Jewish knowledge?
>
> Lately I've noticed that some Day Schools think of themselves as "private" schools. I'd rather they thought of themselves as the "public" schools of the Jewish people. Public schools have a responsibility to educate every child who comes to them—private schools don't. Some private schools have a like it or leave it attitude, especially where there is a waiting list. Some private schools keep parents at arm's length because they are wary of parental interference. All that is antithetical to the reverence in which our tradition holds parents and children, and shouldn't be part of the culture of our schools.

Chapter 2
MONEY IN THE BANK

In this chapter we are going to explain one "behaviorist" metaphor for family systems called "Money In The Bank." We learned it from Dr. Carlfield Broderick in a seminar given at the Whizin Institute for Jewish Family Life. It teaches a lot about the ways that people get other people to trust them—and overcome fear and suspicion. If you've read chapter one, then you understand why that is an important part of the family education process.

Ethan and the Power of Shame

[Joel's Story]: *I want to begin this chapter with a complicated story that will take a while to unpack. It teaches more than one point.*

This year I was privileged to teach 14-year-old Ethan. From day one, Ethan was difficult. He was hostile to other students. He talked almost constantly over everything everyone else said. Much of his language and imagery was sexually charged. He was a pain. Interestingly, I also had Ethan's parents attending an adult class I was teaching. But, I didn't make that connection until later. I was using all my best classroom management stuff on Ethan, getting somewhere, but never getting far enough. I could "suspend" his behavior, but never really get it to stop or to be more than temporarily under control. The first week of class, Ethan and I had a battle over wearing a *kippah*. (It seemed to be that ordinary old battle that one faces in Conservative schools.) On the second week of class, he wore a fez to school—I had my camera with me. I credited him with a very funny over-the-top *kippah* protest. I took a picture, put one on my wall, and mailed him a copy—with my appreciation for the laughter. We made a human connection, but the behavior was still generally unacceptable. I thought he was just angry and 14—and needed some attention.

Next week, almost in tears (I realized later), his mother came to me after class and said, "If you need any help in dealing with Ethan, you can call me." She didn't make eye contact. I didn't get it then, because I still labored under the illusion that I could control Ethan. He was, for the most part, controllable. I tossed him out most weeks at the hour-and-15-minute point in an hour-and-35-minute double period class—BUT—that is not unusual for 14-year-olds. There are always one or two who are like that. And, I had a good and patient class who tolerated most of what Ethan did, and never got distracted from the lesson.

A couple of weeks later, Ethan went on the school retreat weekend and wiped out. His behavior there was completely antisocial. No one could control him at all. Later, in conversation with the parents, the school was finally given a technical diagnosis of Tourette's syndrome, something which had been missing from all Ethan's forms the family had filled out. [I used to joke about this in workshops, "What, they thought we might not notice?" It gets a big laugh.] The truth is, this is a story which was too painful for Ethan's mother to tell us. She has had to share her embarrassment and failure with a lot of teachers and a lot of schools—each time he wiped out. Each telling is a reopening of the wound. In not telling us, she was doing what all of us do—delaying the pain.

This is the *shame* part of this story. Ethan's parents are not responsible for his behavior. They are good parents. They try hard. They do more than their best. The truth is—nothing else they can try can ever "make him," or probably even "help him" control himself. He's got therapists. He's got the right drugs. He's got their love and their limits. Yet, time after time, they've walked into schools and been told in one way or another, "If *you* don't do something about *your* kid, *we're* not going to be able to keep him." When a kid is in trouble, parents tend to feel responsible and feel guilty. Sometimes that guilt and sense of responsibility cause them to shut down; other times they erupt as blame and anger. While Ethan's parents retreated, many others would come out swinging, blaming school and teacher for failing to stimulate or manage their child appropriately. *Shame* often becomes *blame*!

Not yet having heard the magic word "Tourette's," and still believing that I could handle Ethan, I told the parents, "He's past bar mitzvah. This is high school—he's responsible for his own actions. If I can't work it out with him (but I think I can)—I'll inform you about what is going on." The truth is, I've never spoken to them again. They stopped coming to my adult class. *[I'll confess, until right now, reflecting on the story—I never realized that I should have followed up about their participation. I hadn't noticed their absence as unique because I always lose about half the parents who start out with the good intention of going to class while their kids are at Hebrew High. Their absence was a detail I missed.]*

Ethan started to get worse. I told my principal that I was running out of ideas. He dropped the "T" word as a way for me to not feel bad about saying this was more than I could handle. I decided to try one more thing. Regularly, I take a number of my Hebrew High kids out for lunch on

Sunday afternoon, after class. Usually, it is a time for good extended intellectual conversation—sort of a salon thing. I took Ethan out to lunch. There, for the first time, I met this amazing, gentle but wounded person. We talked music and travel. We told family stories. He and I shared both trust and pain. The miracle was simple—no one else was there. When he didn't have to compete, when I didn't have to juggle him and 16 other kids and could just listen to him, he was a wonderful person. At the end of that day, we had a bond, not just a relationship.

Here are the two resultant truths. One, Ethan's behavior went downhill from that point. It wasn't me. It was the craziness of the post-February schedule where you never get more than two Sundays in a row, followed by three weeks off. It was puberty escalating. Puberty on Tourette's is real hell. It was a half dozen other problems not to be gone into here. But, here is the good thing. I often asked Ethan to leave. I more often told him that his behavior was beyond what I could handle—and that he would have to control it or leave—and usually he sort of handled it for most of the time. Sometimes, he told me he was getting out of control and asked to leave. The good part was, even though I had to work with Ethan's inappropriateness for the rest of the year, I never had to fight him about it—once I had enough *money in the bank*.

Here is the second truth. Two weeks later, Alan started dropping into my class. He was another 13ish-year-old. He was an angry, short kid. Basically, Alan was in everyone's face just because he was short. He was the kind of short kid who gets very good at basketball—just because of the contradiction. [If you teach—you know the type.] Anyway, he had been in another teacher's room, and had been getting thrown out of there ('cause he deserved it) almost every session. All of a sudden, each time he got thrown out, he started showing up in my room, rather than walking the halls. The first time he walked in and said, "If you let me stay, I promise not to cause any trouble—please?" He behaved like an angel. Afterwards, I asked if he needed to be covered from getting in trouble for not being elsewhere. He said, "No. I just figured out that this was a safe place to be." It happened twice more, and then we moved him into my room permanently. And, for the rest of the year he was a pretty reasonable class member. As near as I can figure it, I took the thorn out of Ethan's hand and also cured Alan's paw. This too is a *money in the bank* story.

> **[Jo Kay's Comments]:** The "money in the bank" concept really works on every level. When I work with PACE teachers, the first order of business is to encourage them to develop regular lines of communication with both parents and kids. Calls before class to let parents know you are looking forward to seeing them in class next week; calls after class to follow up; notes home as updates; calls when parent or child misses a class to find out why and to tell them they were

missed, etc. What happens is loads of "money in the bank." One parent once said, "We know you care about all of us and that's what is important. We wouldn't want to disappoint you."

[Cherie Koller-Fox's Comment]: Hebrew school is too short. We need to spend one-on-one time with each student and each parent. How can we make that happen?

[Shirley Barish's Comment]: From listening to the kids over the years, I have a fortune (money in the bank). I will never forget the kid in seventh grade who was a terror until I sat with him while the rest of the class went to services and found out more about him. We had a nice long talk and one thing I found out was he liked to draw cartoons. Yep, I had him drawing cartoons in the next class and he was no longer a terror. And, he was a good artist!

Another kid in the eighth grade wasn't too interested in what was taking place in class. Another long talk and I found out he played the guitar. The next week I brought a NFTY songbook with chords and a tape and gave it to him. Asked him to learn some of the songs and even made a few suggestions. Next thing I knew he was the song leader of the local youth group, then regional song leader, and just for closure, he is now a rabbi and sings with *Beged Kefet*. (I'll let you try and guess who it is).

Money in the Bank

Money in the bank is an abstract metaphor for a reality we all know. Think: "I owe you one." Sometimes we can get away with a request that would never be honored for anyone else. Why? Because the other person "owes us." What they "owe us" is an abstraction. Perhaps we have done a favor and the "currency" is actually being repaid. More often, we are "trading" on a connection, a sense of caring, knowing and understanding.

One secret of working with students, working with adults, and especially working with families—is that it is good to have *"money in the bank."* The rest of the secret is that showing we care is usually the best way to make a deposit.

My friend and teacher Seymour Rossel began his book, *Managing the Jewish Classroom*, with a chapter called *Remaining Relevant*. He begins by stating:

> Capturing the student's attention is essential. Even the work of motivation cannot begin if the student and the teacher are not on the same wave length. And the transformation of teaching into learning depends on teachers, students, and parents working cooperatively. This chapter contains a series of simple and tested activities [techniques] which help teachers, students, and parents interact in useful ways.

Seymour then goes on to suggest a number of strategies that allow the teacher to gather information about student (and parent) interests, starting with an index card which they fill out with a favorite book, movie, album, hobby, TV show, etc. The value of the technique is not only in the "data" which is collected, but in the caring demonstrated by the act of collection. Seymour is very much a behaviorist as a teacher and a teacher trainer. Even though I am more humanistic in my orientation, I use all of his techniques—they put *money in the bank*.

I often tell the story of my friend Joyce Seglin who is a truly great school principal. When she was the principal of Temple Emanuel in Beverly Hills, she used to stand on the steps every day and say hello and good-bye to every student (and parent) who came or went (before or after school). Every before-school meeting ended in time for Joyce to stand on the steps. Every after-school meeting started after step patrol. These hellos were more than "What's Up?" and a nod. Once, I saw this little 11-year-old kid mope up the stairs—his eyes were on his shoes—and he looked on the edge of tears. Joyce asked him, "How are you doing?" And he said, "My mother kicked my father out of the house again." Joyce looked at him with a great big smile and said, "And things are much better now, right?" The kid's head lifted, and with a big smile he said, "You bet! A lot less screaming!" You have to know kids really well to be there like that.

> **[Treasure Cohen's Comment]:** This story is confusing. I'm not sure I get it.
>
> **[Joel's Response]:** Thanks for pointing out the need to clarify. The kid was really confused. He was actually relieved to have his father out of the house. But, he thought that he was supposed to feel bad. Joyce knew the family well enough to know what was happening. By voicing the positive, she liberated his true feelings from the projected ambivalence. The message of this story is that she knew the kid and the family well enough to speak the unexpected truth. That takes real CONNECTION.

Seymour's behaviorist techniques represent one kind of "fund raising." Joyce's spontaneous knowing and responding represents another kind (*I-Thou*-ish) form of putting money in the bank. Regardless of your teaching philosophy—*we need to put money in the bank*. In order to work the whole family, we need to make deposits into the kids' accounts (which are double credited to our credibility with parents) and we need *money in the parent's bank account*, too (which can also be double credited back to the kid's account). Do it with techniques. Do it with your whole self saying "I"—whatever—but do it!

Meet Mama Bear: Thinking States—Emotional States

When a teacher communicates with a parent it often feels like an angry Mama Bear has gotten on the phone or walked in the room. We see the claws. We hear the growls. This is one angry creature, and she is out to defend her young....Hold that image.

One of my new heroes is a parent and teacher trainer named Jim Fay. I learned this insight from a great tape set he did called *How to Handle Difficult Parent-Teacher Conferences*. Mama Bear is my image. (She's eaten me in too many parent-teacher conferences I've run.) Fay says that when parents walk into a parent-teacher conference, "usually they are drunk on emotion." He explains, "They are in the emotional state—not the thinking state." Like Ethan's mother, they feel *shame* over their child's behavior—and because *shame* is unacceptable in our culture (and not generally a good feeling)—they are looking for a "responsible party" to *blame*.

Hear is the Fay truth: "When someone is in the emotional state—you can't talk to them. You need them in the thinking state. You need them sober. Only one thing gets them into the thinking state— Words. NOW LISTEN CAREFULLY—this means *their* words—not *your* words." In other words, the best thing we can do when we work with parents is listen, and demonstrate that we are listening. Listening empties the emotional state, and *listening* puts *money in the bank*.

Later in the book, we'll deal specifically with parent-teacher conferences and issues of shared management of student behavior, but *money in the bank* is the insight we need right now.

The progression of this book is very simple. We will use **techniques** and **attitudes** to invite families to be part of our classroom—and to show them that they can "trust" us because we will listen and we do care. *This makes an initial deposit.* Then, as we get to know them better, we will listen and share and be there (in a real relationship) *putting more money in the bank,* so that when we need them—or when they need us—we have the currency to work on the problem.

Sometimes the bear eats you. Sometimes the bear buys you a drink. That is the story of Brett and you'll hear it later in this book.

[Jo Kay's Comments]: I would agree on the need to listen, which can help diffuse a tough situation. I also try to disarm hostile parents by agreeing with them on their primary argument. For example, "We're sorry Andrew was made to feel that way," or "You are right, you should have been notified first, and for that I apologize." Now, there is no longer any reason to argue. I then try to present the issue from the perspective of helping the child—and the parent usually begins to HEAR the problem!

Chapter 3
FIRST CONTACT

In this chapter you are going to learn one basic strategy:

It is good to begin a school year by writing a letter which aggressively and proactively communicates with parents (and directly or indirectly with children as well).

We are going to try to convince you that this is a good thing and worth taking the time to do for two reasons:

- It gives you lots of credibility as a teacher because it makes you look professional.

- It begins to build relationships with parents which will contribute to your long-term success.

Class Begins in the Foyer

[Ron's Story]: **Introduce yourself to your students and their families:** Parents often do not feel welcomed by the school or synagogue. Think about it. How are most people greeted when they call or stop by the office? These are the same parents who shop at The Gap and The Disney Store and Wal-Mart who, when they first walk in the door of those establishments, are warmly welcomed by an employee whose only job is to greet you.

But, we are interested in more than selling products. We are interested in enlisting parents as partners in the Jewish education of their children. Ironically, then, the next step is to talk not about the kids, but about yourself and themselves.

As you will see in many of the sample letters that follow, you can enhance the message to parents that you are a real, caring person by telling them something about yourself. Share your own story—where you come from, your educational background, your teaching experience. Tell your Jewish story—why you are so committed to Jewish education, why Judaism is so important to you. And, what you hope to share with their children. Invite them to tell their story to you—by letter, by phone, in person. Ask about their Jewish journey—what was their Jewish education as a child (if any—remember we have many parents who were not born Jewish), or their Jewish experiences as adults. What do they hope their children will gain from participating in a program of Jewish education? Do they have any particular talent or expertise they are willing to share with the class? Tell them how they can reach you—if you are comfortable sharing your phone number, by all means do so. Tell them when "Open House" is and invite them to meet you. Offer to meet them by appointment. In short, open the lines of communication. Without it, you cannot possibly expect to motivate them to the next level of involvement.

For many parents, you are the most visible and accessible person representing the school they are likely to meet. You are literally on the front-line. How you make this first contact with parents can determine the tone and quality of your future relationship with them. That is why the first meeting, the first letter, the first phone call needs to be carefully considered.

These letters are our way of standing in the foyer, introducing ourselves, inviting their stories through our stories, and opening the access.

The Hillel and Shammai of Parent Communication

There are a number of "schools" (points of view) about how to start communicating with families:

[*Bet Hillel* and *Bet Shammai* were rival schools back in the time of the Mishnah, circa 100 BCE. They always took opposite positions. Here they are being used as a metaphor].

- *Bet Shammai* says that a teacher should call every family in his/her class before the school year (or at least during the first two weeks).

- *Bet Hillel* says that a teacher should send a letter to every family in his/her class.

- *Bet Shammai* says the letter should be addressed to the parents with the understanding that they will share it with their child.

- *Bet Hillel* says that the letter should be sent to the child with the knowledge that the parents will read it over the child's shoulder.

- Some workshop participants suggest that two letters should be sent. Some workshop participants suggest that the age of the child is a determining factor.

- All agree that initial communication is critical.

The Guidelines

We have intentionally built this chapter around a number of real letters which actual teachers have sent to actual parents. We believe these examples will teach an experienced teacher more than the set principles we have included. Good teachers see a good idea and then begin a process to find their own way of adapting it. We invite you to be a good teacher and do the same thing.

We suggest that an "ideal" parent contact letter contains three elements:
- a personal introduction
- a statement of expectations
- an invitation to ongoing communication.

Also learn The Law Of The Refrigerator Door: The earliest mailing received gets precedence in the family calendar. What this means is if you ask in August or early September—your *requests* are highly likelier to be considered reasonable and be met. If you ask in February—your *demands* are going to be considered unreasonable. Therefore,

- any dates, any supplies, anything "extra" you want from families *needs* to be in your opening communications.

The three elements we have suggested were culled from studying a series of such good letters. The truth is, most examples we have chosen to include here don't include all three of these elements, but they are great examples nevertheless. Each of our samples does at least one of these things really well.

[1] A Personal Introduction:

Introduces yourself as a unique, caring individual (with some vulnerabilities) who really wants to succeed.

One of the prime goals of this letter is to establish communication—a relationship. In person, we establish a connection by making eye contact. In a letter, we do it by breaking through the anonymity of the mail and revealing something personal and unique about ourselves. Our job in this letter is to begin to become a person, and not just a warm body filling the given teaching slot.

The first task is to let them feel a little bit close to you. You want them excited that their child will get the privilege of spending time with you. While each of us will do this in our own way, it usually will include (a) some background, (b) a statement of your vision or goals, and (c) and acknowledgment that teaching their child is both a serious responsibility and a privilege.

[2] A Setting of Expectations:

In advance you want both parents and students to (1) know what you expect from them, (2) know how you will deal with exceptions (because in Jewish schools there are always exceptions), and

(3) develop a vision of the rewards they may expect if they actively participate. You are going to be sharing with them what they will have to do and what they will get out of it.

Here is the reality. There are two goals here, one is "legislative" and one is "motivational"—but they are related. As a teacher you are used to doing both. With one hand you are "shaking a ruler" and saying these are the rules and standards in my classroom. I expect x, y, and z out of you. This is what you need to bring. This is when you need to be here. This is what I expect you to master. This is how we will deal with it if you have a problem. With the other hand you are tousling their hair, and saying if you do well in this class, you will achieve amazing things.

When you are writing this letter to parents who will also be involved in the educational process (as we hope many parents are), you need to tell parents both what you expect of their kids, and the times, materials, and efforts you expect from them, as well.

Most families will do almost anything, if it is formally part of the program. The big problems come when you "change the rules" and introduce a new expectation mid-process.

The second need is to establish a vision of benefit. Every effort needs a motivation, a reward—in this letter you are "selling" parents on their involvement using the "reward" their "efforts" will produce. Real advertising agencies call this "reason why," and you need to do it, too.

[3] An Invitation to On-Going Communication and Involvement

The ultimate goal of this letter is to establish a "contract" between the classroom and the home. You want to agree to be a "team" which works together on the student's Jewish education.

In this contract, you are asking for their concern, involvement, support, and willingness to solve problems. They need to be able to ask you for the same. In the future, if a child is having difficulty with the material, not conforming to classroom behavioral standards, having trouble interacting with peers, etc., you want to be able to call parents and ask them to collaborate with you in solving this problem. You don't want them to feel that you are either "blaming them" or "making them responsible" for their child's behavior. You want to be able to establish a confrontation-free "parent-teacher committee" to collectively work towards the child's success.

Likewise, they want to be able to do the same. If their child is confused, angry, unhappy, bored, etc. they want to be able to work with you in improving the situation. If this contract is properly established (and one letter won't do that, it will only begin the process), such calls won't feel like they are "blam-

ing" the teacher, or "holding the teacher responsible" for all the child's experiences. Rather, the parent-teacher committee can work together on solutions which will improve the situation.

If we can take away the guilt, the blame, and all the defensive reactions from parent-teacher contacts—it makes the work much easier.

You want to set the modalities by which they can actively participate in shaping their child's education.

- If there are volunteer roles which will be important to your classroom's success, solicit participation.

- If there are legitimate skills you want—carpentry, cooking, art, etc.—now is the time to ask.

And if you are really brave, this would be a great time to invite participation in a classroom advisory committee.

The Rationale: Why Take the Time?

As you will see in the following examples, writing a good letter of introduction takes time and planning. It represents a lot of effort. The work of mailing such letters also takes time which often you, and not the school, will have to expend. These letters also contain a future risk—promises you must keep. Committing yourself to goals and procedures always carries a risk. So why is it worth it?

Because if you do it...

- parents will respect you as a "professional" teacher, one who invests time, plans ahead, is thoughtful about his/her classroom, and cares about their child.

- parents will trust you to work with their child and feel more ready to be partners in making education effective.

- parents will know the obligations and most of them will find a way to "back you up" by working with their child to meet the reasonable expectations you have set.

- parents will know they have an invitation to communicate back, verbalizing their needs and desires, too. With these on the table, you have a common bond and a basis for shared problem solving.

REAL PARENT CONTACT: LETTERS FROM REAL TEACHERS

Andy German

All we know about Andy is that he taught a 6th grade Israel class and a 7th grade Judaics class at Temple Sha'ary Shalom Religious School, in Springfield, New Jersey. We've never met him, but his principal, Irene Bolton, was so proud of this letter that she sent it to her favorite publisher, Torah Aura Productions .

P.S. This is a great letter, but it is actually an early-in-the-year letter, not a before-the-year letter.

Dear Parents,

Shalom and Blessings!!

I am writing to you from my incredibly messy dormitory room, a labyrinth of Jewish books, unwashed clothes, and pounds of Chips Ahoy cookies, the food on which all students survive (even when they tell their parents that they are eating healthy). Besides teaching your children, the only other things I do here are make a colossal mess, accuse everyone of being messy, then clean everything up, never forgetting in between all of this to remind myself that I should, theoretically speaking, be going to class.

Ah, college. Or more appropriately, oy college.

Well, I didn't write to tell you of my life, but rather to tell you of your child's inner Jewish life. Teaching your children is a distinct and humbling honor. It is also a great *mitzvah.* As it is said, "And you shall teach them to your children…" (Deut. 6:7)

In each of my students, your children, I have seen sparks of brilliance and future glory as Jewish adults. No matter how discouraged I may get after a hard day in the classroom, this knowledge gives me strength to go on. It should give you as parents great pleasure.

But just the existence of a potential commitment to Judaism is not enough, it is merely a challenge. We now know that these sparks, these *nitzotzim d'kedushah* (sparks of holiness), as the Kabbalists called them, can be lost to the ravages of assimilation, gone forever. We must guard them, and be as miserly as we can.

In this matter then I need your help. As parents you can fight on the second front, as it were, by taking an interest in your child's education, by bringing Jewishness into the home, by helping me to inspire within them a healthy warmth and love toward our ancient Tribe, whose history has covered more then 2/3 of recorded time. Most importantly, you can discuss with your children what they've learned, and discuss with me what is yet to be done.

In my class only one rule exists. In Hebrew it is called *kavod* (respect). Everything falls within that rubric. Teach that word at home, as I will in class, and a great leap toward learning will have been taken!!

My college dorm number is (908) XXX-XXXX, and as a college student, I am officially forbidden to sleep normal hours, so you are welcome, nay encouraged, to call me at any and all unseemly hours. I would like to hear from you so that together we can make great Jewish adults out of your children. It is not an easy task being a Jew, but, since we are free to say what we want, is it not a most splendorous adventure? 4,000 years!! Surely there must be some great drama at work here. It is that great adventure and drama that we can hopefully use together to inspire your sons and daughters, my students.

Ah, well, I've chewed your eyes off enough. It's a Jewish disease I think, excessive verbosity! Until we meet, may The Holy One bless you and yours (and my Dodgers) this New Year and write us all in the Book of Life.

Shana Tova u'Mivurechet,

Shalom, Andy German

Susan Fish et al

Susan Fish is a second-grade secular studies teacher at The Jewish Day School in Seattle, Washington. Each year, she and her co-teachers choose a theme and center the opening of school around it. They use this theme for their opening communication with both parents and students. One of Susan's big tricks is having parents help students prepare for the first day of school by pre-assigning student to bring to class some introductory items that all but certainly require their parents' help. Without being very explicit about it, Susan and team start school by involving the whole family in the preparation.

For the School Year 1992-1993

Three elements were sent home to the family: a note to parents, a letter to students, and a student task sheet.

This note was handwritten and then photocopied:

Dear Parents,

The theme in 2nd grade this year is *Yad b'Yad*—Hand in Hand. We would like to invite **you** to join us in "lending a helping hand" in our class. In these busy first days of the school year, and of course during the year, we would appreciate any time you could give. (We even offer a wide variety of projects to choose from!)

Please stop by our classrooms or call at your convenience and we can set up some great "hands-on" activities for you. We appreciate your time, support, and generosity in giving us a hand.

Thank you very much.

Morah Sara, Morah Susan, Morah Vered.

P.S.

Please remind your child to bring his/her Siddur to school on Tuesday. Thank You!

This letter was typed and then photocopied with a border of hands being shaken. Each student's Hebrew and English names were handwritten into the blanks.

Dear _____ ,

Yad b'Yad means "hand in hand."

In 2nd grade together we'll stand.

Yad b'Yad, we'll learn and grow.

Hand in hand, we'll make it so.

Yad b'Yad, in all we do,

Torah, Hebrew, science too!

Yad b'Yad we'll meet each day.

Hand in hand, together we'll pray.

Yad b'Yad—one people, one heart—

We'll get the year off to a wonderful start.

So join our class—a circle of friends

Yad b'Yad from beginning to end.

Please let us get to know you! Please bring the following things to school Tuesday, September 1.

1. Your hands drawing (See below)
2. 2 photographs of you (and your family, pet, etc.)
3. Your Hebrew name
4. Your smile!

We can't wait to meet you!

A hand written worksheet with a picture of hands at the bottom and the label: Example.

Hand Instructions (see example)

1. Trace your left and right hands on the colored paper. (You may want to ask someone to help you.)
2. Write your name in English.
3. Write your name in Hebrew.
4. Bring your hands, photographs, names and your smile to school on Tuesday!

What needs to be understood is that because this is a Day School, the school culture shapes major aspects of the classroom. These teachers really can be reached daily through the school (and so extra contact information isn't needed). And, because of secular academic issues, the school handbook is a much more substantial document than those supplemental schools produce (when they produce them) and clearly states the expectations for families, the academic parameters, and other such information. In other words, even given those expectations, Susan's team still actualizes a personal contact with the home.

For the School Year 1993-1994
A typed letter with a "tool" border .

OUR CHILDREN, OUR BUILDERS
BANAINU, BONA'NU
OUR CHILD, OUR BUILDER!
We're glad to meet you!
Together we'll BUILD a year really fine.
Preparing Shabbat,
And blessing wine.
We'll BUILD Noah's Ark,
With the animal zoo,
While BUILDING good friendships,
Here in Grade 2.
Hand in hand we'll create
In Hebrew and math.
Using new tools
On the learning path.
So, come to be a BUILDER,
It won't take you long
To make our "foundation" mighty and strong.
Just think of a "tool" for your year in Grade 2,
Something to BUILD a wonderful you!
It might be a crayon, a pencil, a book
Be creative and take a look!

PLEASE THINK OF A "TOOL" TO HELP BUILD A TERRIFIC YEAR IN 2ND GRADE & BRING IT THE FIRST DAY OF SCHOOL FOR OUR "TOOLBOX." (Please label your tool with your name.)

HAMOROT SUSAN, SARA, AND VERED

Ellen Abrahams Brosbe

Ellen Brosbe is a family educator living in Santa Rosa, California. These days she works for the Jewish Family Education Project in San Francisco. As we were starting this book, she was the director of the Santa Rosa Jewish Community Center Nursery School, Congregation Beth Ami, Santa Rosa, CA.

Bubbe Helen tells a story. It seems her great niece, age 4, was taken to the restroom at a restaurant and saw a double roll of toilet tissue stored on the dispenser. "What's a Torah doing in here?" she asked. This story, for those of us in early childhood Jewish education, says the best and worst about Jewish education in the early years. If toilet paper roll *Sifrei Torah* or *Megillot* are the only *Sifrei Torah* these children know, we are failing. As Jewish resource persons for a preschool staff of 50% non-Jewish educators, we are constantly evaluating "What's Jewish about early childhood Jewish education."

The year 92-93 marked the third of the first three years of family programming for the Santa Rosa Jewish Community Center Nursery School and Congregation Beth Ami. We have come to the conclusion that the most important part of our job is getting to know our families. The diversity within our community goes beyond interfaith, gay or lesbian, single parent, or Jewish at birth but ambivalent. Our most frequent request isn't simply "Jewish how-to" but how families are managing in this day and age.

We are now seeing that upwardly mobile preschool program families need a tremendous amount of support in their daily lives. As resource person and family educator, I needed to listen more intently when a parent says, "We can't get it together to 'do' Shabbat." I needed to push for a team approach among the nursery school staff, director, Rabbi, board, and synagogue administrator.

The two biggest changes to our school included two programs. The '*ḥesed pram*' is the blue baby buggy used for ongoing donation of clothing, food, and other items (anyone can donate or take what they need) and the participation of nursery school children in collecting items. ("Where is the 'toilet tree?'" asked Zoe, when we collected personal hygiene items.) The creation of an intergenerational read-aloud program for preschoolers by seniors, called the Grandparent Connection (BJE, Boston) arose from a need many of our families have for adopted grandparents because their grandparents live far away.

These programs are significant because the families created the momentum to keep these programs going. The teachers support the programs willingly, and the Jewish content is an easy introduction to *gemilut hasadim* and the Jewish love of books.

Ellen Abrahams Brosbe,
Santa Rose Jewish Community Center Nursery School,
Congregation Beth Ami, Santa Rosa, CA

[Esther Netter's Comment]: There is another similar story about a conservative rabbi who went to visit the classes in his Hebrew school. It was the beginning of the school year just before Sukkot. The rabbi went into a fourth grade class and asked, "Who knows what holiday is coming next?" Several students responded, "Sukkot." "And who knows what a sukkah is?" the rabbi asked. A hand shot up in the front row and the 4th grade student said, "A sukkah is a shoebox."

Same thing; that kid never saw, built or visited a real sukkah. The closest he got to a sukkah was the annual sukkah shoebox art project.

Elise Cohen

This letter was sent to us from Temple Ramat Zion in Northridge, California.

Dear Students and Parents:

Welcome back to religious school and welcome to Kitah Hey. I would like to take this opportunity to introduce myself, my expectations and the curriculum for this year.

First of all my name is Elise Cohen. I am a graduate of the University of Texas, and I am currently working on my Master's degree in education at the University of Judaism. I am new at Temple Ramat Zion this year, but I have been in the field of Jewish education for over eight years. I believe that religious school can be a fun place to grow, learn and make friends. I also feel that it is important for religious school teachers to be available to their students and their parents; therefore, please feel free to call me at home—my number is (XXX) XXX-XXXX.

After teaching for many years, I have found that it is important to spell out our expectations. By doing this everyone has a clear understanding of what is expected of them, and discipline problems are minimized. Therefore, the following is Elise's Four Answers to religious school's four questions.

1. What do I need to bring?

   Everyone needs to bring their Religious School books, notebooks, *Kippah*, pen/pencil and a positive attitude to class. Yes, attitude is required. I realize that some days it's just not there, but it's much harder to enjoy something if you have already decided to hate it.

2. Do I have to do my homework?

   Yes, I would not assign it if I did not want you to complete it. However, I am well aware of the amount of homework you receive in public school, and I will keep mine short and to the point. Remember my goal is to have you like coming to religious school.

3. Do I have to raise my hand?

   I do not make you raise your hand in class discussion, but I do require that you be mensch-like. Therefore, you must listen to each other and you must show appropriate behavior in class and in services. Remember, you are the class the school looks up to.

4. Is there ever make-up work?

Of course, there is make-up work. You missed class. We did something during the time that you were not with us; otherwise, why would we have to come at all? Make up work is due within a week. You are to ask me before class or at *hafsaka* about your assignment.

I am very excited about the curriculum this year. We will be completing the *Master of Mitzvot* series. Our topics will include *tallit* and *tefillin;* the synagogue; holocaust; personal identity; life cycle, marriage, divorce, old age and death; and history. We will continue our study of tefillot and holidays. My hope is to spend less time reading about Judaism and more time experiencing Judaism. Therefore, we will be making our own tallitot, building a synagogue, holding a mock wedding and much more. We have also added a new program. This year on Sundays the *Hey* Class will work with the *Alef* Class. This will give us a chance to give information rather than just receive it at Religious School. This will definitely be a year to remember.

L'Shanah Tova,

Elise Cohen

Hey Teacher

I have read the above letter. I know what is expected of me for the coming school year, and I am willing to meet those expectations.

_____

Student Signature

I have read the above letter, and I know what is expected of my son/daughter. I am willing as a parent to help my child meet those expectations.

_____

Parent Signature

Joel Lurie Grishaver

A few years ago, as part of a 40th birthday reflection, I took a part-time sabbatical from Torah Aura and went back to teach a three-day-a-week 7th grade afterschool Hebrew School class. Before my 7th Grade class ever met, I mailed this letter of introduction and expectation to each family. It is not the one I would send today. For me, it is now too much in some areas, too little in others—but that year was my first attempt at teaching this way. This letter was intentionally sent on my corporate letterhead. Knowing that I would be facing puberty head on, I wanted all the respect I could muster.

Dear *Dalet* Parents,

My name is Joel Lurie Grishaver and I am privileged and challenged to be your children's Hebrew School Teacher. I am proud this year to serve as your **agent** and as your **baby-sitter**. I am excited about our partnership.

The Talmud makes it very clear that it is a parent's responsibility to directly provide their own child with a Jewish education. They take this directly from the book of Deuteronomy where in a familiar passage the Jewish people are taught: "AND YOU SHALL TEACH THEM (the words of Torah) TO YOUR CHILDREN." While parents are empowered to hire a teacher, and while Jewish communities are obligated to provide such teachers, these teachers only act as the **agent** of the parents. I am looking forward to being a partner in the sense of Jewishness and the depth of Jewish understanding you are conveying to your child. As your **agent**, I am always interested in evaluation of the job I am doing—and in your sense of what we can accomplish together.

In a very famous Jewish legal ruling in the middle ages, it is stated that all Jewish teachers should be paid as **baby-sitters**. This ruling is not intended as an insult, but rather both as an insight and as a solution to a legal problem. The legal problem involves a Talmudic text which states: "One should not make a spade out of the Torah." It means the Torah is too important to become a tool by which one earns a living. Torah should be a life process which one shares. Therefore, it is wrong to charge money for Torah teaching. And consequently, in looking for a way to compensate teachers (who indeed deserve compensation for their time and effort), the rabbis chose to look at Torah teaching as high quality **baby-sitting**— again a temporary serving as *in loco parentis*. In real life, I earn my living by being a co-owner and serving as the creative chair of two companies, and by teaching at the University of Judaism. I have chosen to allocate some of my time this year to learning from you and your children, while sharing some of my skills and knowledge—I think of it as a wonderful opportunity to provide high class baby-sitting for my neighbors' children, and to be able to share a small part of the responsibility for raising Jewish children. I thank you for the small way in which you have made me part of your families.

For you to share and review with your child:

The Basic Rules

1. Be here. Have your books—have something to write with.

2. Do not hurt or harm or bother anyone else.

3. Do not interfere with anyone else's ability to learn or Joel's ability to teach.

4. Expect to learn—a lot.

Included in the packet was a letter to the students which included these details:

Academics

1. We will be studying three subjects this year: Jewish History; selections from the Torah (in Hebrew); and the daily/Shabbat service with a central focus on the *Amidah*. Much, in fact most, of what you will be studying will be brand new material which I am presently writing or thinking about writing.

   This means: (a) you will need a three ringed notebook, and you will need to bring it each and every time. (b) you will need to take notes and do written work every session—bring a thing to write with. I may keep some pencils in the room, but I will not worry that you have one. You are now old enough to be responsible.

2. There will be homework from almost every session. In history, there will be a weekly reading assignment. (Yes, there will be a quiz.) Your history book stays at home. I don't expect to use it in class—but I do expect you to do the reading.

   In Torah, you will not have a lot of original work to do at home, but you will have vocabulary to work on, and translations to review and fix. I already know from last year, that the language side is going to be our big focus. You can expect a lot of vocabulary and translation of texts!

   In Siddur, we will do almost all of the work in class. However, you will be expected to "perform" specific prayers with a reasonable fluency.

Tzedakah

I will not pass a brown envelope around the class and watch the games it creates. You are now ready for a more serious lesson, and you are now ready to make a more serious commitment.

There are twenty-two sessions between now and our first family education day on November 18th. I want you to make a pledge to Tzedakah for that period. I want you to talk with your parents and decide how much money is appropriate for you to pledge. (As a guideline, if you were to bring 25 cents a session—your pledge would be $ 4.25.) All monies are to be brought on that day, in cash—no checks will be acceptable. No one will know the amount of your pledge. I hold your parents responsible for seeing to it that you set an obligation and keep it. On that day, as a group of families, we will allocate the monies collected. We will do this twice more during the year.

Family Education

Six of the Sundays in the year will be set aside as family learning days. On those dates, which will also be included in the letter to your parents, parents will be invited to join us in class for some special learning experiences. Some of it will be stuff we do with everyone—some of it will be some parent learning which will happen separately.

It is your job and privilege to *make* them come. In the same way that they *make* you come to Hebrew school—this is your chance to get even.

Discipline

1. Everyone is human. Everyone has bad days—that goes for the teacher, too. In most cases, I expect a reminder or a warning to be enough.

2. I do not yell (except as a way of getting excited about material we are studying). I will not kick you out of class. I don't write names on the board, give rewards—or have any fancy system! Rather, I expect to solve all problems.

First, I will talk to you. If you and I can work out the problem—it is over.

If you and I get nowhere, then I'll talk to your parents. If, together, we can work it out, then it's over.

Otherwise, we'll solve the problem another way.

P.S. Expect me to call or write your parents when I catch you doing something good—as well.

Attendance

1. No one drops out! Don't even think about it! If you start to disappear, I promise to go looking for you and make a fuss! I think it is critical that you continue your Jewish education by taking Hebrew and Jewish studies in college. I might settle in a few cases for finishing your formal Jewish studies in twelfth grade, but there is nothing negotiable for me about being 13. You are now just ready to begin some real Jewish learning.

2. I don't need this job. I own two companies and teach at a University graduate school. They all pay a lot better and give me a lot more respect. I am taking time out of my busy life to be here for three reasons: (1) I like this class—I asked for it—I chose it—don't change my mind. (2) I believe that this year of learning is so important, and you guys have so much to learn—that I was even willing to teach it myself. (3) I like stories, and I expect to be able to tell a few more good ones after this experience.

The bottom line: If I can find the time to be here, so can you.

If you are absent, getting the work is **your** responsibility. If there is a handout or some new material, I will have the office mail it to you. Otherwise, finding out what you missed and what the homework is, is your responsibility.

Call someone else, or call my office, or have your parents call it: xxx-xxxx. The person answering the phone will have the daily assignments.

Parties

1. I like parties, too! We will have them often—as often as you earn them. Every time we finish a major unit—especially a Torah text—we will celebrate.

2. Bonus party. You can expect a weekly quiz or test. Any time the whole class scores B or better on a quiz, the next session will have micro-party (a little one). Any time the whole class scores perfect papers—there will be a macro-major party.

3. All parties are the responsibility of your teacher, Temple Beth El Religious School, and its staff. You **need** not contribute anything to them—you **cannot** contribute anything to them. Suggestions can be made—but we will decide what and how much is consumed at each event!

Love, Gris

P.S. I am sure that we will add and change things as the year goes on!

Sharon's Story: An Epilogue

Sharon Lerner is a 5th grade teacher at Temple Beth El in San Pedro, California. She also was for a while part of the Torah Aura Productions design team. The school year 1992-93 was her first time in a classroom. Her first introductory letter asks parents to join her and their children for the first fifteen minutes of class. About 70% of parents showed up, most of those missing were those not driving the given car pool.

Dear Parent,

Congratulations! Sunday, September 20, 1992, is just ahead...the day that your child will begin Kitah Gimmel here at Temple Beth El Religious School.

My name is Sharon Lerner and I will be the Kitah Gimmel teacher. I returned to California this past after spending 5½ wonderful years learning, working, and living in the land of Israel. I am excited about joining the faculty of Temple Beth El and I am looking forward to meeting your children and you.

We have a full, challenging, and fun year ahead—a curriculum I am certain the children will enjoy learning.

Looking into this year's 5th grade, Kitah Gimmel Class—we will be busy with our lessons in Hebrew: We are beginning with learning our *Brakhah System* and moving on to *The Shema and Its Blessings*. Each week we will take a look at our Torah portion and talk about the commentaries as well. Certain to be thought-provoking and fun is our "What Shall I do?" curriculum—a book of ethical problems and Jewish responses. As we move further into the year we will begin a newly developed curriculum about Israel that promises to be very fun and interesting.

There you have it, all the ingredients for the coming year, sprinkled with Music, Dance and Art—a winning recipe!

I feel very fortunate to be teaching at Temple Beth El under the guidance of Debi Rowe, our Principal, who has provided such a terrific curriculum and atmosphere for both the children and the educators.

Shanah Tovah,

Sharon Lerner

P.S. I would like to remind you to see to it that your child does show up on time to class sessions with his/her books, learning materials, pencil, writing paper, and homework assignment when appropriate. Also, I would like to extend an invitation to the parents to join us for the first 15 minutes of our first class session so we can all meet one another, and I will hand out copies of our "Class Rules" at that time.

This year Sharon composed a new letter, but in the chaos of starting school, the synagogue never mailed it. Wonderfully, parents still dropped by the room to introduce themselves, Sharon quickly "networked" and when the dust settled, 80% or more of the parents were present, including one mother whose son was absent.

In these opening sessions, Sharon had parents and children introduce themselves, then she passed out and explained her classroom rules (based on derekh eretz), described the syllabus and curriculum, and set her expectations. At the end of the session, Sharon was asked the one question every teacher wants parents to ask, "What can we do to help!" All of this took fifteen or twenty minutes; then the parents left and the first lesson began.

Learn from Sharon's example; consider parleying a "opening letter" into an "opening event."

Also for consideration: This suggestion came into the Torah Aura Bulletin Board and seemed to fit here:

In my *Rosh ha-Shanah Seder* course at CAJE 17 and CAJE 18, several teachers mentioned that they create contracts with children at the beginning of the school year. A child's educational goals are drawn or written, depending on abilities and sealed envelopes of a child's goals are then slipped, like wishes and prayers, into a mock Western Wall... to be opened and discussed at *Shavuot.*

This year I'm teaching ongoing *Ethical Wills.* I call them *Leaves from the Tree,* to help families create Judaic goals together, reflecting on the Judaism they want their children to experience and learn—and why. If a program like this were to be run for parents and kids on the first day of school, perhaps students would feel more compelled to try to learn from their Hebrew school sessions.

Like states building new prisons while abandoning their public school systems, personalized attention for the class clown at the expense of others neglects the very students who enter the classroom hoping to gain an education. B'shalom, **Hasta CAJE, Steffi Aronson Karp <shalom-bk@treelife.com>**

Chapter 4
ONGOING COMMUNICATIONS

In this chapter we are going to expand the basic truth learned in the previous chapter. In this chapter we will discover:

If it is good to begin a school year with direct contact with the parents of the students you are teaching, it is even better to continue that communication on a regular basis.

In communicating with parents, we teachers have many objectives and are meeting diverse needs. These include:

- **Making the parents feel involved by empowering them with a working knowledge of the material being covered in class.** This allows them to effectively "interview" their children on the way home, and establish follow-up questions when "Nothing" is the answer to "What did you learn in school today?"

- **Let them know about the progress and experience of their own child.** If you are an effective communicator, you can let them know things a report card can never accomplish—they will not only know (1) what they can feel proud about, and (2) what they should be concerned about—but will have stories to tell and questions to ask.

- **Give them resources for extending and adapting the classroom experience in their own family context.**

- **Remind them, and prompt them**, about the expectations for their and their child's ongoing involvement.

- **Build a sense of team, community, and collective accomplishment.** The bottom line is this: *This communication is not designed as your shot to "bitch" about how your expectations are not being met, or how disappointed you are—rather you are the coach in the locker room at half-time, building team confidence, team spirit, and team energy.* This is not to say that problems can't be shared, but they should always be things we are going to work on together.

Four Unconventional Classroom Tools

[Joel's Shtick] : When I walk in to do one of my **"Jewish Parent"** workshops for teachers, I bring four things I always have in my classroom. They are not particularly logical things. But, I always have: (1) **postcards**, (2) **business cards**, (3) a **cellular phone**, and (4) these days— my **"Voice Organizer"** [though it used to be a small pad of 3" x 5" *Post-it Notes* inside my attendance book]. I hold each object and make the following explanations. Here is what I do with each.

The **postcards** I fill out after every class. (Confession: I am better at this at the beginning of the year, than the end!) I try to pick out one or two kids with exceptional moments in the lesson and either (a) share the good thought/activity/moment with parents, or (b) follow up on a thought with the kid him/herself. With my high school students I sometimes send questions about great statements. This is an idea I got from Seymour Rossel (see Chapter 2, *"Money in the Bank"*). Often, on my drive home, when my mind is replaying some part of the class, then my attention focuses on some insight I missed during the lesson. That generates another postcard the next morning.

The **business cards** are my first line of defense. I give them out a lot. (1) I want my kids sending post cards and e-mail back at me—if they want to comment or follow-up. (2) If I ever have to call a parent, I never want to "cold call." I learned this many years ago. It is easier to give a card to kids and tell them to have their parent call before they come back to class again. I want the kid to "improvise" his/her own version of the story first, so the parents already have some details and some doubts before I talk to them. They call, I listen, then share, then ask for collaboration. In my life, the business card makes sure that I deal with this during my office day, not at home. That's the way I want it. If I wanted it at a different time, I'd buy a rubber stamp and indicate that on the back of the card. [*In chapter 6, you'll hear the story of how the business card strategy got Brett's father to buy me a drink.*] I'll say this again later as well, but I think that problems are a great opportunity for connecting to parents.

The **cellular phone** I got for Avi. (That is not his real name, Julie is not his mother's, and their family name I won't bother to invent.) Avi was a very bright, very manipulating 13-year-old. He would sit like a vulture, silently well behaved through most of class, and then drop the bombshell at about fifteen minutes before the bell. He was the kind of kid who, no matter how much class he missed, always "aced" every test I would give. It was hard to get too mad because, once Avi was caught, he smiled politely and then accepted responsibility. There was no wrestling to the mat, no jailhouse lawyering over the incident. Besides, who could hate a 13-year-old who understood classroom dynamics well enough to know the precise moment to shatter a lesson, and who also quoted from *Catcher in the Rye*? It got to be a habit to "throw Avi out" of class—in a branch where there was no one to supervise him—because we were two teachers and no administrator. So, I got the cellular phone, entered his mother's car phone as speed dial 15, and got to say, "Julie, Avi is ready for pick-up, again." The good news is that Julie was a former graduate student of mine and we collaborated on dealing with Avi. The bad news: Nothing we did was going to alter his behavior, which was annoying, not evil. Together, we lived with it. Since then, I've usually saved a speed dial button or two on the phone for a "special" student. It is really powerful, the first time you pick up the phone, hand it to a kid (having already set it to ring at his home) and tell her or him, "Tell your parents I want to talk to them." It is one of those Clint Eastwood teaching moments. [The whole thing is equally powerful when you get a kid to call a parent to share great news—right in the classroom—like a good score or a great insight!]

The **Voice Organizer** is this little electronic box they sell in all the catalogs and airplane magazines. It is basically a digital tape recorder that stores each message on its own. I bought it because life got overwhelming between work, traveling, and teaching. But, I found that in class, it was an amazing device. Here are some classic messages: "Find the Artson article on vegetarianism for Lindsey." "Bring three extra copies of the Pirke Avot text for the VBS second period." or "Michelle said, 'You can't judge a book by its movie!'" The class would regularly shout at me to add things to the tape—it made them official. I also used it privately to annotate the follow-ups I needed with individual kids or families. [Before the machine, I made the inside cover of my attendance notebook a mass of post-it notes to follow up.] Here is the message: Part of being a great teacher—especially a family teacher—is a running "To Do List."

Now here is my favorite part. I was doing this *shtick* at an LABJE workshop at the UJ, when a woman whom I had never met before in my life, stood up in the room and said, "He really does it," holding up the card I had sent to her son earlier in the year. That single moment built the rest of my credibility in that workshop and hammered home the point.

Categories: (Names of...)

Among the kinds of ongoing communications we have collected in our research are...

Small Byte Communication

• **Good News Post Cards:** This is as simple as it gets. (1) Keep a stack of postcards in your school materials. (2) After class, write to the families of one or two kids and tell them something wonderful their child said, did, created, etc. in class today. (3) For those of you who are record keepers, you can have fun making all kinds of checks. For those of you who are more spontaneous, have fun your way. This one we first learned from Seymour Rossel in *Managing the Jewish Classroom*, though we have no idea where it began. Joel's Caveat: Before Bat/Bar Mitzvah I send them to the parents. After Bat/Bar Mitzvah, they go directly to the kids.

• **E-Mail:** The new technology for all of this is "e-mail." This year in Joel's Hebrew High classes, individual sessions were often followed up by a flurry of e-mail messages back and forth between teacher and student. The e-mail parents who attended his parent-child class regularly commented on the goings-on that way as well. These are the postcards of the future. It was a great moment when David Tytell E-mailed Joel that he (David) got into Cal Tech. It was a virtual *simḥah*.

• **Sunshine Telegrams/Esther Karten's Shalom-a-Grams:** Once these were dittoed. (Remember dittos?) Often they are Xeroxed. More often they are now run on NCR (the stuff that makes copies without carbon). These are "cute" forms teachers can fill out and either send or mail home. These can cover good news, absences, missing school work, need for extra help, etc. (You'll see a collection sent in by Nachama Skolnik Moskowitz from her tenure at the Minneapolis Jewish Day School at the end of this chapter.)

By the way, the reason for the NCR paper copies is: *pink* goes into the *permanent record*, *yellow* is *signed* and returned, and *white* is kept at *home*). Some people keep compulsive records. Some don't. Some worry about lawsuits. Some don't.

• **Jane Golub's Weekly Calendar:** Jane Golub is a partner in Torah Aura Productions and a veteran Hebrew school teacher. She was facing a classic Hebrew school problem, sporadic attendance. She was endlessly dealing with make-up work (and all that). Her solution was to print out a weekly calendar of material that would be covered in the next week, and the assignments which would be given. That solved her problem. But, especially given all the design-your-own-calendar computer programs, we can do a lot more with a calendar—think about matching assignments with Shabbat and holiday annotations—and other goodies.

And while we are talking about Jane, she is also the one who figured out that rather than just asking her students to "drill" reading prayers at home, asking them to make a tape was better. It did three things: (1) Encouraged more practice than a classroom reading test would have, (2) took up a lot less class time than the test where everyone had to read, and (3) as the kids "cheated" and over-dubbed their tapes, they really worked on perfecting the passage. Finally, the process often provided an extra gift of making parents co-conspirators.

- **Instant Cellular Phone Calls:** (See the story of Avi, above.)

- **Situation Letters:** These are just like postcards, but longer. Several examples are included at the end of the chapter.

Regular, Periodic Communication

- **Periodic Letters:** A lot of teachers write letters home two to ten times a year. Sometimes these letters are just an "update," sometimes they are the sharing (or the clarifying) of expectations, sometimes they are a sharing of resources. Ironically, day schools and once-a-month schools (opposite ends of the time spectrum) are the most frequent practitioners of these letters. (A number are in the collection at the end of this chapter)

- **Classroom Newsletter:** These tend to come from day school classrooms because of the time commitment, and are also, often, a way of sharing student work as well as teacher work.

- **Regular Phone Calls:** This one is easy—(I've [Joel] just never done it)—let your fingers do the walking. (I also don't know anyone who does do this—though I know a number of schools who suggest/urge/insist that their teachers do this.) My own experience is with absence phone calls. They are something that I always resist (because of the embarrassment of interrupting a household at whatever, but that has usually been rewarding). Even with a successful track record at this process, I still find myself avoiding the "cold call." Print works much better for me—even though I love talking on the telephone. Alan Rowe, another Torah Aura Productions partner, suggests that if you time it right, you can talk only to answering machines. Despite my cynicism, this might be your best way. Here is one more truth: The later in the year it gets, the more I consider the "target" parents people I actually know, the easier and the more rewarding calling becomes.

And here is yet one more truth. The real purpose and the real advantage of "phone calls" is not talking but listening. Verily, the more you have had the opportunity to listen, the more the experience is to be praised.

> **[Cherie Koller-Fox's Comment]:** The idea of regular phone calls is commendable, but at Eitz Chayim, we've mandated a mid-year phone call. We've asked our teachers to time their calls and on the average they are ten minutes long. They come immediately after the mid-year report card and are a good way for us to learn things that people thought were too insignificant to bring to our attention on their own. We answer their questions and listen to their concerns. The teacher lets the parent know if he/she has concerns about the child. They dialogue and problem solve together. Each teacher fills out a written response sheet chronicling the conversation and from that I know which parents I need to call directly. (See the "forms" in the appendix to this chapter.)

- **Creative Use of Report Cards:** Less and less are "Jewish" report cards about grades. That went as the rise of GTHBA (see chapter one if you've forgotten) came into Jewish education. With the de-escalation of grades, we lost one "controlling factor" and gained an opportunity as a trade. Today, there are two report card trends: less or more. In the less report card (practice by most public schools), report cards are reduced to letters, numbers, check off boxes and stock phrases. In a certain sense, to "protect the school" and to minimize teacher burdens, the least possible information is communicated.

  The other alternative is using a report card as an extended and personal communication with each child or family. (Included at the back is the first semester report Joel wrote for Avi of the cellular phone story.)

- **Surveys and Focus Groups (the Fantasy Advisory Panel):** We don't know any classroom teachers who have actualized this fantasy formally, but we like the idea. Marketing people have learned that the act of asking for feedback is always a way of investing people in the product. Therefore, sending home surveys on various past and future activities should (in theory) be a great way of involving parents. All the more so, inviting them to participate in an advisory board (which meets) or a focus group should generate amazing results.

Enrichment Communication

- **Discussion starters:** "Ask Me About...." Some parents actually want to know what their kids are learning in Hebrew school. Some parents want better questions than "What did you learn in school today." Therefore, some teachers provide parents with content summaries and/or specific questions like: "Tell me the story of the Rabbi who told the family to bring a cow into the house."

- **Questions for Family Discussion Built Around Curricular Goals:** These are resources which extend the classroom to the dining table, rather than "interviews" which drill and extend a single child's lesson. This is when you can invite the whole family to wonder: "Does God actually ever give us the things we ask for in our prayers?"

- **Holiday Resource Kits:** Many schools prepare (or purchase) resource booklets for families—especially for the holidays. These contain table services, customs, sukkah blueprints, recipes, read-aloud stories—all kinds of stuff which empower and enable families to live the life the school is teaching about. We particularly like the attitude of Edith Feingold, a teacher in Atlanta, who said in one of our workshops, "I get to families via their stomachs. I am always sending recipes home, especially for the holidays." The same could easily be said of stories, texts, etc.

F2F (Face to Face Stuff)

- **Carpool Confabs:** Ron has already suggested that it is a good idea to welcome families on the way in. Joel favors working the pick-up line. Joel's practice is to always walk out the door with his students, hang around talking to them and their parents, and then go back into the room to gather his things and pack up. He says it serves two purposes: "First are the snatches of conversation I pick up. (See the letter to Bruce in the back of the chapter.) Second, when parents are late picking up kids, the ten minutes of waiting is often good bonding time with a child." Harlene Appelman teaches that some of a parent's best conversations with their children take place when the parent is driving a single child somewhere. Both the shared space and the limited time frame make the conversation possible. Waiting with a single kid, or one carpool's worth, is the same kind of moment for a teacher. Plus, parents who know that you have waited often appreciate the gesture. It is a way of putting money in the bank.

[Joel's Story]: One day when I was teaching the Adam and Eve story, my eighth grade class asked a whole bunch of "sex" questions fairly seriously. Why does Judaism allow you to have sex only when you are most likely to get pregnant? How come guys in the Bible could have more than one wife? (As if it was theology.) Did you know there were gays in the Israeli military? And Avi (whom you've already met) asked about Judaism's view of oral sex. Rather than use the cell phone, I answered the questions—teaching all the right texts. It needs to be pointed out that this was a small branch (only 15 or so kids) and I knew every family, every parent—well. At this branch, we were the only ones there on Wednesday nights, so parents regularly held "a tail gate party" while they waited for their kids. I walked out with my class, saw Daniel's mother, and said, "Guess what we got to study about today." Daniel was shocked. He said, "You can't talk about that stuff with my Mother." She said, "Why not?" I said, "If you are here, she knows about it." It was a good class; it was a great half-hour discussion with five or six families in the parking lot. One can only imagine the rides home!

- **Go to Shul:** If you want to get to know the families in your class, if you want to be a real person (not just a "teacher"), go to shul. Special events like picnics and Purim are important—regular Shabbat services are more impressive. You won't see everyone, but you will connect with the core families—which in turn often gives you a lot of access to the others.

    [RISA GRUBERGER'S COMMENT]: When I taught 7th grade it was a monthly chore (but one worth all the effort) to send home testimonials from the kids. Instead of sending home my letter describing what we had studied, through testimonials, the students were the tellers of what went on in class. All comments went home. Caution: Make sure to send at least one comment from each child throughout the year. Parents will eagerly await the comment from their child. This is nothing sophisticated, rather a new and different type of letter for parents to receive. I believe parents are interested in what kids have to say.

A COLLECTION OF SCHOOL-HOME COMMUNICATION PIECES

Here is a classic—institutional—"You were absent" postcard from our collection. We include it in the "better than nothing" category. On the positive side it (1) notes the absence, (2) makes a statement, and (3) invites the parent to respond. On the other side, it feels like one of those postcards you fill out at the dentist so they can bug you in six months or a year. Ask yourself two questions: "What do parents feel like the third time they get this card?" And, "How could we do better?"

Date _____

We have missed _____ from Religious School on _____. We are very concerned when one of our students is "missing" for any period of time and would appreciate your letting us know what's happening and how much longer (we hope not at all) your child will be absent. Repeated absences disrupt the educational experience for your child. Please contact the teacher so that work missed can be made up. We hope there is no long-term health problem which is preventing attendance. If there is, the teacher will be happy to send home some assignments so your child can still participate in learning and in the class.

If there is some other problem which is causing the absences, please contact me so we can talk and, hopefully, resolve your difficulty. We appreciate your help in the process of providing a good Jewish education for your child.

Shalom!

Here are four "forms" from the Minneapolis Jewish Day School, shared by Nachama Skolnik Moskowitz. While we've only recorded the text here, each of these comes with a cute drawing. Each one uses up 1/4 of a page of 8.5" x 11" paper:

Minneapolis Jewish Day School

Mensch Memo: It is with great pride that I tell you your child did the following wonderful deed:

_____

_____

_____

Signed _____

Date _____

I'm proud too!
Parent signature _____

WOW! This is a great piece of work because....

_____

_____

MAZEL TOV!

I saw my child's great work!

Signed _____

OOPS! This work is not up to the standards we expect at MJDS. Please take some extra time and:

____ Redo your work neatly
____ Check spelling
____ Check for punctuation
____ Check for capitals
____ Redo the incorrect answers
____ Put more thought into your answers

Thank you for taking the time to do your best!

Signature _____

Date _____

I checked my child's corrections.
Parent Signature _____

Help Wanted! Your child could use some extra assistance with:

_____

Could you please help out by

_____

Thanks! Please sign and return this note indicating you're aware of this request. If you have questions please call me! I'll keep you informed of your child's progress!

_____ Date _____

I read this request for help and I will do my best.

Parent signature _____

This form, also from MJDS, was set up for a teacher to fill in and then photocopy for the entire class:

Shabbat Schmooze:

Sent each Friday:

This week in school we... _____

_____

Be sure to ask your child..._____

_____

General information: _____

_____

Sometimes schools have cultures which encourage parent-classroom cooperation. Terry Kalet, Director of Education at Temple B'nai Torah School in Seattle, WA, sent us this wonderful collection of things. Alone, each is impressive. As a school portfolio, amazing.

TEMPLE B'NAI TORAH SCHOOL GESHER PROGRAM

It should never be "too late" to begin a Jewish education. For some families the beginning of a Jewish Education has been delayed. For these families, there is a risk that they will never begin due to the difficulty in catching up and feeling like they are not a part of the life of the community. To overcome this barrier, we have implemented a program that includes parents and students learning together.

The *Gesher* (bridges) program at Temple B'nai Torah takes students entering school after 4th grade with no or little religious education and enables students to cross the bridge from their point of entry into the Temple B'nai Torah School curriculum. This includes areas of prayer skills, synagogue skills, comfort with Jewish identity, knowledge content in areas of *Humash, Tanakh,* Shabbat, holidays, rituals, life cycle, history, ethics, mitzvot and Hebrew.

During our Sunday School program parents attend a two hour class with their students throughout the year. This class covers *Alef* and *Bet* Level Hebrew in the first hour and Judaic Studies in the second hour. After a short lunch break, students attend regular Judaic classes based on their public school grade level. For parents wishing to continue studying, they join an adult education class during the time when their children are in the Judaic classes.

Parent participation in learning has been critically important in successfully integrating late starting students into school. Students tell me they appreciate having their parents with them to feel at home in a new school, and help them with their Hebrew homework. Students especially enjoy seeing their parents struggle to learn Hebrew along with them. Discussions that begin in class continue at home and result in a fuller participation in Jewish learning.

This program has also assisted parents in getting to know other families in the congregation and becoming an active part of the community. Parents tell me they wish Hebrew school has been this much fun when they were young.

Terry Kalet, Director of Education, Temple B'nai Torah School

Dear 6A Students and Parents,

It's difficult dealing with the Holocaust, but we've begun our study in the best possible environment: a classroom full of interested and caring learners. I sincerely appreciate the privilege of learning with your children. I believe parents need to know what's going on, too. Under our "Class Goals" section of our notebook so far we've written: "I want to know why I should study the Holocaust." The answers will be forthcoming all year. Please be sure to write in a second goal before the next Sunday: "I want to know what the lessons of the Holocaust are."

One lesson we started studying last Sunday is that each one of us must be responsible for one another. We need to remember that this is a Jewish value. Ask your child about Cain and Abel and the famous "Am I my brother's keeper?" in Bereshit, the first Torah portion. Look together at the *Haftorah Bereshit* to see Isaiah's vision of the Jewish people's purpose of being a "light of the nations." (It's our homework to understand it.)

I came face-to-face with the importance of this Jewish value in a diary entry preserved in *Through Our Eyes: Children Witness the Holocaust* by Itzhak Tatelbaum:

I ask you not to forget the deceased. I beg and implore you to avenge our blood, to take vengeance upon the ruthless criminals whose cruel hand has deprived us of our very lives. I ask you to build a memorial in our names, a monument reaching up to the heavens, that the entire world might see. Not a monument of marble or stone, but one of good deeds, for I believe with full and perfect faith that only such a monument can promise you and your children a better future.

I am seeking your cooperation in helping your child to focus on some projects that will allow him/her to work on building such a memorial of good deeds or "mitzvot." The mitzvot would really be personalized tzedakah (justice) and gemilut hasadim, deeds of lovingkindness. They would give your child an opportunity to do something positive and focused as a result of our study of the Holocaust. The following are only some possible suggestions for projects; you and your child may think of others that would work better. The important thing is to do something. I am not setting any minimum standards; you and your child know your own time and energy levels best. These Mitzvot projects will be ongoing though we will periodically call for reports. We will have such a meaningful Yom ha-Shoah (Holocaust Remembrance Day) at the end of this year!

Project 1: Befriending a new student or someone who seems to be alone whom you encounter on a regular basis. This means more than just saying "Hi." (Last Sunday almost everyone said he/she had felt like an outsider at a new school. This is a chance to make a difference for that new person.)

Project 2: Standing up for an issue. This means speaking up or writing your opinion if you strongly believe something is right or wrong. (We will be discussing the tragedy of remaining silent while six million died in the Holocaust.)

Project 3: Involving a non-Jewish friend(s) in celebrating Hanukkah or any Jewish holiday. (Some students also said they felt like outsiders at Christmas time.)

Project 4: Buying Trees for Israel. (Later this year we will learn about the important of the formation of the State of Israel for Holocaust survivors and for all Jews who are oppressed.) This Sunday I will pass out Blue Boxes from Jewish National Fund. The traditional time to drop coins in is just before lighting candles on Friday night, but anytime is fine. We will all bring our Blue Boxes Friday night, January 13, 1995, our 6th grade Shabbat, as it is just a week before Tu B'Shevat, the Birthday of the Trees. A tree costs $10.00.

Project 5: Fighting hunger. (I know the students were all moved seeing the pictures of children and adults starving in the ghettos and the concentration camps.) People are still starving today. Perhaps your child could pledge a part of his/her allowance or earn some extra money for this project. MAZON is the Jewish response to hunger. Or, your child might want to donate food to Jewish Family Service or the charity of his/her choice.

Project 6: Fighting disease. (Very soon we will hear about the terrible diseases the Jews suffered from in the Holocaust.) Children's Hospital has a Thrift Shop in the Overlake area that accepts clothes and toys in good condition; all proceeds go to the Hospital. I will also be getting patterns for making finger puppets for the patients who have their fingers pricked for blood samples; these puppets actually make the small children feel better faster. There are also "Hero" badges to make. Or your child may have his/her own "cause."

Project 7: Caring for those less fortunate. I am interested in having each of our 5 table clusters "adopt" a family for Hanukkah through the Jewish Family Service Hanukkah Tzedakah Project. We will talk about this in class on Sunday as Hanukkah is next month.

Once again, these are voluntary projects and these are only my suggestions. I'm very interested in hearing your ideas. Thank you for taking the time to help your child grow more and more into a "mensch."

Sincerely yours, Ettie Davis

P.S. Please bring this letter Sunday. We will punch holes and keep it under "Projects."

Here is the actual classroom newsletter.

2nd GRADE SCHMOOZE

An Update

We're almost finished with *Bereshit* (Genesis) in our "Torah and You" book. When school resumes on January 9, we will review the rest of the Jacob stories. Please ask your children sometime during the break if they have read through the story called "Esau Forgives Jacob," which is on pages 60-61.

I think the answer from most of the children will be, "Yes, I read that ages ago." What a smart, enthusiastic bunch of Second Graders we have!

We're a little behind on our paper Torah, which is the beautiful review project we do every few weeks in class. For every story in our book, we will have a giant picture to illustrate what we have learned. You'll see our Torahs in progress at the class Shabbat on January 8.

The finished Torahs will be used as scenery for our puppet show, which is tentatively scheduled for March 13. Our puppets have painted heads (except for a few that need to be painted by the students who were absent on painting day).

The next steps in the puppet-making process are gluing on hair and making clothes. Thanks to parental donations and leftovers from last year, we have plenty of yarn for hair and fabric, too. I'll call the sewing volunteers soon.

PLEASE JOIN US JAN. 8 FOR 2ND GRADE SHABBAT

Saturday, Jan. 8, is Temple B'nai Torah's Second Grade Shabbat. It will be quite an exciting religious experience this year, as we have the largest Second Grade in Temple history.

That means there won't be a lot of room for individual contributions to the service. We plan to have ALL the children upon on the bima at the same time to sing a few Shabbat songs they have learned in music class with Morah Marla. I think music is one of the favorite parts of school for my students, so it should be a beautiful service.

This also will be an opportunity for all Second Grade students and parents to meet each other for the first time. I hope you'll plan to bring your entire family to Shabbat morning services and a lovely Oneg Shabbat afterward.

Please try to bring your children to Temple by 10:00 a.m. for a short rehearsal before services begin at 10:30 a.m.

Tzedakah Update

Both my morning and afternoon classes have voted about where to send their tzedakah money. The discussion before the vote was lively and intelligent. I think the students learned a lot about informed giving.

The morning class (2AX) has decided to send all their tzedakah to the Temple B'nai Torah building fund. The afternoon class (2BX) is sending its tzedakah to the Kline Galland Home and the World Wildlife Fund.

Isn't it interesting that neither class stuck to the suggestion list when they made their decisions?

Tu B'Shevat

Tu B'Shevat, the birthday of trees, falls on Jan. 27 this year. To commemorate the holiday in school, we will be studying about Tu B'Shevat traditions, one of which is the planting of trees in Israel.

The Department of Education of the Jewish National Fund is distributing a series of educational materials for the holiday and the inevitable tree order forms. Students will be encouraged, but not forced of course, to plant trees in Israel. Last year I think it cost about $10 to plant a tree. I expect the price to go up this year.

As you may remember from your days in Sunday School, tree certificates make nice birthday presents for grandparents or mother's day and father's day gifts. When I went to Israel in 1978 with the NFTY Summer in Israel program, I planted a JNF tree myself. That was one of the exciting moments of my trip. Any one who asks can see a picture of their then 17-year-old teacher planting a tree.

Our book called, "My Jewish Year," has a short chapter on Tu B'Shevat that you may find interesting. This can become a fun family holiday, by doing an environmental mitzvah project or planning a Tu B'Shevat seder.

OUR 15 MINUTES OF FAME

One of our students won The Jewish Transcript's Kids Color Hanukkah drawing contest. Rebecca Miller, who is in the afternoon session, will be rewarded by the newspaper with a giant chocolate chip cookie. Several other students had their drawings reproduced in the newspaper (Zoe Davis and Jessica Stein of the afternoon session and Rachel Dedrickson of the morning session) and many children got their names in the newspaper.

I'll reproduce some of the pictures here. If you didn't get a chance to see the actual paper, please call and I'll try to get you a copy.

CALL THE TEACHER: MORAH DONNA

If you would like to talk to me for any reason, you can reach me at my home at XXX-XXXX. Because I work at home as a freelance writer, you can reach me there during the day or evening or leave a message. Parents of students in my morning class should call if they would like to see copies of the first two issues of our newsletter, 2nd grade schmooze. B'Shalom, Donna Gordon Blankinship

Dear Parents:

I wanted to bring you up to date on what we have been studying over the last 2 months. We spent time during December learning about Shabbat: when it's celebrated, how different families observe, and the blessings that are said on Shabbat. We also read some Shabbat stories and made our own Shabbat books. December was the time to get ready for Hanukkah as well. We learned the story with books and the children helped retell it using the flannel board. We made our own menorahs to take home to use (unfortunately the clay was not the right kind and our menorah got a little blackened...next year I'll know better!). We also learned about different customs of Hanukkah; making and eating latkes (the children were wonderful cooks!), playing the dreidel game and identifying the Hebrew letters on the dreidel, and singing Hanukkah songs and blessings.

We started 1994 off by adding a new component to our morning... circle time with the weather, seasons and calendar...all done in Hebrew. The children are used to having circle times in their kindergarten classes and are able to remember the Hebrew words within a familiar context which they seem to enjoy and look forward to. We will be learning songs at this time as well as joining Josee's class for music with Marla on a weekly basis. Ofrah will be teaching Hebrew in our class on a bi-weekly basis, and on the weeks she is unable to be with us we will be working on our personalized Alef-Bet books. Since we only do a few pages at a time, the books will probably not be completed until close to the end of the year.

Our themes for the month of January were Tu B'Shevat and learning about the different prayers and blessings (specifically the Shema and ha-Motzi). The children made their own mezuzot after we discussed the meaning of the Shema and practiced saying it together. We took two weeks to learn about the Arbor Day holiday of Tu B'Shevat; the children came up with many good ideas about things they liked about trees and different ways of taking care of trees and the earth. We made tree mobiles, bird feeders and paintings of trees, planted seeds that they can take care of on their own (I tried so hard to find saplings and unfortunately it's the wrong time of year!), and went on a walk around the school to pick up litter as a way of helping the earth.

Approximately every other week we also study a parashah that the entire school is learning about at the same time. In December we studied the story of Noah and the Ark and in January we discussed the story of Exodus (how the Jews left Egypt to wander in the desert) and also how they received the Ten Commandments.

It is challenging and fun to work with such a lively group of 5-6 year olds and I truly enjoy every Sunday morning. If you have any questions or wish to visit class please don't hesitate to call me or drop in any time (but you will be put to work!).

Shalom, Robin XXX-XXXX

P.S. If your child has a Hebrew name could you please send it with him or her next week? Thanks.

Dear 6th Grade Parents:

Our class is well into the first half of this school year. I am honestly impressed with the cohesiveness of our group and the commitment to Jewish Education and mutual respect that I have witnessed in these first 10 weeks. This letter is an overview of topics and activities covered so far, and **an announcement of future events including the upcoming "Voices..." video and oral presentation December 11th at 11 A.M.**

Topics covered:
Biblical story of Creation, Biblical story of Noah
Spanish Expulsion/Inquisition
Roots and comparative cultures of Ashkenazic and Sephardic Jews
Three movements of Judaism
Jewish laws (Mitzvoth, Belief in God, Study of Torah, Kashrut, Circumcision)
Defining Race, Racism, Discrimination, Stereotyping
Activities:
Music
Art Project (Wall Hangings decorated with symbols of Judaism)
Tzedakah Drive ($10/wk goal. Class chose Nat'l Holocaust Museum. and Local
  Food Bank)
Future Topics, Activities and Events

Topics:
Geographical study of pre-W.W.II Europe
Comparison of Governmental Systems
Racism and Social Action
Historical Overlook of Events leading to Holocaust
Process of Concentrating Jewish Communities in camps

Activities:
Gemilut Hasidim—pet food project for Humane Society of Bellevue.

Upcoming Events:
12/11 "Voices" Holocaust Presentation for Parents and Students 11a-12p
1/13 Shabbat Services featuring participation and art of the 6th grade 8p
1/15 Dor L'Dor intergeneration day for Parents and Students 11a-1p

These 3 events are for Parents as well as Students. I look forward to your participation.

Sincerely, Craig Lini

Laura Harari was the education director of The Jewish Reconstructionist Congregation in Evanston, IL. Once again, she sent us a collection of monthly letters sent home by the cadre of teachers in the school. Once again, a school portfolio is a wondrous thing. The picture of the collective school culture and the unique qualities of individual teachers play off each other and teach much about the nature of schools today (and about how to do really solid communication with families).

Jewish Reconstructionist Congregation

Shalom:

It has been most enjoyable and gratifying for me to see how the children have expressed their thoughts about Mitzvah (Mitzvot). Their pictures regarding this subject are hanging on the second floor! Their exhilaration in making their own Tzedakah boxes was great to observe! I will be giving out Mitzvah Certificates through this month! As we spoke about doing Mitzvot—here are their thoughts:

Reading the Torah—Eric
Singing Jewish songs—Levi
Saying prayers—Josh
Planting trees in Israel—Ayal
Drawing a Menorah and giving it to someone—Kimberly
Giving Tzedakah to people—Maggie
Lighting Shabbat candles—Samara
Going to JRC Sunday School—Stephanie
Making Chanukah presents for someone else—Laura
Putting napkins out for Jewish Holidays—Samantha
Sharing one of my Chanukah presents with a friend—Max
Buying my Dad a present when he was sick—Rachel
Giving my brother a treat when he was sick—Isabel
She comes to JRC Sunday School because she wants to learn about Jewish things—Joanna
She helps mom set the table for Shabbat—Julia
Comes to JRC for services—Eric
She gave a dollar for Tzedakah and that's a lot of money—Alexandra

I hope you get as much nachas (pleasure) out of these as I do! Your children are wonderful!

We saw a movie about Israel with the first grade class—which we enjoyed. We will now proceed with studying about Israel and familiarize ourselves with the Hebrew letters!

March will bring the fun holiday of Purim. On Sunday, March 12 each session will have a Primary Purim Workshop (for students only). Sunday, March 19 will be our annual Purim Carnival—fun, fun! See you all there!

Happy Purim, Elaine Rubinstein

Dear Parents:

During January and February the children have been busy learning the stories of Abraham and Sarah, Isaac and Rebekah, and Jacob, Rachel and Leah. They acted out the stories, discussed their meaning and made beautiful cut-out pictures of their favorite story. The children wrote and attached to their artwork a story describing the event depicted in their scene. Please come upstairs to admire their work which is being displayed on the bulletin board next to our classroom.

The children have also worked hard learning the aleph-bet up to the letter "Ayin!" They now know 22 letters and 10 vowels! They have learned quickly and are almost finished with the entire aleph-bet!

During the next months we have many exciting holidays to celebrate. We will learn about Purim, make Mishloach Manot, noisemakers and our own Megillot. We will also begin learning about Pesach and the parts of the Seder. Following Pesach we will observe Holocaust Memorial Day, celebrate Israel Independence Day and learn about Shavuot.

Shalom,

Ziva Green-Kredow

Dear Parents:

L'Shanah Tovah Tikatevu! I hope you enjoy the New Year card that your child has brought home for you and that you will enjoy even more hearing from him/her about all the exciting and interesting activities that went on in second grade today at JRC.

I plan on writing to you at least once a month in order to give you details on what has been and will be going on in your child's class each week. Please look for all school correspondences in the homework folder that your child will bring back from school every Sunday.

Please see to it that each week's homework assignment is completed and returned by your child the following Sunday in his/her folder so it can be checked. Work that is satisfactorily completed will receive a grade of _____ (tov)—good. Work that is well done and reflects considerable effort by your child will receive a grade of _____ (tov m'od)—very good. Once homework is graded, your child may remove the assignment from the folder and keep it at home.

Each homework assignment will be accompanied by a card from the "Jewish Experiences Together" program. Your entire family will enjoy participating in your child's religious studies by getting involved in the activities described on these cards. After your family has completed a card, please sign it and have your child return it in his/her homework folder.

Please support our weekly classroom collection of Tzedakah. Details on its eventual use will be forthcoming.

Again, I'm looking forward to meeting you and sharing in your child's religious educational experiences this year. If you have any questions, comments, or concerns, please feel free to contact me at (XXX) XXX-XXXX.

Ralph Moses

2nd Grade Teacher/ JRC

Dear Parents:

I would like to take this opportunity to thank you for all of your support in helping us get off to such a great start in second grade this year at JRC.

Our first three weeks of the new school year were spent studying the holidays of Rosh Ha-Shanah, Yom Kippur, Sukkot and Simchat Torah. This month will be devoted to learning about the traditions of Shabbat, the meaning of the Shema, and the significance of the synagogue in our lives.

Other classroom activities will continue to include our introduction to Hebrew, the acting out of Bible stories, class discussions, and art projects.

Our students have been doing an excellent job with their homework assignments so far, and I appreciate your encouragement and commitment in seeing to it that their work is completed and is returned to class the following week. Also, we have gotten a very good initial response to the Jewish Experience Together activity cards, and we hope that all families will be participating in this program very soon.

I realize it is sometimes difficult to get your child to class on time, particularly on Sunday mornings; however, it is absolutely essential that class begins promptly at 9:00 a.m. and 11:15 a.m., due to the very busy class schedule we maintain. Therefore, in the best interest of your child, I ask that you make every effort to have him/her in class on time every Sunday. Thank you so much for your cooperation.

Also, I appreciate those of you who have already introduced Tzedakah into your child's life as an important aspect in understanding that we have a responsibility to help those who are in need to help themselves. Tzedakah is collected in class each week. Please encourage your child to become an active participant in giving Tzedakah in class and throughout his/her life.

I have enjoyed meeting many of you already and I look forward to talking with all parents throughout the school year. As always, if you have any questions, comments, or concerns, please feel free to contact me at (XXX) XXX-XXXX.

Shalom,

Ralph Moses

2nd Grade Teacher

Dear Parents:

School has been in session for four weeks, and for this short time we have managed to go through a substantial amount of material.

The first hour of each class is always dedicated to the Hebrew language. I feel that the beginning of class is the best time to teach new material. We begin with a review on the board of all the letters studied in previous classes consequently adding another new letter or vowel. Until today, we have learned to write in print the following letters: XXXX. At this point we read all possible combinations with the letters and vowels, play games with them and have also been able to learn a few vocabulary words. The class has also used this first hour to read and work in the workbooks.

Regarding the Holidays:

For Rosh Ha-Shanah and Yom Kippur we made our own "Scales of Justice" reflecting our good and not so good deeds from this past year, and also had the chance to create a time capsule including all our different good wishes for the future generations.

For Sukkot: we learned about the four species and had the opportunity to hold and shake the Etrog and Lulav. The students were given work sheets which included material about the holiday. For Simchat Torah, we explained the holiday, and made our own Alef-Bet scrolls with the same type of letters as in the Torah.

In honor of our first three letters—which add up to the word Shabbat, we created a Shabbat table, spoke about the meaning of Shabbat, how it is celebrated, learned the prayers and made our own Shabbat plate.

Through our "I live in Israel" book, the students learned what life is like for young people their age living in various settings in Israel. We have been learning about life in the Kibbutz creating our own Kibbutz in class.

Please feel free to call me with questions or suggestions.

Sincerely,

Dorit Lehavy

Dear Parents:

I would like to share with you what we have been doing in class in the past few weeks, and what we are going to do in the next few weeks.

I. Hebrew

We've finished Lesson 9 in our book and I'm very happy with the children's Hebrew vocabulary. Nearly all members of the class are able to write nice and meaningful Hebrew sentences. I hope that by the spring vacation we will finish our book (through lesson 12) and will have time to review our Hebrew Skills—reading and writing from then through the end of the year. I would like to remind you that every week we have a vocabulary and sentence writing quiz. Please check with your children to be sure they have prepared. Also, I encourage you to ask to see their quizzes and have them share their results with you.

II. Pen pals

In the past month we've received letters from Israeli school children, and each child has received a letter. We asked the children to respond and they wrote beautiful letters. I hope that we will hear back soon from the Israeli children.

III. Torah

We are now learning the Abraham and Sarah stories. I have been emphasizing the covenant that God made with Abraham. I feel that the children are involved with the text. The Abraham and Sarah cycle will continue for the next few weeks.

IV. Purim

The holiday of Purim is approaching. For Purim we will be looking at some aspects of the Megillah and making the connection between these ideas and our everyday lives.

Next week we are looking forward to having Alan Amberg, our drama teacher, do a workshop with our children about Torah stories. Naomi Sondak will be doing an art project with the children.

Happy Purim,

Orna Levinson

Dear Parents:

First of all, I would like to thank all of you for your participation in the recent Family Education program. I hope you enjoyed it.

You child's class is doing great in Hebrew. We have already finished Lesson 9 and have only three more lessons to cover before we finish our Hebrew book. The students still have a weekly quiz and they have been doing very well. We had a test on Lessons 4–8 last week and all the students passed.

In our book *Being Torah*, we covered the story of Noah and the Flood and the covenant between God and Noah. We are now talking about Abram's leaving home. We discussed in class the meaning of leaving home and what are the three items they would take with them if they needed to leave their homes. The students shared very interesting thoughts with the class and it was an enjoyable lesson. We have also learned about Lot leaving. We discussed why he left his uncle Abram and went to live in a different city. This week we started to learn about the covenant between God and Abram. We saw that Abram was very patient with God and he did everything that God told him to do. Now Abram asks God to let him have children and God blessed him and promised Abram that he will have children soon.

I would like to remind you that I will be available for parent teacher conferences on Tuesday, March 7th from 6:15–8:15 p.m. I will be more than happy to meet with you during this time to discuss your child. Please call Ilene Cutler in the school office at (XXX) XXX-XXXX to schedule your conference with me.

I am enclosing recipes for the dishes we served at the Family Education program—Hummus, Malawach (the Yemenite dish) and Baklava. Enjoy!

Sincerely,

Sima Cohen

This page was attached to the previous letter.

HUMMUS (chick-pea Dip)

2 cups canned chick-peas, drained
juice of 2 lemons
1 tsp. salt
1/4 tsp. cumin
3 tbs. pure tahini paste or 1 cup tehina
2 garlic cloves, mashed
2-3 tbs. oil
parsley (for garnish)

Like tehina, hummus was brought to Israel by Jews from Arab countries, though today it is everyone's favorite. It tastes best when eaten with fresh, warm pita bread.

Place all the ingredients in a food processor or blender, mix until chick-peas are smooth. Refrigerate hummus in a covered container. Serve well-chilled, with chopped parsley on top. If desired, reserve 1/4 cup unmashed chick-peas and sprinkle on top. More garlic may be added, if desired. If pita is not available, crackers or thick slices of French or Italian bread may be used.

MALAWACH

4 cups flour
1-1/4 cups water
12 tsp. salt
1 stick margarine
tomato sauce (optional)
sour cream (optional)

Malawach is one of a number of dishes brought to Israel by the Jews from Yemen. The popularity of this versatile dish, which may be served with a variety of fillings and toppings, testifies to the love for Yemenite food which Israelis have acquired.

Mix flour, water, and salt until dough becomes soft. Add more flour if dough is sticky. Cut dough into two sections. Knead and roll each section into a 20x20 inch sheet. Spread margarine on the sheets. Fold each sheet like an envelope with ends meeting at center. Repeat folding process to get two layers of folds. Cover with a paper towel, let sit for 1/2 hour. Cut each sheet into 10 parts. Form each piece of dough to the shape of your frying pan and fry until golden brown on both sides. Serve with tomato sauce or sour cream.

BAKLAVA (Honey and Nut Pastry)

Pastry

1 lb. phyllo pastry sheets
1/2 cup chopped almonds
1-1/2 cups melted sweet butter
Dash of ground clove
5 tbs. sugar
1 tsp. cinnamon
2 cups walnuts, pistachio nuts or hazelnuts, roughly chopped

Syrup

2 cups water
2 cups sugar
1/2 cup honey
3 slices orange and lemon rind
1 cinnamon stick
3 cloves
1 tsp. lemon juice

Baklava is a delicacy found throughout the Arab world. The Jews who came to Israel from Arab countries continue to prepare and enjoy the taste of baklava. This sweet pastry is sold in both Jewish and Arab markets, and comes in a multitude of varieties.

Pastry: Place sheets of phyllo pastry in a 13 x 9 x 2 inch pan, brushing every other sheets evenly with butter. When ten or twelve sheets are in place, combine walnuts, sugar, cinnamon, and clove, and spread 1/3 of this mixture over the sheet. Place another five or six buttered sheets of phyllo on top of nut mixture. Repeat another five or six buttered sheets of phyllo on top of nut mixture. Repeat this process two more times, alternating nut mixture with five or six sheets of buttered phyllo. Preheat oven to 350°. With sharp knife, cut baklava into diamond-shaped pieces. Heat remaining butter (there should be about 1/2 cup) until hot and light brown. Pour evenly over the baklava. Sprinkle a few drops of cold water on top and bake for 30 minutes. Reduce the temperature to 300° and continue to bake for one hour.

Syrup: In a saucepan combine water, sugar, honey, lemon juice, orange and lemon rind, cinnamon stick and cloves. Heat mixture until a drop forms when placed into a cup of cold water, then simmer for an additional 20 minutes. Strain. When the baklava is baked, pour syrup over it. Makes 30-36 pieces.

Dear Fifth Grade Parents:

The year is more than half over and we have covered a nice amount of material. *The Lifecycle Book* has nearly been completed, and we are at about the halfway point in Hebrew and in our Judaica books.

Wonderful discussions have emerged surrounding the Purim holiday and we encourage your children to share with you what they have learned about the holiday.

On the subject of Purim, it was discussed that in addition to the regular Tzedakah (charity) that is given at the beginning of class, we would have a supplemental program. From suggestions by your children, it was decided that we would organize a bake sale to be held during the Purim carnival at JRC. The attached list reflects the TENTATIVE commitments made by your children. Any additions, deletions or questions should be directed to Rosanne or Allan (XXX-XXX-XXXX) and this list is by no means final. Clearly, the parents have the final say in what you feel comfortable (in quantity and in substance) having your children bring.

The children in general have grown and matured considerably this year. This is definitely reflected in the feedback and discussions in class. Overall, we are very proud and pleased with their achievements and efforts.

We look forward to seeing you at the Purim carnival and, as a reminder, Parent-Teacher Conferences will be held on March 5.

Sincerely,

Rosanne Arnet   Allan Arnet

P.S.: Another nice topic for discussion at home would be to talk about the differences among Tzedakah (charity usually involving money), Gemilut Chasadim (acts of loving kindness) and Mitzvah (commandment).

Dear Parents of 6th graders:

November was a busy month for the sixth grade, and I hope you're aware of the progress that the children are making. There was actually one day a couple of weeks ago when all of the students (barring those who were excused for one reason or another) brought in their completed homework. I wish it could happen every week! Even the students who feel put upon by the homework assignments have been coming to me to say the reading is getting easier and taking less time to finish. This delights me, and makes the class a better place for everyone. We can play games to speed up our reading and comprehension, but we don't have to wait painful minutes just to get through single syllables.

Speaking of games, here are some of the ways we have used games to practice Hebrew language skills:

Team games like "Baseball" and reading races (including the malformed horse race called "Dock da soos"—don't forget to ask your child about it) give the kids the opportunity to read quickly and to define the words that they read. There is usually a winning team, and the competition encourages the students to plow through difficulties they might otherwise give up on.

Scavenger hunts through magazines for pictures of study words, and through stories for words and sentences provide active companionable small team activities in which the students work at their own rate to achieve a particular outcome. These also leave tangible evidence of the activity, since when they're finished, the students have created some kind of artistic masterpiece that can be hung on the walls. They're decorative and they help the students to review.

Movement games and activities get us up and moving. Games such as the color search game, in which the students had to find something in the room for each specific color called, and "Cham/Kar" (warmer/cooler) in which students help other students to guess the location of a missing object are invigorating and fun, and provide a really good review, too.

In our history and Judaica sections, we've been studying the effects of assimilation on ancient Judaism, and examining our current traditions for rituals that may have been adopted from other ancient religions. In our discussions about Torah, the arguments always flow fast and furious as the students seek to interpret what they read, and to understand other students' interpretations. One week, we read a book of children's bible stories, and examined the differences between the actual text from the Torah, and the short, easy stories. The students were amazed at how much richness and depth there is in the original stories. I hope you will come to see the pictures they made (hanging up on the southern wall of our classroom) to illustrate the stories we read.

Coming up in the next few months, we'll be donating our dreidel game winnings to the winners' favorite charities, and we'll be writing and rehearsing a Purimspiel to perform both at JRC for the other classes, and for the folks who live at North Shore Hotel. The latter builds community in the classroom, throughout JRC, and in the wider Evanston community, while also giving the children the opportunity to engage in a creative, experiential program which culminates in performance.

As always, if you have any questions and concerns, please feel free to call me at (XXX) XXX-XXXX.

Sincerely,

Claudia A. Shafto

Dear Seventh Grade Parents:

The past few weeks in class we have been concentrating on developing the tools to analyze Jewish prayers and holidays. In class we have been discussing prayer and worship, the different types of prayers and ways of finding relevance in historical events that happened in far off lands long ago.

Based on a matrix that Rabbi Richard Hirsch developed with the students, we have begun to analyze different relationships in prayer. How does the text reflect the different relationship? What makes a prayer special? When do we pray? How do we pray? What do we use to accessorize worship (How does the use of tefillin, tallit and kippah change the way we pray?)?

We have reviewed different prayers to see how they can be categorized. What language makes a prayer a prayer of asking, remembrance, blessing or thanks?

Recently, we have reviewed the history of the holiday of Purim. The class has tried to define what constitutes a minority. What forces act upon members of a minority? How do the actions of individual members of a minority have bearing on the rest of the minority?

As usual, material is presented to the class and is discussed openly. I have tried to develop the tools that each student should use to explore meaning individually.

Over the next few weeks, I would like to work on exploring the various on-line computer services with the class. There are a variety of Jewish forums on both AOL and Compuserve. If any parent has any suggestions on this subject—or would like to join us—please feel free to contact me at home or work.

Please feel free to contact me if you have any questions or comments.

Sincerely,

Vic Levinson

Here are two ongoing parent letters shared with us by Harriet Hunter, Temple Israel Religious School, Westport, CT. Included is a noble attempt to make even the Hebrew curriculum accessible to parents. (We've had discussions among the contributors to this book—each guessing how successful or unsuccessful it was—but the truth is all of us are guessing. And, all of us know that Hebrew is hard.)

Dear Parents:

I've enjoyed meeting you over the last few weeks, and especially seeing your children each Shabbat morning. They are all very sweet and a delightful class. I hope they've enjoyed our Saturday get-togethers as much as I have!

Our Saturday morning schedule typically runs like this:

09:00–09:20	Shabbat greetings
	First activities, i.e., baking holiday goodies, learning a new Hebrew letter
09:20–09:40	Circle Time
	Introduce a new Hebrew letter or Jewish holiday
	Read a story
	Do finger plays or sing a song related to a Jewish theme or holiday
09:45–10:00	Service with the Rabbi and cantor in the sanctuary
10:00–10:15	Kiddush in our room with a Bible story
10:15–10:30	Movement and dance with lots of Hebrew words and Jewish songs
10:30–10:55	Arts & Crafts

I hoped you enjoyed all our high holiday baking and crafts!

Today we played with peanut butter playdough and formed the letter "Aleph." You can make peanut butter playdough at home! It's very easy:

1 cup creamy peanut butter

1 cup light cornstarch

1-1/4 cup powdered milk

1-1/4 cup powered sugar

Mix well. Mold into dough. Add warm water if necessary until pliable yet not sticky. Have fun!

Your child is bringing home the first of our *Aleph-Bet* books. Practice using these words during the week. Soon you'll have a large Hebrew vocabulary.

Here are some other Aleph words we're learning:

Ach	brother
Ah-chote	sister
o-nee-yah	ship
ahv	father
ah-good-dai	thumb
ah-vahz	goose
o-fah-nay-yeem	bicycle

Dear Third Grade Parent,

I have now met with the children six times and can tell that this is going to be a very good year. This is a very alert and keen group of children.

We start each morning in the sanctuary with a service led by either Rabbi Orkand or Rabbi Cohen. This is followed by one of the activities the children enjoy most, Kiddush time, when we take a break, relax and share.

In third grade, we will continue in celebrating the Jewish holidays together and learning about our Jewish world. The children will be introduced to the Torah with stories from Genesis. In addition, a lot of emphasis will be put on acquiring a good basis for Hebrew.

Learning a new language requires regular attendance in class. It is very difficult to read without the full complement of letters and vowels. If your child misses a class, please have him/her call a friend to find out the class and homework, both of which should be made up.

We have music twice a month and periodically art. This year I would like to make our library more accessible to the children. I have arranged with the librarian to have books available in the class for borrowing. This can be done before class begins.

Thank you for your cooperation so far this year, especially for the three-hole puncher, that is helping us be organized. I look forward to meeting each one of you in person.

Shalom Ve Litra'ot, Reilly Coleman

These two kindergarten letters are wonderful examples of how teachers communicate to involve families in the classroom process. They were both actually sent to Ron and Susie Wolfson when their child was a student in Janine Jacob's class at the Abraham Joshua Heschel Day School in Northridge, California. What is interesting is that Kindergarten teachers do this so well—and the older kids get, the less we think it is either necessary or advantageous. Perhaps that is an assumption we should rethink.

Abraham Joshua Heschel Day School

Dear Parent,

We hope you had a wonderful vacation. It's school time again and we have a lot of new and exciting things planned. This folder is filled with things we've been studying and we want to share them with you!

MATH

Least-most, and small-medium-large, are both concepts of ordering. Ordering by size is important for making comparisons and judgments and developing logical patterns. We also introduce words which will expand the child's vocabulary.

Sequencing (Thanksgiving story and alfalfa sprouts) involves interpreting pictures and details. The child cuts out the pictures and puts them in a logical order with a beginning, middle and ending. This also strengthens left to right progression.

Numeral writing (whales and oceans and counting book) requires concentration and time. We are just beginning to work with the children on correct formation of numerals. In addition, these centers further reinforce numeral recognition and one-to-one correspondence.

Patterning can be a complex concept. We have included a shape pattern and a Thanksgiving character pattern. Each strengthens the skills of matching, learning to think ahead and predict, and also develops memory ability.

LANGUAGE ARTS

We are using letters and words every day within the program. We continue to isolate some letters in particular and strengthen consonant recognition and letter/sound relationships. In this folder, you will find Ll for library, and Tt for turkey. As a reinforcement of Bb, Mm, Tt, and Ll, there is a market center with foods beginning with the letters indicated.

The "take me home" with mammals and their homes was designed as a "tracking center." Tracking is following the path indicated. This strengthens a child's eye/hand and fine motor coordination in addition to matching the correct mammal to its home.

SCIENCE

Mammals have taken up much of our science study. The children have observed, asked, answered, researched and enjoyed. They are eager to share their warm-blooded, born alive, hair or fur facts with you. The "color the mammal" was designed as an opportunity for the children to check their knowledge of mammals with nine animals, only five of which are mammals.

Puzzles of the man and/or the dog were part of the study of mammals and were also used to strengthen their matching abilities.

Until the next folder, enjoy-enjoy! Please remember, you are welcome to come in, browse, see what is going on in the "Magic Kingdom" of the Heschel Kindergarten!

See you soon, Kindergarten!

Dear Parent(s),

Here come "the seeds." This is not a new musical group but a small booklet indicating that we kindergarteners are familiar with some of the insides and outsides of what we eat.

Some time back, we cut, felt, smelled, looked at, paper mache'd and, of course, ate many fruits in an effort to conduct seed investigations. (When the mold obscured the identity of said fruits, the investigation ended.)

We played games of "concentration" to further reinforce the names of the fruits in Hebrew. We also found that some peculiar "fruits" are fruits—for instance—green and red pepper, tomatoes and cucumbers and other so called "vegetables" which contain seeds within the edible, fleshy portions. In Hebrew, *peyrote* are fruits and *yirakote* are vegetables... thus: *peyrakote z'raheem* (the "h" is silent) are seeds—the growing kind. We found all shapes and sizes in *avahtiah* (winter melon), *meloon* (melon), *m'lahfeh'fone* (cucumber), *pipel* (pepper—green, red and ground), *tapuah* (apple), and *tapuz* (orange).

Now we know that you would think of using these words to drill your children. We introduce language in a way that insures some success for every child. These words are for you. You can remind your children with phrases like, "How interesting! I didn't know that apple was *tapuah*." Or something like that.

We're also sending home a game that we made to help reinforce the names of people in the family and family pets (not all pets were included—we wanted to restrict the vocabulary).

Both the seed booklet and the *mi babayeet* (who's at home) game utilized phrases which ask questions and phrases which explain answers so that Hebrew language as an expression of simple ideas, is used right from the start. (Lists are good for shopping.)

Question Phrases for *mi babayeet*?

Mi babayeet?

Aba babayeet..................................Dad's in the house

Ima babayeet..................................Mom's in the house

Ah name babayeet..................................Brother name's in the house

Ahote name babayeet..................................Sister name's in the house

Tinoke name babayeet..................................Baby (M) name's in the house

Tinoket <u>name</u> *ba-bayeet*...............Baby (F) <u>name's</u> in the house

kelev ba-bayeet...............a dog's in the house

hatule ba-bayeet...............a cat's in the house

dag or dageem ba-bayeet...............fish are in the house

tziporah ba-bayeet...............a bird is in the house

As each character leaves the house they are *bid "shalom* _____."

The last picture may be: *Mispahah ba-bayeet*—a family is in the house

And finally: *Af ehad ba-bayeet*—no one is in the house

There may be some reluctance to play this game away from the security of the class.

Please be assured that these and other games will be repeated and reintroduced throughout the year. Remember, the primary purpose of language in the kindergarten is ear training. Becoming familiar with sounds when representing ideas. Verbal participation is NOT a primary goal. Some children will try. Some children like to gather a great deal of information before they are willing to risk a syllable.

Enjoyment and feeling comfortable and unpressured are very important for those who are uncomfortable in new situations. So with everybody's help and understanding, we will have started our children along a secure, fun-laden road to Hebrew, the language of the Jewish people.

Love, Kindergarten

> **[Joel's Comment]:** I like this second letter a lot because of its noble failure. Here, the kindergarten team tries to empower parents to help with Hebrew homework. They do it with transliteration (because they suspect that parents will not know Hebrew) but the transliteration fails if you don't already know the Hebrew. It is a noble effort to solve rather than just give up on a difficult problem.

> **[Ron's Comment]:** I don't think that it failed.

> **[Sharon Halper's Comment]:** Always send home Hebrew, transliteration, and translation—to provide multiple points of parent entry. I think the best format is interlinear. (1) Hebrew, (2) Transliteration, (3) Translation. You don't get coherent English, but you get a whole lotta learnin' going on.

The perpetual motion machine, Susan Fish, (who is a wondrous second grade teacher at The Jewish Day School in Seattle) sent us four of her one-page classroom newsletters.

THE DAY SCHOOL DISPATCH
Vol 1 Issue 1 1993-94
WELCOME TO SHALOM TOWN! WELCOME TO 2ND GRADE!

THE DAY SCHOOL DISPATCH is a weekly publication that communicates information across the curriculum, featurs examples of student work, highlights the *"Child of the Week,"* provides opportunities for parent feedback and communication, and allows for upcoming events and classroom needs.

The *SUCCESS* edition and other special editions circulate every other week. The *"Child of the Week"* edition circulates on the opposite weeks. *Tzedakah Times* circulates once a month and highlights the integrated 2nd grade curriculum and its connections to our monthly/daily Tzedakah curriculum. ENJOY!

THE DAY SCHOOL DISPATCH—
SUCCESS EDITION 5754-5755

WORD STUDY

The Power of Light

Sun

Moon

Stars

heat

reflect

candles

electricity

flashlight

oak

wood

Can you add to the list?

RESEARCH

The Power of Light:

- science textbooks
- Chanukah books
- library books
- magazines
- science investigations

RECREATIONAL READING

- Quiet Reading—15-20 minutes
- chapter books
- city kids
- class books
- The Power of Light
- *The Odd Potato*—I.B. Singer, E. Sherman

WRITING

- Source of Light
- Candle Questions
- Chanukah Math Stories

- Latke Recipes
- Science Investigations

CLASSIFIEDS

Thank you to all of our wonderful parent helpers! We couldn't do all we do without you!!

-kippot making

-Thanksgiving with council house

-Q.F.C. and Lake Hills Library trips

-Seattle Jewish Primary school—"The Power of Light" with our 2nd graders as hosts

NEWSBEAT/PARSHA

Today we celebrate "Chanukah—The Power of Light" with the 2nd grade Seattle Jewish Primary School. We invited them to be our guests as we:

- lit the Chanukah candles
- explored eight "light" stations from science investigations, art, math, Hebrew, reading and writing
- ate latkes
- Potato Pancakes All Around
- Uncle Willie In the Soup Kitchen
- Parsha-Miketz
- "Feeding the Hungry"
- Kosher Food Bank

Write an addition to the story about Chanukah. Write a number model. Write a label in the unit.

today is Chanukah. The gusts learn thay brot 20 hanleas 20 mor gusts kam and brot 20 mor hanleys htar or 40 hankays 20 x 20= 40 masha

THE DAY SCHOOL DISPATCH— SPECIAL MATH EDITION

TEKIAH...SHEVARIM...TERUAH...TEKIAH GADOLAH

Usually these notes are sounded from the shofar, but not in 2nd grade! We shared a story called "The Announcing Tool" from Marc Geller's book, *Does God have a Big Toe?* In the story, Enoch searched for the perfect announcing tool for the new year. God suggests certain requirements as to what makes a good announcing tool. We listened for messages about tools and what makes the best tool for the job. We looked at a shofar and made an "Announcing Tool Quilt" which will be on display in our "Hardware Store!"

We then explored the "inside" of the shofar—the sound patterns it creates and the messages it sends through its notes. We also found these notes in patterns built with "tools" of Unifix cubes, links, chips, and color tiles! We used information about patterns, tools, and the shofar! We built in cooperative planning teams using color, size, shape, and imagination as our "blueprints." We recorded our information in our writing journals by drawing, labeling, and writing about our designs. Here are our findings...

Sneakers to Shul is a traditional tale told at Yom Kippur in Kitah Bet. It is the story of a family preparing for the holiday. One of the things they do is prepare their sneakers for shul. The child in the story tries to understand why his parents are doing this. At the end of the story, he understands the message. We shared this story and talked about the tools we need to get ready for Yom Kippur and the new year—ways we want to "hit the mark."

We also played a math game called, "Shoes!" The children took off their shoes and put them in the circle in which we were sitting. We grouped our shoes by tens and ones to find out how many pairs of shoes we had. We then did the same thing on paper with drawings of shoes. The children shared ideas and information about how to solve the problem put before them. We then designed special shoes for Yom Kippur where we included messages we would like God to hear.

The Day School Dispatch comes out once a week. The Tzedakah times is a monthly supplement.

TZEDAKAH TIMES
Kindness, Caring, and King County Humane Society!

Rachamin and Chesed were key words to our visitors from the King County Humane Society. Carol and her very "special guest"—Ginger—talked to us on Monday, October 24 about caring, kindness, and respect for animals. We learned about pet care—grooming, food and water, toys, rest, exercise, homes, and love for our furry (and non-furry) friends. Carol and "Ginger" (a beautiful Lab/Golden Retriever) demonstrated an animal-friendly way to meet and greet someone's pet. She also talked about ways to keep animals healthy and safe with appropriate immunizations, vet visits, and proper identification tags.

We not only had an opportunity to be learners, but teachers as well! We explained the meaning of Chesed and Rachamim, Tzedakah, and mitzvot. We used our Heshvan Tzedakah to purchase dog food and cat food for senior citizens who own pets and may not be able to afford food for the animals. Carol told us that their cupboards at the animal shelter were bare and our pet food would be most welcomed. It was a wonderful way to celebrate "OPERATION: COOPERATION"—2nd grade-style and a great connection to parshiot "Beresheet" and "Noah"—the Creation of the World and our responsibility as HaShem's partners to care for it. She sincerely appreciated the food from our "Pet Food Drive" and was very impressed with the work of the 2nd grade "Mitzvah Monkeys!"

To follow up on our role as pet educators, we are busy planning to welcome guests (1st grade) to our PET SHOW on Friday, October 28. We are getting our pets ready with the information provided from the Humane Society and we are preparing for our guests using the guidelines from last week's Torah portion "Va-yera" which focuses on Avraham and Sara welcoming guests! We learned how to create a poster to advertise, how to prepare refreshments and be a good host and hostess, and how to prepare the room!

The enclosed article is from *MetroWest Jewish News* in New Jersey (Hamorah Sara's subscription)! It highlights some of the same messages our 2nd graders are learning about. Enjoy.

Susan, Sara, and Vered

From Beth Shalom Congregation, Kansas City, MO, courtesy of Patti Kroll

NEWSLETTER of the FAMILY EDUCATION CENTER OF CONSERVATIVE JUDAISM

Sunday, October 31, 1993 *Parashat Ha-Shavuah—Chaya Sarah*

JEWISH VALUE WORD OF THE WEEK

BRIT—Covenant, valuing community; a contract.

WHEN 3 STARS COME OUT

This is just a reminder that if you have not made your reservations for Ohev Sholom's upcoming program on November 6th, it is not too late to call the office (XXX-XXXX) with your family's RSVP. Families will meet at the Jewish Community Campus at 6:00 p.m. and then travel together to Powell Observatory. Don't miss out on this family education program.

MAZEL TOV

Mazel Tov to our upcoming November Family Education Center Bat Mitzvah, Sarah Orlovick, Nov. 27.

3RD & 4th GRADE JR. CHOIR

Everyone is invited to Sunday morning services in the Katz Chapel on November 14th to see the first "public appearance" of our 3rd and 4th Grade Jr. Choir, *Kol Shalom*. They will perform selections from the Hallel service, a joyous service celebrating *Rosh Hodesh Kislev*. Jr. Choir is an integral part of our 3rd and 4th Grade fine arts program. Students in these grades meet with Cantor Barash each Sunday from 11:30 until noon to learn new material and to rehearse. Watch this newsletter for announcements on other upcoming performances. If you have not turned in your RSVP yet for the Jr. Choir family breakfast on the 14th, call Jill in the office.

BETH SHALOM SISTERHOOD NEWS

Sisterhood invites you to join them for a cooking demonstration by Patti Shapiro of Bagel & Bagel on November 16th at 12:15 p.m. at Beth Shalom. The cost is $5 and includes lunch, the demonstration, and babysitting. Reservations are required—call Sunni at XXX-XXXX or Hannah at XXX-XXXX.

6TH GRADE HAPPENINGS

Mrs. Cohen & Mrs. Shalinsky's sixth graders (those not participating in the current B'nai Mitzvah Seminar) capped off their study of *tzedakah* this morning with a visit/work session at St. Mary's Food Kitchen. Students helped to prepare and serve lunch to the homeless community of Kansas City. Last

week's *tzedakah* project was one bene-
fiting the synagogue. *Yasher Koach* to
the participants.

SCHOOL CALENDAR

Sun. Nov. 7   8th grade has class

Fr. Nov. 12-13   9th Grade Shabbaton

Sun. Nov. 14   Jr. Choir Hillel
                        performance

                        8:00 a.m.-Katz Chapel
                        Jr. Choir/Family
                        breakfast

                        9:00 a.m.-Commons Room
                        10th Grade has class

9TH GRADE SHABBATON

Don't forget—your permission slips and
money are due into the Education
Center office by November 7th for the
9th Grade Shabbaton which will take
place on November 12-13 at the B'nai
Jehudah Retreat Site. If you need a new
form, please call the Education Center
office. Remember, this is a required part
of the 9th Grade curriculum.

K-2ND GRADE FAMILY PROGRAM

On Sunday morning, November 21, families and students in Grades K-2 at the
Hyman Brand Hebrew Academy and
the Family Education Center have been
invited to participate in our first
Family Education Program of the 1993-
94 school year. Age-appropriate activities focusing on Jewish Book Month
will be led by Fran Wolf, Marlene Katz,

Linda Salvay, Larina Gebhard and Rosa
Fish. Please see the attached flyer to
make your reservations and arrange
for baby-sitting for younger siblings.

EDUCATOR'S CORNER

On Shabbat and holidays, it is traditional to eat braided loaves of bread called
hallah which means sanctified dough,
and refers specifically to the bread
from which the dough has been separated. In the Torah, there is a mitzvah
that the rosh (head) of the dough be
separated and given to the Priests.
Today, we symbolically fulfill this mitzvah by removing from the dough a
small piece, about the size of an olive
and burning it in the oven before baking the rest. There is a special blessing
which we say when separating the hallah.

Two whole hallot are used, which correspond to "remember" and "keep" the
Sabbath day, and as a reminder of the
double portion of the Mannah which
was provided for us in the desert for the
Sabbath (Exodus 16:22-26). The loaves
are covered because the Mannah was
covered by the dew (Exodus 16:13-14),
and because we recite kiddush first and
it is not right that the bread be exposed
when it is not being used, and not
rejected in favor of the wine. This is a
Jewish idea of extending the concept of
fairness, and might be a topic of discussion for you and your children. (More
on hallah next week.)

From Ron's Collection of Classroom Samples:

What's Happening?

Shalom Parents:

Here are some ideas for enrichment activities that you and your child might enjoy this coming month:

1. The synagogue is sponsoring a Purim carnival on Sunday, March 7, from 1:00-5:00 p.m. Fun for all!

2. On Monday evening, March 15, on KCET, Channel 28, at 7:00 p.m., a special documentary on Israel will be televised. Watch it together and discuss.

3. The children's Symphony presents a concert of classical music on Sunday afternoon, March 21, at the City Auditorium. Tickets available at the Auditorium box office for the 1:00 p.m. concert.

4. Have you seen *"Raiders of the Lost Ark?"* Take your upper elementary kids and older (there are some horrific effects too intense for little ones). After the movie, look up the description of the real Holy Ark in Exodus, Chapter 25. Or, using the *Encyclopedia Judaica*, find out what you can about the ark. The film is now showing at the Plaza Four Theater.

Enjoy! Ron Wolfson

The Harvard Hillel Children's School Phone Call:

I: Introduction: You Clearly State Your Name And Purpose Of CALL

Introduce yourself. I am (name of student)'s Hebrew, Bible, or Projects teacher, at the Harvard Hillel Children's School, Nina Glassman.

Instead of a written midyear report card, we are calling each of our students' homes to tell you how he/she is doing in school and to hear from you how you and Plonit FEEL that the year is going. (If there are two parents, ask if the other one would like to get on the phone as well.)

Are there any problems?

Do you have any concerns?

II. Academic progress and report of subject matter studied

(This is meant to be as positive as possible.)

In the past few months in my class, _____ has been studying about (here give a summary of the subject matter. In Projects, please refer to the specific ones that they have done so far.)

Academically in my class, _____ seems particularly to be (e.g. improving his/her Hebrew reading, enjoying working on her Golda Meir project, participating in our discussions about creation, etc.)

Do you have any suggestions or questions about what we are teaching in class?

Do you have any questions or concerns about her progress in Hebrew, Bible or projects? (Name other two teachers.) I have spoken to them both and they have told me that _____ is (basically doing well in each of these areas, or doing about the same in those areas as in the area I can speak to you most directly about since I am the teacher.) I can ask one or both of her other two teachers to give you a call. Who would you like to call you?

III. Social Progress

(This is meant to be as positive as possible.)

Socially, _____ seems to be making (or has some or many) friends here. He/She and _____ like to spend time together in school. Would it be possible for them to spend some time together outside of school? It seems to help them feel more connected to the school if a personal friendship is developed.

IV. YOUR CONCERNS

* We have been a little concerned because _____

Examples:

- has been coming very late
- has missed a number of classes
- seems to hesitate to participate in class discussions
- seems to ask a lot of questions about _____
- seems to have trouble concentrating on a class discussion
- has trouble finishing his/her work
- is not doing homework regularly

* If a child is having a behavior or serious academic problem please consult Cherie BEFORE the phone call.

** IF there are two asterisks before a child's name, please tell the parent that we would appreciate

- a conference at 1:00 on a Sunday. What dates would be convenient for them? Or they could suggest an alternative time. Conferences will be without the student.

- Can you give me any ideas why this might be happening or how to handle it? Does _____ have similar problems in other settings?

IV. CHERIE CAN FOLLOW UP

Cherie wanted me to ask you whether you have any concerns relating to your child's progress or about your family's participation in the community.

Cherie would be happy to give you a call to discuss these concerns. Would you like me to ask her to call you?

REPLY FORM FOR MIDDLE SCHOOL

You can use the back—write legibly!

TEACHER:_____

NAME OF STUDENT: _____

PHONE NUMBER:_____

Please call people by their last names unless you are on a first-name basis with them.

With whom did you speak?
q Mother   q Father

How long was the phone call?_____

Did the parents express any concern about what the children were learning in school? If so, what?

_____

_____

Did the parents seem to know generally what is being taught in your class, or did the information you gave them seem new to them?

_____

_____

Did you offer any negative comments about the child, either academically or socially? If so, explain what and say how the parents reacted or what follow-up you suggested.

_____

_____

Do the parents seem, on the whole,
q satisfied? q dissatisfied?

What kind of concerns did they express?

_____

_____

Did the parents express any feelings of isolation from the community for themselves or their children? Did they talk about not having met other people, or not knowing the names of the other children or parents?

_____

_____

Did the parents express any positive feelings of being part of the community, such as liking Adult Ed or Family Events?

_____

_____

Did the parents want Cherie to call?
q Yes q No

Why?_____

Do you think Cherie should call this family? q Yes q No

Why?_____

From Joel's Collection of His Teacher Letters

Even though I now use postcards a lot, these "letters" were banged out on my office computer the next day; that is why I can call them up.

Dear Jim and Barbara:

On Tuesday, Kent entered my pantheon of folk heroes.

It was the end of our pizza party for finishing a Torah chapter. The kids were sitting around and shmoosing—and the conversation turned to that great twelve-year-old topic: "Who are you going to invite to your Bar Mitzvah?" This of course gave students a chance to make a point to carefully list who was not going to be invited. It was prime meanness.

Just before I stopped the conversation, Kent broke in. He said, "I am going to invite the whole class to my Bar Mitzvah." When someone meanly asked, "Even the two Shanes?" Kent didn't miss a beat, with a sneer worthy of Clint Eastwood, he shot back: "Of course, more gifts." It stopped the put-downs cold—and he walked away with all his cool intact. I was really impressed. Good values. Good skills.

I am looking forward to seeing you on October 21st.

L'hit, GRIS

cc: Kent

Dear Jon and Susan,

Today, Ben somehow lost his Jewish star during class. That will clearly be his major memory of the day. I'm sorry it happened. I don't have any major insights into the process since Ben was relatively stationary the entire day.

However, I do want to share with you one of my major memories of the day. We had a two-part quiz on the first two verses in the book of Genesis—material we had studied the week before. I had the class read the material from Torah script (without vowels) for the first time. Ben did a really excellent job. Given my work with the class last year, I was surprised by the progress. It was really nice. Please feel free to share this note with him.

L'Shanah Tovah, Joel Lurie Grishaver

I sent this letter the week after Bruce's conversion. His son BJ was a 12-year-old at the time. And in an informal way, this was my welcome to a new investment in Jewish parenting.

Dear Bruce,

After Hebrew school on Sunday I was out in front of the Temple and did some eavesdropping. I heard you and BJ do the usual father-and-son routine about "How was Hebrew School?" Abbott and Costello were the ones who invented it originally, but they found that "Who's on first?" was funnier than "Boring" and "Nothing."

I want you to know that (1) you did a good job in trying to pry information about class out of BJ, and that (2) even though it is ritually required that he fail to acknowledge anything significant, the interest you demonstrated will make a difference in his motivation—even if he will never admit it. Thanks.

By the way, half the day was devoted to mastering the Hebrew in the first paragraph in the Torah. To the best of my knowledge, it was the first time this class actually experienced understanding something in Hebrew. Most of the class was actually able to work out their own translation for the first five sentences in the Bible without any dictionaries or worklists, etc. I think that's pretty exciting.

In the second hour, we started talking about how Israeli geography has influenced Israeli history, but got sidetracked into talking about the Dead Sea Scrolls, Carbon 14 dating, and the Shroud of Turin. All in all, it was an interesting O.K. day.

Thanks for the interest you showed.

L'Shanah Tovah, GRIS

Avi's First Semester Report Card

The year Joel only taught thirty students, he took a lot of time to write personal report cards to each. Because they were Hebrew High School students, the cards were addressed to the kids, though the school addressed the envelopes to the parents. (When he taught lower grades, the same kind of report was written directly to parents.)

Three pieces of "back story" to understand this card. (1) Avi's father was a Jew by choice who was related to Thomas Jefferson. (2) Daniel, another student, was a direct descendent of Rashi (the French Biblical commentator). (3) Every time Joel mentioned Rashi, Daniel would affirm his lineage, then Avi, with a smile, would point out his connection to Thomas Jefferson. This became a classroom ritual.

Dear Avi,

Technically, your grade is an incomplete—but I can say a lot in this letter, and then let you complete the academic process later. Let's start with a story. There was one night when the two of us were at the *shul* a good half-hour before anyone else. You were shooting hoops. I joined you. I think I missed every shot for fifteen minutes while you had a pretty good shooting average. We didn't say a word to each other. You never threw me a ball. We didn't communicate at all. (But you didn't make fun of me at all, either.) We tolerated each other being there—and it was okay. The funny part I can't explain is that there was something warm in sharing the time—despite the complete lack of communication. I think our classroom experience is a lot like that.

You are smart. Your Hebrew is good. You've scored well on each and every academic piece—yet you seem to float outside the active class. I know you hear most everything. I know you do well when called on. I know you understand most of it—but I have this unrealistic fantasy about your taking a more aggressive role as "learner" rather than as "student"—as a seeker of knowledge rather than of "correct answers."

Now let's talk about behavior. I know that I am the last hour. I know you "cool it" most of the time. I know we understand each other—but I need you to make it through more of those last fifteen minutes.

Finally, I love having Thomas Jefferson in my room every week. I appreciate your conjuring him. Having Rashi on one shoulder and Tom on the other has enriched my life. Thank you. I look forward to seeing you and old Tom and your complete midterm in January.

L'hit.

GRIS

[Cherie Koller-Fox's Comment]: These letters to parents are all sweet and informative. I saw a commercial from the phone company a few months ago that caught my attention. It was selling voice-mail. It suggested that each day the teacher record a message with the homework assignment and a little tid-bit about what happened in class that day. It takes the teacher less than five minutes to do—if parents called in to listen it would be great. Maybe the same thing could be done on e-mail or on a system that broadcasts a message to everyone's answering machine.

Jane Golub, Tifereth Jacob, Manhattan Beach

The culture of Torah Aura is that just about everyone who works in our shop teaches. Jane Golub, one of our founding partners, holds the company record for most years of regular teaching while trying to run a business. She is a coauthor of Being Torah *and many of our other publications and brings her "classroom eyes" to bear on everything we produce. She is a master and beloved teacher who—like most long-term teachers—has her own collection of tricks. Every two weeks Jane sends home an agenda that outlines material to be covered, homework assignments and special events. Here is an example.*

BET CLASS: Sunday, October 22-Sunday, October 29, 1995

SUNDAY, OCTOBER 22

Torah	Noah, Part 1: Introducing Noah *Being Torah*—pages 38-41 *Being Torah Student Commentary*—pages 15-17
Hebrew	*Ot la-Ba'Ot*, Book 3, pages 9-14 New Letter—ה, New Words—הַבְדָלָה, הַגָּדָה
Homework	Hebrew Reading #7. Due 10/29

WEDNESDAY, OCTOBER 25

Torah	Noah, Part 2: The Flood *Being Torah*—pages 43-47 *Being Torah Student Commentary*—pages 18-19
Hebrew	*Ot la-Ba'Ot*, Book 3, pages 15-20 New Letter—ר, New Vowels—רָ, רֶ New Words—רֹאשׁ הַשָּׁנָה, רִמּוֹנִים, רִמְבָּם
Homework	*Being Torah*, page 48—Cubit Department. Due 10/29

SUNDAY, OCTOBER 29

Torah	Noah, Part 3: After the Flood *Being Torah*—pages 49-54 *Being Torah Student Commentary*—pages 20-21
Hebrew	*Ot la-Ba'Ot*, Book 3, pages 21-24 New Letter—כּ **Party Time!**

THE SPECIAL NEEDS CODA

The CAJE Explosion

[Joel's Story]: This "coda" exploded in my face at the 1995 CAJE conference in Amherst, MA. Often failures are great learning opportunities. I was doing the **"Jewish Parents"** workshop and we were having fun. Actually we had just gotten past the "Family Homework" blow-up which is chronicled in the next chapter when I opened this box and it exploded in my face.

I said, "It is good to send a letter home at the beginning of the year to establish a relationship with kids and their families." One participant stood up and said, "I have a Down syndrome child and I refuse to tell the school about his condition." She went off for a while about their letters and forms and how they confuse a "condition" with a "special need." (*Remember: "Yesterday's language can be today's offense"—I almost got lynched in St. Paul this year for saying "Special Needs Kids" instead of "Children with Special Needs" because they are not problems inside of children, but children with challenges!!!!*) Finally she concluded, "I don't trust the teacher to have this information—it will influence the way they will treat him." I wanted to say, "What, do you expect them not to notice?" But, I never had the chance. The room exploded. Of the 80 or 90 people in there, 20 or so must have told stories about how teachers mistreated their child with a special need.

What freaked me out completely were two things. First, was the number of parents with these issues. Second, was the fact that a room full of teachers and educators were complaining about the way teachers and educators treated their kids—and each stating they do not trust teachers. When teachers fail to trust other teachers to work fairly and effectively with their children—what does this tell us about the mass of "civilian" parents out there?

Three lessons became instantly clear. (1) Teachers need to work on **credibility** with parents and children. (2) We in Jewish education have to begin to take special needs far more seriously, and (3) Jewish family education needs to take into consideration families with special needs members. This book is about the first. That day has generated a Torah Aura Productions interest in the second (and a book in progress and this coda), and the work that Whizin hopes to do in the future will begin to address the third.

> **[Michelle Stansbury's Comment]:** Credibility is the key to being trusted and respected by parents and kids alike. Saying what you mean, and doing what you say you're going to do will reduce or eliminate issues like favoritism, and inconsistency.

Here is the bottom line—then the rest of this coda follows. **In public education, IEP or ILP (Individualized Educational Plan or Individualized Learning Program) are the hottest and latest jargon and truth.**

It references a number of insights:

- All learners have different learning strengths and weaknesses and teacher sensitivity to them can create environments and processes which maximally enable student success.

    [Michelle Stansbury's Comment]: Teachers need to teach students via their strengths and then use this teaching to strengthen the weaknesses.

- Inclusion is "in." More and more students with special needs now "belong" in "ordinary" classrooms. This creates some positive opportunities and some real challenges.

- ADD and ADHD are the *"syndromes du jour."* We are seeing (according to some studies) upwards of 30 percent of student populations with these "designer labels." Some of our schools have reported close to 50 percent of their students in some grades are receiving Ritalin (and four or five other stimulants). According to the experts (a) some of this is real ADD and real need, (b) some of this is pseudo-ADD and a quick chemical cover-up for a more complicated problem, and (c) the whole culture is ADD-o-genic, reinforcing short attention spans and high anxiety. Who are we to judge each case?

- Dealing with more and more of our students requires greater collaboration with parents— when they often trust us less—and when we often fear their placing greater and greater demands on us. (For the untrained, underpaid, two-hour-a-week teacher to face six different individual learning programs is a real nightmare—and it is a nightmare we really face!)

Being a teacher today means working with parents (and often with therapists and doctors) in order to create a learning environment resulting in the greatest possible success for each student. In that universe, clear, caring and open communication with parents is critical—it is the life-line.

AND THE CAVEAT: Until you have "money in the bank" they are usually not going to trust you—and they are usually not going to take the first step. More and more schools are going to have to find ways of asking each parent, "Help us to maximize your child's success by partnering with us—helping us to learn your child's needs and desires." This is new ground which must be broken soon.

The ADD Forum from the TAP-BB

After CAJE, Joel and the Torah Aura staff, the Torah Aura gantze mispahah and dinner companions, along with Deena Bloomstone, a San Antonio principal and the 1995-1996 editor of the **Torah Aura Bulletin Board,** *had a series of discussions of the "blow-up" over special needs at that CAJE module. It resulted in a two-month discussion in the Torah Aura Bulletin Board and on the Torah Aura Cyber Circle (list). Here are some excerpts from that conversation. Family based conclusions will be found at the end. Meanwhile, enjoy this jumpy—ADD-like—collection of reflections about ADD. It will provide some context to this conversation.*

BUT DO NOT THINK that all special needs are "ADD" and do not think that everyone with "ADD" has a big special need!

Why are we seeing more of these children? Didn't we all have special needs when we were in school? Do we now define different learning styles as special needs? How much of the difficulties these children experience is caused by ineffective parenting, e.g., no boundary setting, etc.? How can we differentiate between "real" special needs and the regular special needs? And, what about the "Ritalin Kids?" Are we raising an entire generation of druggies?

Now for an answer to the question about what we do. A number of years ago, we tried a special Hebrew class for certain learning disabled kids—there seemed to be a high percentage of them in one age group. On Sundays, in the Religious School they were integrated into the regular class. Despite the increased learning that took place for those kids, some of them felt stigmatized and never became socially connected to their peers. Currently, and only in the Hebrew program, we use post-Bar- or Bat-Mitzvah teacher aides to work with two or three students for 10 or 15 minutes at a time, mixing special kids with regular learners, or just to sit during the class with a child who needs help focusing. As a last resort, we encourage private tutoring for children who are becoming totally frustrated (and frustrating) in the classroom. **Joan Carr, Director of Education, Congregation Sha'aray Shalom, Hingham, MA. <Dcjpcarr@aol.com>**

Yes, we are seeing more children with special needs, but I've always tried to individualize my program as much as possible, so in a way it doesn't matter. On the other hand, I do wish parents were more forthcoming about their supplemental school children with special needs. There's so little time, and I want any advance help I can get! **Jessie Kerr-Whitt, <Kerrwhitt@aol.com>**

I've been reviewing the health and personal concerns of the students enrolled in school. There are 23 known students whose parents listed them as ADD or ADHD on our registration form. Of those known students, only four were listed as taking Ritalin, and only one of those parents noted that her child is not on Ritalin during the weekend. I know my students. I know I can at least double the figure of 23 students who are ADD or ADHD for the school. I also know that I can easily quadruple the number of students who are taking Ritalin at least during the week. How to get parents to share information about their children with the school is another article entirely. Knowing that there are at least two children per class who are diagnosed ADD or ADHD leads me to two immediate concerns: (1) How do we teach these children in a personally meaningful manner so that they are on a par with the rest of the class? And (2) What do I do to train the faculty so they can work effectively with these students?

Karen Traeger, Director of the Jewish Education Department in Dallas, has helped me deal with my two concerns. She has taught me to teach different learning styles (visual, auditory, kinetic/kinesthetic). Every student has a preferred learning style. Our challenge as teachers is to make sure that our teaching involves those different styles. If we vary our teaching strategies so they incorporate different styles, we reach a greater number of students, whatever their situation. Over the next few weeks, as the faculty learns who their students are, they will find me sending them a variety of information about learning styles as well as explanations of ADD and ADHD. Empowering the teachers with knowledge about their students will help them meet their challenge to teach.

The faculty and I met after school this week to discuss our students and how best to reach them. We will shortly have an in-service session on these things called ADD, ADHD and Ritalin. With the help of the parents, we are learning to distinguish behavioral problems from learning challenges. Parental help has been made possible by a number of phone calls home asking parents about their children and why they do or don't do thus and such. What is fascinating about these phone calls is that parents have provided us with some very insightful information about how to work with their children, none of which was ever written on the registration form or told to us directly. Parents have shared what their children's secular school teachers are doing with them in class and I know we can adopt many of these strategies. I know as the faculty continues to get to know who the students are and which ways they learn best, we will be successful. Our first problem is ignorance. Having found a way to get parents to share information about their children through these phone calls, we can now work on the child in the classroom: moving his seat closer to the front, encouraging oral reports rather than written, giving certain children longer amounts of time to deal with an issue, having a child work one on one with a teaching assistant are just some of what we can do. **Deena Bloomstone**

The kids on Ritalin or with so-called ADD—are these the same kids that can be found sitting in front of the TV for 3 or 4 hours at a time, mesmerized by the action taking place? Are these the same kids that go to a movie and when you ask them about it, can repeat almost line-by-line the action which took place in the movie? I bet they are! I've had some long talks with my daughter who is worried that her son, my grandson, might be ADD, but, when she sees him engrossed in watching TV, or telling about the action of a movie he just saw, she has second thoughts. Instead she makes more demands on him. Instead of TV, she has him spend more time at the school books and she even sits with him to help him concentrate on the subject at hand. Remember, she is a single mother and works full time! Where there is a will there is a way. She is determined that her son will not be "labeled" and won't take any "chemicals."

Karen Traeger hit the nail on the head. Children learn in different ways, just as teachers teach in different ways. The most recent material I have read says, "give the students choices of not only what material to cover, but how to cover it, how to display they have learned it." The child will choose the option that lends itself to their way of learning. It is true that I don't work in a classroom anymore, but that doesn't mean things have changed that much. Many times we do not give them credit for the intelligence they really have. Yes, they like to sit in front of the TV, but, if you challenge them, if you give them options, if you identify their learning skills, you will have less and less so-called ADD and ADHD kids in the class. And, of course, somehow we have to reach the parents—and I am not sure how that can be done. **Shirley Barish, <BarishS@aol.com>**

I agree that there are many children with special learning needs in our classes who do not get diagnosed or addressed adequately. However, I strongly believe there is another learning disorder that I never hear about at conferences or read in special education articles, "Motivational Disorder." This seems to especially affect Hebrew school kids. They are quite capable of learning if they want to, but, they often don't. If they are turned on by an exciting teacher, activity, trip or program, they may do very well, but generally they show little interest, often arrive late, are weak in several skill areas and even have other physical problems on Sunday mornings and Hebrew school afternoons (stomachaches, headaches, blurry vision, etc.) This disorder may be genetic. Often the same children have parents who hated Hebrew school (and often tell their kids that), never attend services, other than Hanukkah and Passover, do nothing Jewish in the home and often give the children mixed messages about Hebrew School: You can miss today because you are going to a ball game or birthday party; we are only sending you so you can have a Bar Mitzvah; or, I don't believe in the religious stuff your mother (or grandfather or whoever) cares about. Is there a prescription like Ritalin that will fix this motivational disorder? If you know of one please share the info! **Cantor Sheldon Levin: <slevin@mciunix.mciu.k12.pa.us>**

> **[Michelle Stansbury's Comment]:** Presenters at several ADD/ADHD workshops I have attended have stated that learning another language is very difficult for people who have ADD/ADHD. Maybe some of the behaviors that accompany Hebrew school students with ADD/ADHD are motivated by avoidance of the task rather than random acts of disruption or inability to attend.

I have been following the discussion on ADD, ADHD and Ritalin with growing concern. As an educator, I have seen too many children put on medication as a first, rather than last option. However, as a parent of an ADHD child, I feel that you need to hear the other side.

My son, Kenny, is an extremely bright child, a talented artist in the making, who has an outrageous sense of humor. When the chemicals in his brain that control impulsivity are produced in the right amounts throughout the day, Kenny is sweet, gentle, loving, attentive, cooperative, motivated, excited to learn, focused, etc. Unfortunately, Kenny's brain does not produce the necessary chemicals in the right amounts throughout the day without the assistance of medication. Without medication, Kenny cannot control his impulses. He cannot stop himself acting before thinking. Once he gets started, he cannot get a grip. He gets into fights, is belligerent, and spends significant time visiting the school principal. Yes, Kenny loves to watch TV and movies. Who can blame him, after working so hard all day at school to keep it together? He also loves to read, draw, play games, work on the computer, and engage his parents in interesting conversations. Most of us are particularly sensitive to the needs of our special students, but few of us understand the needs of their parents. How can one understand the blame parents assume, the doubting of their parenting abilities, and the embarrassment parents suffer when their child has an episode in public unless one is that parent?

My husband and I agonized over the decision to medicate our child. We first engaged in family counseling for one-and-a-half years, trying to deal with Kenny's problems behaviorally. Although we all made great strides, it became evident that Kenny's difficulties stem from a chemical deficiency and imbalance. We could no longer bear to watch our precious child suffer. Our choice was clear. Kenny still has difficulties. We are still working to find the right medication and the right dosage for Kenny. We are still working with the therapist to help Kenny learn coping strategies and to help us learn how to be the best parents for Kenny.

Our story is a deeply personal one. So is the story of each and every one of your families who has a child suffering from ADD or ADHD. Rather than blaming the parent for not giving their child quality time, or condemning the parents who label their child with the purpose of getting that child the help he/she needs, try understanding the needs of those parents. There is a tremendous amount of pain, embarrassment, guilt and hard work associated with ADD/ADHD. We need your understanding, your patience and most of all, your compassion. What we do **not** need is your judgment. **Lisa Goldstein, Director of Education, Congregation Solel, Highland Park, IL.**

"Many adult drug addicts report having been put on Ritalin as youngsters. Does this mean that Ritalin predisposed them to later addiction? Does it mean that hyperactive or attention deficit disorder kids are prone to addictive disorders? Is the problem psychobiological or are these children children who "hear a different drummer" from the attentive "good" children who sit and listen?"

There are many opinions as there are questions. Research is mixed in this area. We are not really sure of the long-term effects of this drug on children and their behavioral and psychological development. Many of the clients at *Gateways Beit T'Shuvah* used Ritalin as children and grew up to be addicted to speed and/or heroin. While I can understand using speed, the use of heroin surprises me. Ritalin is a form of speed or amphetamine so the continued use of it is understandable. Does this mean that Ritalin causes people to go to drugs? The answer may be yes—when it is prescribed in error. The fact that many heroin users were treated with Ritalin is a puzzle. Heroin is a depressant and the recommended drug for ADD or ADHD is amphetamines. I believe many children were misdiagnosed. In our need to put labels and fix everything for our children, we may be acting prematurely.

The largest challenge ahead of us is to do long-term studies. Manage the use of Ritalin and therapy for the child and family very closely and not label our children because they are different. I believe while there are many children (and adults) who suffer from this illness, there is also a great deal of misdiagnosis happening because doctors and therapists and parents need labels and cures. **Harriet Rossetto, licensed clinical social worker and Director of Gateways Beit T'Shuvah, a Jewish recovery house.**

My name is Dan Nussbaum. I am a developmental pediatrician. My wife, Alice, is a Judaic needlework designer and the director of the Educational Resource Center at the Bureau of Jewish Education here in Rochester. The fact that many adult substance abusers were treated with Ritalin as children can be interpreted many ways. The obvious interpretation is that Ritalin leads to substance abuse. Another one is that most children with behavior problems wind up being treated with Ritalin eventually and many adult drug abusers start out with behavior problems, so naturally one would see a high correlation between adult drug abuse and early Ritalin usage. Remember, correlation does not prove cause and effect.

Yet another interpretation is that adult substance abuse could be a form of attempted self medication, because the abuser realizes he has a problem that requires medication but does not know what to use or how to obtain it. An item pointing to this third interpretation is the following: Researchers in Detroit are now successfully using Ritalin to treat adult substance abusers (Schubiner et al., J. Clin Psych, 56; 4, 146-150). Most of these abusers were never exposed to Ritalin previously. The whole question of the relationship between neurochemistry, medications, drugs and behavior is unresolved. The easiest way to solve the immediate question we are discussing would be to take two groups of children with behavior problems. Put one group on stimulant medication, keep one off, and follow them for twenty years. For good measure and scientific accuracy, one should probably take a group of normal children and put them on stimulant medication also and follow. However, there are practical and ethical problems with such a study. Until someone comes up with an adequate research paradigm and does the study, those of us in the trenches will have to plod along doing the best we can and not listen to the scaremongers led by the Church of Scientology. Should people involved in Torah education be listening to them anyway? **Daniel Nussbaum II, MD, FAAP, Developmental Pediatrician, Oak Orchard Community Health Center, Brockport, New York.**

In many ways, if we focused less on textbook learning and more on experiential programming, it would be a great deal easier to teach all children. Hands-on projects, cooperative learning, allowing children to choose a modality to work with to demonstrate their skills and knowledge gained, and presenting information in a variety of ways all assist our learners in their efforts to achieve success.

Gardner's theory of multiple intelligences (linguistic, logical-mathematical, spatial, musical, bodily-kinesthetic, interpersonal and intrapersonal) builds upon what we, as special educators, have been taught for years. People learn in different ways, and to best meet their needs, material needs to be presented in different ways.

So, don't "ditch" the textbooks, but provide greatly expanded teachers' guides with activities that lend themselves to the above. Create, if possible, kits with hands-on activities—learning centers beyond the *Ha-motzi Kit*. Provide suggestions for specific music teachers can access—and tell them where to access it! When teaching Torah, though you want to get into personalizing the material, provide multiple access points. Suggest teachers offer a variety of entry activities—some kids could be using math skills to determine ages and timelines of events as they read, others could be looking for family conflicts as they role-play in small groups, some could be learning appropriate music to present to the class, etc.

Our teachers are too busy, too poorly paid, and not necessarily skilled enough to create these options on their own. They need to be handed the ideas and the resources to make it work. As to children with multiple and more severe disabilities, if you have multiple *madrikhim*, have them work within classrooms. Supporting children as needed will go a long way, and that is also where serious discussions with the child's family and public school teachers will help prevent the "reinventing the wheel" syndrome. **Deena Bloomstone**

It is a wonderful thing that we are seeing more children who have disabilities in our Religious School and Hebrew classes. In the past, the majority of Jewish parents kept these children out of Hebrew schools because they didn't want people to know that their child had a "problem" or they felt that a religious or Hebrew education would be too much for their child to handle. With increased awareness of and sensitivity to special needs, we now see more of these children in Hebrew and Religious schools. This is a great victory, but it presents us with a great challenge. As has been mentioned, parents can be a great resource in recommending strategies for children with special needs. There is a wealth of resources available in our own Jewish communities! Since 1987, there has been an annual colloquium of the "Consortium of Special Educators in Central Agencies for Jewish Education." This consortium was founded by Sara R. Simon, Director, Special Needs Dept., BJE of Greater Washington; Rabbi Martin Schloss, now Director of School Services, BJE of Greater New York; and Caren Levine, Coordinator, Central Agency Services and Networks, JESNA. The members of this consortium are the directors of special education departments or services in Bureaus or Boards of Jewish Education across the country. Formal special education services are available through many BJE offices throughout North America. A call to a BJE would verify whether they have a special education department and would connect teachers to JEWISH special education resources in the areas of ADD as well as other disabilities. In addition, there is a national group called Ch.A.D.D. (children and adults with attention deficit disorder.) There are chapters in many cities, and they publish wonderful materials for teachers and parents. They also have support groups, educational programs, doctor referral services, and much, much more. I'd be happy to give you more information. I can be reached at the Bureau of Jewish Education, 639 14th Ave. San Francisco,

CA 94118. Tel. (415) 751-6983 ext 122. My e-mail (at home) is kupfermn@ix.netcom.com. **Flora Kupferman, Special Education Consultant at the Bureau of Jewish Education.**

Also available: *"How Difficult Can This Be?"*—a 70-minute video produced by PBS, is an excellent introduction to learning disabilities for teachers, parents and administrators. As stated by the producers, "This informative and entertaining film allows the viewer to look at the world through the eyes of a learning disabled child. It features a unique workshop attended by parents, educators, psychologists and social workers. They participate in a series of classroom activities that cause frustration, anxiety and tension... emotions all too familiar to the student with a learning disability. Following the workshop, the participants enter a lively discussion of topics ranging from school/home communication, sibling relationships and social skills." An excellent teaching guide (including reproducible handouts for parents and teachers) is included as well as guidelines for conducting a discussion after the movie. For information call PBS: 1-800-424-7963. It may also be available at local libraries. **<MARGOLD2@aol.com>**

The last issue of TAP-BB gave me a lot to think about. The issues presented to us by children diagnosed as ADD or ADHD are complex. They cannot be reduced to poor parenting or low motivation. I spoke with Cherie Weiss, a counseling supervisor for one of the school districts in San Antonio. Cherie explains that people often want to categorize children by their abilities and inabilities. Many people prefer to believe in the brat hypothesis. And many, who accept the idea of a chemical imbalance, have legitimate issues about putting children on medications such as Ritalin. Is it not our responsibility as educators to find the methods to work with these children on their terms? I asked Cherie about the television phenomenon, why these children who can't stay seated in a classroom, can sit and stare at a television for hours. Cherie explained that when a child sits in front of a television at home, the interaction is one-on-one and the distractions of the family television room are minimal. The same is true for a child's ability to sit before a computer, to read a book, or other one-on-one activities. Put that same child in front of a television in a classroom, and that child will act differently, stimulated by the other activities or people found in that classroom. When Shirley spoke of her grandson's ability to sit with his mother and work, her example demonstrates that with less distractions, working one-on-one, a child with ADD or ADHD can function normally. Ritalin and medications like it, are not the only solution for all. When parents make the decision not to medicate, or to medicate only on weekdays, we need to respect that decision, whether we agree or not. As educators, we need to know more about what affects our students. We need to learn more about the teaching techniques that have been successful in secular education with this population. We need to become partners with the parents of our students, for they often can tell us what works with their children. We also need to be there for the parents, helping them with the issues they confront.

Hawthorne Educational Services, Inc., is a publishing company devoted to education and intervention of learning challenges such as ADD, ADHD, learning disabilities, giftedness and so on. It is an invaluable resource for those wishing further information about ADD and ADHD, publishing books for educators as well as parents. If you would like a copy of their catalogue, you can contact Hawthorne Educational Services by calling 1-800-542-1673 or fax them at 1-800-542-1673. **Deena Bloomstone**.

At CAJE three summers ago (San Antonio), there was a four-hour session on Learning Disabilities, the goal of which was to try to give the participants (Hebrew School/Day School Teachers/Administrators—and one lawyer) an idea of what it would be like—and what it would feel like—to be LD. Among the things they did:

- They strictly enforced otherwise simple rules that they hadn't told us about, or that they had told us about differently from the way they were being enforced or that others of them had told us differently.

- They quizzed us about otherwise simple material they had covered "last time."

- They made us read flash cards really fast—even though some of the letters had been substituted with other symbols. Like c&t for cat, only the words were longer. Or where the p's, q's, b's and d's were all mixed up.

- They made us read paragraphs really fast—without using our fingers as pointers—where the above "stick and bump" letters were mixed up, where all the writing was mirror writing, and where the letters were mixed up *and* there was mirror writing.

- Then they gave us otherwise simple *reading comprehension* questions *about* the paragraphs—when we had spent all our concentration just decoding the words.

- They had us copy simple geometrical diagrams while looking only in a mirror.

- They had us follow otherwise simple directions given to us through headphones—with some words indistinct, others coming into only one ear or the other, different words coming into each ear at the same time or other distractions/interferences.

Oh Yes. I nearly forgot…

- They *berated* us for not trying hard enough, paying attention, studying hard enough, caring, etc. and *threatened* us with the dire consequences of telling our parents (again), tossing us out of class (again), not getting into college, etc.

The reaction of the "class" was amazing. Some (like guess who?) got real competitive about the challenge, buckled down and tried to figure out systems to deal with the problem. Others tried and gave up. Others made jokes or otherwise became behavior problems. Others ganged up on the ones (guess who?) who were able to figure out more answers than they were.

But it was demoralizing and demeaning for all of us. Even the ones (guess who?) who got pretty good at "reading" mirror written paragraphs with letters mixed up got a flat 1 or 2 out of 10 on basic comprehension questions like how many characters there were in the paragraph or even the simplest questions about what happened. At the end of the session, my thumbs were both raw from where I had picked at hangnails from the tension.

In the evaluation afterward, they told us that people like me (who had figured out compensatory systems to try to deal with the situation) were the *most* at risk—because sooner or later all systems would inevitably fail. But ours would fail later than those of others. Others would be identified earlier and have a better chance of receiving help. We might not be noticed until later when it would be much harder to intervene. **David Parker <Parques@aol.com>**

ON THE ROAD, DENVER: Two things. First, working for Stan Beiner's central agency is Linda Forest <jsfamf@aol.com> who does special needs work for the community. Here are two lessons she had figured out that I had to learn. (a) Support coffee for parents of special needs' children. (b) A "sibs'"club for siblings of kids with special needs. In special needs, like so much else, the whole family needs treatment. She will be sharing this work with us later in the year. Dan Bennett, principal at Congregation Emanuel, set up a dinner for me and some of his faculty to talk ADD/ADHD. Here are two smart things he did: (a) Invited Linda and an amazing woman named Michelle Stansbury, who is a public school special needs consultant, to join us. (b) Invited the director of Camp Sweider (whose business card I have lost so I can't drop the name), because he handles the same kids under very different conditions. Together, teachers, informal educators, consultants and I ate greasy appetizers and shared feelings, experiences, stories about our kids and classrooms, and tricks of the trade. It was a conversation all needed and none of us had ever had before. There is a lesson here, I think. **<gris@torahaura.com>**

PARENTS WANTED: *"Parents of children of all ages accepted—kids may even be grown! Attempting to raise children in a Jewish environment—all levels of spirituality accepted. Willing to listen patiently; able to share innermost feelings; can laugh hard and cry just as powerfully. Should be an active thinker; able to offer suggestions; knows when there are no suggestions to offer; must be comfortable with a warm hug; experience helpful, but not necessary; on-site training provided."*

"Education: Masters in rushing out the door with only the most essential tasks completed; Ph.D in negotiating; R.N.(M.D. strongly suggested!); Advanced degrees in Physical, Occupational and Speech Therapy; J.D. specializing in taking on the system! Teaching certificates in all subjects; weight training—in many cases, parent must be able to bench press 150 lbs of uncooperative weight and equipment; Dietician's license; juggling class strongly suggested; must be willing to take crash course in any and every new situation that may arise where expertise is needed (could be daily!)."

So should read a "want ad" for new participants in "Kibbitz, Kvell and Coffee," a parents' coffee klatch that meets once a month in Denver. At first it appears that no one could meet the above requirements, but the parents in the group find themselves using many of these skills. They are the parents of children with disabilities! They are strong individuals. They have to be. They have learned to be.

They keep most of their extraordinary talents hidden from view to the general public, and function just like the parents of typical children do. They work, drive carpools, cook, clean, make minor and monumental decisions for their children in the blink of an eye. Just when life seems to be running smoothly, they slam into a situation that requires them to find a phone booth, and quickly change costumes. In goes plain parent, out steps "SUPER PARENT": advocate, rescuer, purveyor of peace, shield against evil, and all around great person! They may have to play this role for only seconds, or it may last for days and weeks. At some point the unrest settles enough for them to change back into their original role, and they trudge bravely on, with their fear hidden just beneath their "plain parent" clothes, just above their hearts.

And so it goes for a couple dozen "plain parents" (if they only knew) in Denver. They get together once a month for "Kibbitz, Kvell and Coffee," a program sponsored by the Special Education Department of the Denver Central Agency for Jewish Education. They "kibbitz" with other parents who experience this unique metamorphosis daily, "kvell" in their children's triumphs as well as their own, and listen, cheer, and encourage each other on.

The mission of the Special Education Department at Denver CAJE goes beyond educating children and adults with special needs; it also includes providing resources and support for their families. The Special Education Office of CAJE has set as one of its goals to develop a cooperative effort between families and the agency. As Linda Forrest, Coordinator of the Special Education Department says, "we need to focus in on the parents of these children. When they approach educators, they are often defensive—looking to do battle to protect their child. We need to enlist these parents, focus on their strengths and support them." Through programs such as "Kibbitz, Kvell and Coffee," "JUST US" sibling support club, family holiday get-togethers, and parent education forums, families can feel a connection not only with their own synagogue but also with other Jewish families with similar needs. "These are not forums for kvetching, and kvetching does not take place. We work to foster a positive outlook, and our programs are seen by parents and children as a positive place to be. Kibbitz, Kvell and Coffee is a program in which parents get together to share, network and mentor each other. It is not a support group, but much more—a havurah in which participants share common concerns and common life situations."

To find out more information on, "Kibbitz, Kvell and Coffee," and other programs offered through the Special Education Department of Denver CAJE, contact Linda Forrest, CAJE Special Education Coordinator, **(303) 321-3191, E-mail: <LFORREST1@aol.com>**; or **Shelley Siegel, "Kibbitz, Kvell and Coffee" volunteer parent coordinator at (303) 220-9743.**

ON THE ROAD, HINGHAM: A pediatrician taught me that Ritalin makes everyone who takes it feel smart, not just ADD kids. **<Gris@TorahAura.Com>**

That's an interesting note about Ritalin. There were kids in my high school who took Ritalin without having to. It made them more alert, and they said they felt smarter. Strange. **<Jeremy Wilgus, 19>**

Your learning in Hingham, Mass. is true but one of the downfalls of this medication is age. Because everyone reacts in a more focused manner, therefore absorbing more of what is going on around him/her, children who are medicated generally have a "positive" reaction. This just confirms everyone's belief that indeed the child has ADD/ADHD and medication is the answer. Unfortunately, most people don't take the time to investigate the underlying issues that could be driving the behaviors that look like ADD because there has been some change in the positive direction. One key question I find people fail to ask in their non-medical diagnosis of children (especially adolescents who all look and act like they're ADD) is whether these behaviors were consistently exhibited at an early age (I believe it's before 8 years old, but I'm not positive). I've had parents tell me that their 13-year-old suddenly developed all of the symptoms and, therefore, their 10-year-old who has just started acting out must be developing the same "disease." Forget the fact that Mom has just started traveling on business and her schedule is out of town for 2 weeks, in town for 1 week. Hopefully, you can share the pediatricians information with people so that educators and parents can make more informed decisions. **Michelle Stansbury <mstansbu@jeffco.k12.co.us>**

FROM DEENA BLOOMSTONE: My friend Cherie Weiss relays the following in regards to teaching students with Attention Deficit Disorder. The most effective treatment of ADD requires full cooperation of teachers and parents working closely with other professionals. In the coordinated effort to ensure success in the lives of children with ADD, the vital importance of the teacher's role cannot be overestimated.

RECOMMENDATIONS FOR THE PROPER LEARNING ENVIRONMENT: [1]
Seat ADD student near teacher's desk, but include as part of regular class seating. [2] Place ADD student up front with his/her back to the rest of the class to keep other students out of view. [3] Surround ADD student with "good role models," preferably students the ADD child views as "significant others." Encourage peer tutoring and cooperative collaborative learning. [4] Avoid distracting stimuli. Try not to place the ADD student near air conditioners, high traffic areas, heaters, doors or windows. [5] ADD children do not handle change well so avoid transitions, physical relocation, changes in schedule, disruptions. [6] Be creative! Produce a "stimuli-reduced study area." Let all students have access to this area so the ADD student will not feel different. [7] Encourage parents to set up appropriate study space at home with routines established as far as set times for study, parental review of completed homework, and periodic notebook and/or book bag organization.

RECOMMENDATIONS FOR GIVING INSTRUCTIONS TO STUDENTS: [1]
Maintain eye contact with the ADD student during verbal instruction. [2] Make directions clear and concise. Be consistent with daily instructions. [3] Simplify complex directions. Avoid multiple commands. [4] Make sure ADD student comprehends before beginning the task. [5] Repeat in a calm, positive manner, if needed. [6] Help ADD child to feel comfortable with seeking assistance (most ADD children won't ask). [7] These children need more help for a longer period of time than the average child. Gradually reduce assistance. [8] Require a daily assignment notebook if neces-

sary. Make sure student correctly writes down all assignments each day. If the student is not capable of this then the teacher should help the student.

RECOMMENDATIONS FOR STUDENTS PERFORMING ASSIGNMENTS: [1] Give out only one task at a time. [2] Monitor frequently. Use supportive attitude. [3] Modify assignments as needed. Develop an individualized educational program. [4] Make sure you are testing knowledge and not attention span. [5] Give extra time for certain tasks. The ADD student may work more slowly. Don't penalize for needed extra time. [6] Keep in mind that ADD children are easily frustrated. Stress, pressure and fatigue can break down the ADD child's self-control and lead to poor behavior.

> **[Michelle Stansbury's Comment]:** I disagree with "Make sure you are testing knowledge and not attention span." As a person who frequently works with students who have ADD/ADHD I believe that we are evaluating both the student's knowledge and their attention span. We often make changes in the student's environment, the task and/or the expectations in order to help him/her be successful. The way the student behaves and "produces" in the classroom is probably as good if not better than the way s/he will function in the real world. We are ultimately preparing them for the real world.

RECOMMENDATIONS FOR SELF-ESTEEM ENHANCEMENT AND BEHAVIOR MODIFICATION: Providing Encouragement: [1] Reward more than you punish in order to build self-esteem. [2] Praise immediately any and all good behavior and performance. [3] Change rewards if not effective in motivating behavioral change. [4] Find ways to encourage the child. [5] Teach the child to reward him/herself. Encourage positive self talk. (i.e., "You did very well remaining in your seat today. How do you feel about that?") This encourages the child to think positively about him/herself.

PROVIDING SUPERVISION AND DISCIPLINE: [1] Remain calm, state infraction of rule, and don't debate or argue with student. [2] Have pre-established consequences for misbehavior. [3] Administer consequences immediately and monitor proper behavior frequently. [4] Enforce rules of the classroom consistently. [5] Discipline should be appropriate to "fit the crime," without harshness. [5] Avoid ridicule and criticism. Remember, ADD children have difficulty staying in control. [6] Avoid publicly reminding students on medication to "take their medicine."

Taken from **The ADD Hyperactivity Handbook for Schools.**

[**Michelle Stansbury's Comment**]: I have found that it helps to change the reward on a regular basis (frequencey will depend upon the age of the student) even if it is successful. Things that are new and different hold the attention of students with ADD/ADHD. It doesn't have to be bigger, just different.

EPILOGUE:

If you made it through the maze of excerpts you'll understand that the present discussion on special needs is both confused and confusing. We have got a lot of work to do, both learning and thinking. Here are the truths at this point in history.

- Families with "special needs" should not and will not go away. Our life will be richer for dealing with them. Successfully including them—as individuals and as families—takes communication and takes preparation.

- The "Denver Lesson" which is a Jewish Family Life Lesson, is important. Parents of kids with special needs, siblings of kids with special needs—have some special needs of their own. These needs are also Jewish opportunities.

- Break-through work on including these families in Jewish family education has to be done—and when you do it, please share—because we need the insights. If you send them to us—they make the next edition.

Chapter 5
FAMILY HOMEWORK

In this chapter we are going to move past communications and family "opportunities" to activities you actually want/expect parents to do:

One of the simplest and most effective things a teacher can do actively to involve parents in the learning process is to create "homework" assignments which actively involve them.

Family homework comes with a number of advantages: Consider family homework assignments because they:

- Create quality "Jewish" time for families.
- Can be the trigger for family rituals.
- Support and reinforce students' Jewish studies.
- Via "Cognitive Dissonance" (the notion that they have already invested the time) bond parents to the education process.
- Vicariously add Judaica to the home under the guise of *"fer der kinder."*
- May actually get homework done.

At the same time, you need to be careful because family homework assignments come with some potential dangers:

- You must not create situations in which parents will fail, or in which parents will be afraid to fail. The age-old "family genealogy" assignment is such a trap for intermarried or families with Jews-by-Choice, etc. Assuming Jewish knowledge or Jewish skills is also a high-risk behavior in most settings.
- There must be a path which allows a child to succeed without the cooperation or involvement of one or both parents.

  [Vicky Kelman's Comment]: Be careful not to send home assignments which assume Jewish knowledge or the ability to read Hebrew.

If such involvement is part of the "expectations" of the class which have been clearly articulated, or even better, discussed and acculturated in a parents meeting, success will be much higher.

[Joel's Story]: This chapter blew up in my face when I taught it at the CAJE Conference during the summer of 1995. It was the second explosion. As soon as I said the words "Family Homework" one father stood up and said, "I hate family homework. It eats up all of our family time. Every teacher gives it (*in public school*) and it seems we never get to do anything else with our kids but their homework."

Before I could say another word, another parent, a mother, stood up and said, "The worst is the math homework which you can never do."

The class was now out of control. I was hosting an anti-family homework riot. The show stopper was the mother who said, "The worst is the drug homework. The school asked me to sit with my sixth grader, tell him every drug I have ever done, and what effect each had on me." With that, the room fell silent.

What I learned that day, and what I told the workshop was: [1] It is clear that family homework has a lot of meaning. For some it is a way of making sure kids do their homework (because parents have to sign off); for others it is a way of providing kids with tutors who reteach the material taught in class, while for others it is a way of creating "sharing" between parents and their children. Each of these has its uses and their abuses. [2] For Jewish schools, family homework is best when it creates moments of sharing and of "handing down" and "handing up" between parents and kids. [3] Even in "sharing" kinds of homework, one needs to be careful that this homework is non-threatening, empowering, and in proper balance. Family Homework should feel like a reward, a privileged moment of quality communication which the school invited.

[P.S.]: *Despite two explosions, it was a great session. The explosions made it. The group went with the interruptive and protesting energy—and then learned from it. Honoring the diverse is an interesting and very Jewish way to teach.*

The Worst (Successful) Family Education Event I Ever Saw

[Joel's Story]: I was once visiting my friend Janice Alper when she was still a school principal. We were going to do some curriculum collaboration. It was Sunday morning, about a half an hour before school. One of her teachers called in sick. That teacher had parents coming. It was that class's family education day. The teacher had left no lesson plan. Janice had to fade back five yards and punt. She turned into a whirlwind of activity. She set up five tables in the social hall. She put a siddur and a Jewish ritual object on each. She pulled out an old ditto with maybe 20 questions on it—and then photocopied the ditto master. (This is an old story.) Only about one parent in three showed up. Janice gave directions. Each team (a parent and three kids), was to complete the questions on the sheet and practice the ritual at each of the five stations. It was out and out one of the worst activities I had ever seen. It was boring. It was mechanical. Nothing significant (other than a few facts) was going to be learned. I waited for the explosion. I was wrong. It was the worst activity—but parents and kids had the best time. GTHBA.

Here is what was happening. The parents were happy. They went into their "help with homework" mode. A requirement for a Jewish parenting license is the skill of sitting over kids while they complete worksheets. Parents liked the fact that they were helping with Jewish learning and were being successful. Kids liked the attention. Rarely do adults pay them that much attention. And everyone had a good time talking to each other about all kinds of things—around the given exercise. I was completely wrong about the day.

This isn't to say that this was an award-winning family learning moment. Just the opposite. What it *does* teach is that parents tend to like helping their kids do their homework—if they can be successful at it.

The "homework mode" gives us leverage into the home.

Kinds of Family Homework

You can ask families to do:

- **Show and Tell:** (The most basic kind of family involvement, whose origins are lost in pre-history.) In the show and tell model, families or children are asked to "bring in" some given object or category of objects from home. They can be given a generic kind of "kindergarten" show and tell task, like bringing some important Jewish object and its story—or it can be course specific: For life cycle have them bring in one invitation to a Jewish event that their family has saved (or received).

- **Family Tzedakah:** (Developed by Joel Lurie Grishaver as part of his 7th grade teaching experiment.) Families were asked to "collect" tzedakah for the class at home, and bring it to school in cash on three set dates. Then, after having researched and presented potential recipients, teams of families followed the "Danny Siegel" model in his essay *The Plain Manila Envelope* and, in a hands-on way, allocated the cash. This made tzedakah a family assignment rather than a classroom task.

> **[Cherie Koller-Fox's Comment]:** Each year our lower school (pre-school-2nd grade students) do home tzedakah projects. It takes some orienting of parents and a lot of nudging to make this happen because people are so busy in their lives. At first parents seem overwhelmed, but when they see what doing this project gives them and their children, they become very enthusiastic, often thanking us for giving them this opportunity to teach their children something that really matters to them. What do they do? They visit the sick, call their grandparents, help their parents around the house. They make money for tzedakah by collecting bottles and cans, selling lemonade, having a bike-a-thon around the block. They buy an extra can in the grocery store, collect clothes and toys and take them to a shelter, and generally participate in the repair of the world. At the end of unit, the parents and kids come together for an honoring assembly where they are recognized for their work.

• **The Parent Interview Form:** (Inspired by a Mother at Temple Menorah, Redondo Beach, CA). Last year at a lecture, a mother handed Joel Grishaver a recipe card for a spinach quiche. On the back were some notes she had made, about the kinds of materials she wanted the school to develop for her so she could more successfully interview her child about what went on in class that day. It included: Ask me about… Discuss with me…. Additional resources…. Extension activities…. It was an invitation to extend the classroom into the home.

• **The Family Project:** (Family projects have been done in many places.) One specific model was developed by Julie Vanek and Rabbi Marc Cutler, Temple Shalom, Newton, MA. They write: "We turned our Social Hall into a "Living Torah" with posters representing each parashah hung around the room. The panels were created by the year's Bar and Bat Mitzvah families as well as by the families studying Torah (using Being Torah) in our Third Grade Family Connection (parent parallel education) class. When the *Hakafot* (Torah Parades) started, the congregation was led into the Social Hall and they paraded around the room in front of the panels. When the music stopped, the families responsible for creating each pane taught the portion to the people standing in front of them. We did this several times so everyone got an opportunity to learn several different portions of Torah."

Similarly: **Pesah Posters** (Sharon Halper and Rabbi Elyse Frishman). Eight days of family activities contained on a colorful laminated refrigerator-sized poster. Each activity builds a contemporary meaning on a Passover tradition and contains questions for family conversations, ideas for social action projects, and other family activities.

• **The Extravaganza:** (In the family education "business" this term is usually applied to the kind of program Harlene Appelman creates. This example, however, was created by Anne Stein, Congregation Etz Chaim, Lombard, IL.) "We made a sukkah on the back of an open trailer U-Haul and sent it around to different neighborhoods. Families signed up to be hosts for a night. The sukkah moved each day to a different home. The whole congregation had a schedule of where it would be each night. Along with the sukkah, we sent a lulav and etrog, along with copies of the various blessings. We draw from a large geographical area so the sukkah-mobile traveled many miles and was visited by over 100 people during the week." Anne & Co., are also working on a "host a Shabbat Dinner kit." Similarly, Sharon Halper has done "create your own Haggadah (then take it home and use it)" programs. Cherie Koller-Fox used to "encourage" at least one family in each class to build a sukkah so each class could have a sukkah.

Rabbi Cherie Koller-Fox believes that homes are the best places to build sukkot. She learned this by accident because for many years her community didn't have a plot of land of their own to build a sukkah on, so they began to build sukkot at people's houses. They build one for every 10-12 families in the congregation. The sukkot belong to the community, not the individual families, and are delivered before Sukkot each year, but the fact of their being built at people's homes makes it feel authentic and important. The children remember building a sukkah with their parents and have warm memories of sitting in the sukkah with their families. Each group decorates the sukkah their own way and they pitch in to buy an etrog and lulav together. The next week they come back to share a meal and a Sukkot Seder together. This does not feel like a class activity even though the teachers are present. It feels like the teacher is a guest and a participant with the families in the building of a sukkah that they will all use.

• **Read something together and discuss it:** Most parents' best "teaching skill" is read-aloud. Most (Jewish) parents figure out a good way to read aloud with their kids and interact with the printed material. We can utilize this a lot of different ways. (1) We can set up book reports which are done by families. (This is the essence of **The Parent/Grandparent Connections** described below). (2) We can send home stories to read and discuss. The Torah Aura Instant Lesson *More than Everywhere* by Bonnie Resnick, follows this model. It is a four-page story about God with discussion questions that follow. (3) Or, we can even grow a whole curriculum based on this model of paired classroom and home reading. The Torah Aura Productions **Building Jewish Life** series, and the Torah Aura Productions **I Can Learn Torah** series are both built around this kind of interaction. **Together,** written by Vicky Kelman and published by the Melton Research Center also represents an exceptional model of inviting parents to read, cook, play, plant, and talk Jewishly with their kids.

• **Have parents "go over" or "monitor" something, just as they would any homework.** Making kids finish homework is the other big parents' teaching technique we can capitalize on. This can be as simple as the "Jet Card Model" where parents sign off (or as Sharon Halper prefers "sign on") on their kids' required tasks. Often, parent help is required to actually complete the task. Behrman House has extended parent help into "Parent Guides" they have produced for several of their books, as well as **Primer Partners,** a pamphlet which encourages parents to help their kids work on their mastery of the Hebrew alphabet and Hebrew "decoding" skills.

• **Visit Someplace.**

• **Interviews (parents of kids, kids of parents).** In A.R.E.'s **Life Cycle Workbook,** Joel Grishaver assigns kids to interview parents about their life cycle experiences. In **My Weekly Sidrah** (Torah Aura Productions) he and Melanie Berman use a "language experience" version of this, asking parents to write down the commentaries created by their kids.

• **Talk about something and report on conversation.**

• **Play a game together.** *Together* series, written by Vicky Kelman and published by the Melton Research Center, has a family game to play at home in almost every booklet. One booklet, *God*, is almost all game.

• Do almost anything else you can think of….

> **[Cherie Koller-Fox's Comment]:** We love to send a ḥallah home uncooked—it does its last rising on the way home. I love to think of that ḥallah coming out of the oven at their house. I imagine how good it makes the house smell and the stories people might tell their children about relatives that made ḥallah. Unfortunately in our calendar, these breads most often come home on Sunday, so we include a recipe and a freezer bag. The choice is simple—either make another one for Shabbas and eat it when it comes out of the oven or put this one in the freezer until Friday. In any case, in nine times out of ten, this ḥallah will guarantee a little Shabbas in each house. Who knows, it could become a habit!

[Sharon Halper's Comment]: Be careful with competition. Parents do not need demonstrations of what they do not know!

[Nachama Skolnik Moskowitz's Comment]: Here's a model I first learned from my child's prechool teacher, Lynda Miller (Z'l) (Beth El, Minneapolis). She had two big stuffed bears which went home with the kids for a week-end along with a journal. A family hosting a bear wrote of the bear's adventures in the journal. Reading the journals was a regular Monday morning activity in circle time. There were often lovely descriptions of Shabbat activities and holiday events. I felt it was also an interesting parent education piece, for often great ideas could be gleaned from reading other families' entries.

[Shirley Barish's Comment]: Send home TV assignments. Teachers prepare a list of questions to be answered after they watch a specific TV show—like Cybill, The Nanny, The Marshall, etc. The questions can cover such areas as Jewish ethics and morals, heroes/heroines, discrimination and stereotypes, etc.

Another idea for sending home material: Send home a question for the week with references where answers could be found. Design it so it can be placed on the door of the refrigerator where everyone can see it—place a magnetic strip on the back so it sticks on easily. Kids bring the answers back the following week. The question can have to do with the lesson, or it can just be a Jewish trivia question. The teacher can write the question the first time, but after that, let the kids write the question—and the questions from the kids do not have to be the same.

Commercial Models:

- **Building Jewish Life** (Joel Lurie Grishaver, Torah Aura Productions) is a series of booklets (in two grade levels, K-2 and 2-5) which include (1) a student text (2) family resources, and (3) activities/homework for the family. An excellent parent's guide, *Step by Step*, was authored by **Harlene Appelman**.

- **I Can Learn Torah:** (Developed by Joel Lurie Grishaver and Ira J. Wise, Torah Aura Productions). I Can Learn Torah is a kindergarten/first grade program, where parents read and discuss Bible stories with their families, following an interview protocol in the read-aloud textbook. Then teachers expand and draw upon that story in their classroom teaching. Parents are supported and enriched in their participation by a parents' guide and a suggested parents' class.

- **JET Cards:** (A Curricular Series by Bruce and Tamar Raff, distributed by Torah Aura Productions). Parents serve as the "merit badge inspectors" for their own children's performance of given tasks. Parents are asked to "sign off" that a given experience has been successfully completed. Often, those experiences (which are chosen from a set of cards) are designed to require adult participation and support. **JET Cards** were developed for kindergarten through third grade and pre bar/bat mitzvah, and a lot of **13 Mitzvot** programs (for B'nai Mitzvah students) also follow this model. Shirley Baum, Temple Shalom, Succasunna, N.J. does a similar program, but tailors it to the third grade curriculum, calling it "**Mitzvah Achievement**." Their program is in six parts: "Holidays, Shabbat, House of Worship, Pioneers, Israel, and Project Ezra." Each has "tasks" which are monitored and signed off by parents. Joan Kaye told us it should be recorded in the oral history of Jewish Family Education, that Dr. Carol Ingall, currently of the Jewish Theological Seminary, was one of the first to utilize this type of format. Dr. Ingalls created a mitzvah program with 32 activites for pre bar/bat mitzvah students to do with their families for Congregation Emanu-El in Providence, RI.

- **The Life-Cycle Workbook:** (Written by Joel Lurie Grishaver for Alternatives in Religious Education). Written originally for 5th-6th grade, but used extensively in junior high school, students are asked to "interview" their parents about each key lifecycle event. In this way, they collect the story of their own family through several generations of Jewish practice.

- **My Weekly Sidrah:** (Developed by Melanie Berman and Joel Lurie Grishaver for Torah Aura Productions). This book lifts technique from good reading instructional practice and has parents of kindergarten and first grade students write down commentaries and stories which their children create as "language experience" pieces.

- **The Parent Connection:** (Originally Developed by Joan Kaye for the Boston BJE). Parents read books with their children at bedtime, or other quality times, and then fill out a brief "book report" card with their child. The number of books completed is monitored and often "prizes" are given. This, too, is a model for children who are below fifth grade. This has been followed by The Grandparent Connection.

- **Primer Partners:** (Developed by Behrman House, no author name included). A series of games (all including transliteration) which help parents to drill the Hebrew reading which their children are learning in *The Hebrew & Heritage Primer*.

- **Shabbat Table Talk:** (Developed by Harlene Appelman for JEFF). Materials are mailed weekly to families. These materials invite families to review and discuss the weekly Torah portion (or a portion of the weekly Torah portion). In the version done by Sharon Halper at Weschester Reform Temple, called **B'shivtekha B'veitekha: When You Sit in Your House**, families get a book for each book of the Torah and a piece of the discussion is recorded (written down) and then brought to the child's class for discussion the next week. Sharon's program has since been published by Torah Aura Productions, as has Dov Peretz Elkins' **Four Questions on the Weekly Sidrah. <shabbas.doc>** a weekly electronic publication doing the same kind of thing directly for families.

- **Together** (Created by Vicky Kelman and published by The Melton Research Center) was a breakthrough collection of family resources. It consists of seven booklets (for 3rd to 5th graders) which provide families with resources and activities.

Esther Netter's Planning Guide:

[Esther Netter's Comment]: I am sending a list of criteria I use in the creation of *Jewish Activity Kits* for My Jewish Discovery Place (a Children's Museum of the Jewish Community Center's Association, Los Angeles). The issues are applicable when teachers design family homework. (A sample JAK is found in the appendix.)

Checklist:

1. Active & Interactive
2. Convenient
3. User friendly—adult and child friendly
4. Self-paced
5. Self-correcting
6. Fun
7. More real, less imitation
8. Use as many senses as possible
9. Durable/replaceable
10. Consumables/non-Consumables
11. Time needed to do/complete
12. Challenging—age appropriate
13. Clean and professional
14. Clear directions
15. Include transliteration if needed
16. Target population—identify in kit
17. And now what…include follow-up and next steps
18. List of what is included in kit
19. Stay-at-home piece
20. Choose container thoughtfully
21. Include Jewish text or quote if suitable

[Joel's Comment]: If you make a list of resources, someone is always mad at being left off. If you don't make a list of resources, people are mad because you didn't provide help. I chose to anger the fewest—whomever I forgot or didn't know about. Sorry!

SAMPLES OF FAMILY HOMEWORK

Joan Kaye, director of the J.E.A., Orange County, CA, shared this "generic" parent homework form with us. It is a good starting point.

HOMEWORK

Quick and Easy Communication

1. What was the funniest thing that happened in school?
2. Show me what pages you read in school today.
3. Tell me three different things you did today.
4. What art project did you do today?
5. What question did you ask today?
6. What question did your friend ask today?
7. Whom did you sit next to?
8. Let's read one of your Hebrew pages together.
9. What prayer did you discuss today?
10. What does that prayer mean to you?
12. Tell me three different ideas you talked about in class today.
13. What story did you read in the Bible today?
14. How would you have changed the ending?
15. Teach me something you learned today.

In this set of materials, like the Ha-Tzofim Curriculum developed by ARE (or like the JET Card series that Bruce and Tamar Raff developed for Torah Aura Productions), students complete tasks on which their parents sign off. Like any good scouting project, signing off is a chance to share involvement.

MITZVAH ACHIEVEMENT

The theme for third grade is Mitzvot. A Mitzvah is a commandment from God—a good deed. "Each Mitzvah is a way to holiness." (Gates of Prayer) Learning about Judaism helps a person to be happy, kind, just, brave and loving. Living as a Jewish student helps a person love and learn about Judaism.

Attached is the packet that you and your children will be using during the year. At the end of the year you will all be participating in a "Mitzvah Achievement Program" to acknowledge the Mitzvot that all of you have accomplished during the year.

We encourage the children to do "Mitzvot" at home as well as in class. You will notice the packet is divided into several different sections and some are sub-divided into "Home" and "Class" work:

- Holidays
- *Shabbat/Havdalah
- House of Worship
- Pioneers/Heroes
- Israel
- Project Ezra

Our hope is that this program will give you the opportunity to share in your child's Jewish education. Help and encourage your children to use their imagination and have fun with it. You have the entire school year to complete the projects. However, periodically we will be checking them. We ask that the completed Mitzvah packets be returned by April 24 so we can properly prepare for the Mitzvah Achievement Program. Please feel free to contact us if you have any questions.

Sincerely,

Susan McDermet, Sandy Rosenfield, Lisa Slobodow, Sally Ann Wallace

House of Worship Achievement

Judaism teaches that people should get together in order to worship. People could get together in each other's houses, but few people live in houses big enough to hold an entire congregation. However, very often temples begin that way and then families help build a special building in which they can hold services, celebrate the holidays and have religious school classes.

In every temple or synagogue there is a special room. It is called a sanctuary. In the sanctuary are several objects: the Ark (Aron ha-Kodesh), the Eternal Light (Ner Tamid) and the Torah.

HOME

- Attend Friday evening or Saturday morning services at Temple Shalom. (Return the attached coupons to your teacher.)
- Talk to someone who helped start Temple Shalom. Write an article for the Menorah.

Signature _____

CLASS

- Explore the sanctuary. Make a list of the ritual objects.

Signature _____

- Think about how you act at home, in class and in the sanctuary. Write some rules about how to behave in the sanctuary.

Signature _____

Pioneers Achievement

Jewish people played an important part in building the United States. Were your parents or grandparents pioneers in their time? When did your families arrive here and from where? How long have members of your family lived in your community?

HOME

- Choose a favorite Jewish hero (family, famous or biblical) and write why this person is a hero to you.

Signature _____

CLASS

- Dress up as your favorite hero (on a designated day).

Signature _____

Israel Achievement

- Israel is the only Jewish country on earth. A visit to Israel would quickly show that Jews come in many different sizes and shapes and live many different kinds of lives. Many will be different from the Jews you have known in your community.

HOME

- Read a book or magazine or newspaper article about Israel.

Signature _____

- Get the Jewish News delivered to your home.

Signature _____

- Purchase a tree(s) from JNF to plant in Israel.

Signature _____

CLASS

- Invite a guest to tell about the lifestyle in Israel and how it compares to our lives.

Signature _____

- Watch a film or video about Israel.

Signature _____

Susan McDermet, Sandy Rosenfield, Lisa Slobodow, Sally Ann Wallace

Risa Gruberger is an outstanding family educator in the Los Angeles area. She is an ongoing consultant to the Whizin Institute for Jewish Family Life, and serves as the director of family education for the co-sponsored pre-school project in the Conejo Valley. She is also part of the Torah Aura team for the development of our new Alef Curriculum. These thoughts and suggestions are her contribution to this work.

Risa Gruberger Portfolio

1. One of my philosophies of Jewish Family Education depends on the metaphor of horticulture—the art of growing gardens. At this point, there are too many greenhouses. Synagogues and schools have replaced the home. The advantage of the greenhouse is its ability to regulate the conditions (temperature and humidity). It is time to let go, protect a little less. The home is the best place for growth and development.

   We have the opportunity to plant seeds for families that will grow and nourish. The seeds may be planted in the school and then transplanted at home, where the potential for growth is enormous and the environment is most natural. Gardens turn into orchards when they grow under just the right conditions. This is all about reaching homes without being in them and reaching families without seeing them face-to-face. The following are ideas that begin in the class and grow at home. Each project must fulfill the following four principles: JOIN

   > **J**ewish Family Time
   > **O**wnership (the family owns and is invested in the project)
   > **I**ntegration of Jewishness into the home
   > **N**atural environment

2. Instead of baking <u>hallah</u> in the classroom, promote something that would excite the child enough to go home and bake <u>hallah</u> with the family. Examples: have the students create sequencing cards of how to bake <u>hallah</u>. a) tell stories of Shabbat that emphasize the smell of <u>hallah</u> (to truly understand you have to go home and experience the smell—send home the recipe), b) have children create pictures of the family making <u>hallah</u>, label all family members (even animals), staple the recipe to the picture, c) create "I like Shabbat" booklets—leave fill-in for Shabbat experiences, "On _____ my family baked <u>hallah</u> for

Shabbat," d) start the process of baking hallah in the class; the finishing touches for baking the dough happen at home.

3. Don't finish holiday cards. Examples: send home a decorated Shanah Tovah card with a space outlined in the center for a family photo. The note home reads:

    Dear parents:

    We need your help. Your child made a New Year card for _____ from your family. To complete the card, as a family, choose a photo that you would like to place in the provided space. Thank you for helping to complete this special card!

4. Send home unfinished projects. Example: In class, decorate a Pesah pillow for reclining during the Seder. Leave empty spaces for family members to write or illustrate their favorite part of Pesah (families can use fabric crayons or permanent markers). When a finished project goes home it is "owned" by the child. Let the family invest in the project by finishing it at home.

5. I think it's a good idea during a child's career in Hebrew school, that it is part of his/her job to enhance the home environment with Jewish stuff. One way to create a Jewish environment in the home is simply to give everyday household items a Jewish touch. The simple fact that things are made at religious school makes them "Jewish." Judaica is not only expensive Hanukkiyot and Shabbat candlesticks. Here is a list of items that can be made in religious school. (Note: not all items should be made in one class or during one year. This may be spiraled into a curriculum. The result is a home filled with things your kids made at the synagogue. Often the things kids make are holiday items and you know where they go when the holiday is over, which is why we need to make places for families to keep them, see #5.) All of these items have a purpose all year long. You can always write the Hebrew word for these items on the project or study Jewish artists and use different art media to create these practical items. The public schools do not have the market on napkin holders!

    [1] a holder for mail, [2] magnets for refrigerator notes, [3] bookmarks, [4] holder for the TV remote, [5] napkin holder, [6] pillow cases, [7] pencil/pen holders, [9] peg board for keys, [10] book cover for the TV guide, [11] container for tooth brushes and toothpaste, [12] magazine stand, [13] newspaper stand, [14] container for CD's, [15] container for computer disks, [16] note pads, [17] calendars, [18] napkin rings, [19] napkins and tablecloths

6. Create special places at home for stuff that is made at religious school. Where and how things are placed in a home is a strong message as to its importance. Kids know the important stuff is in the top drawer in the office or up high in the closet. Some things, like medicines, even get their own cabinets. When things are real important they go under lock and key (safety deposit boxes). Where do we put (plant) the things children bring home from religious school? Rather than answer that, here are some ideas. Remember: A box or a "space of its own" delivers a message of importance and meaning. a) At an "opening school family day" ask each family to bring a large rectangular storage box. Decorate the box in a mosaic with all the Jewish holidays, include the family's last name on the box. This is the place to keep all items for holidays. Some schools have made boxes for individual holidays. Pesah needs a box of its own. b) Create file folders for holidays, mitzvot and other subject matter. This is an easy way to organize papers coming home from school. c) Another family day project is to construct a special container for Shabbat items. (I once saw a three-part family project which was a wooden box with stained glass windows which had compartments for candlesticks, kippot, kiddush cup and havdalah set.)

Lisa J. Goldstein, education director at Congregation Solel, Highland Park, IL, shares this amazing set of family homework pieces created by one of her teachers, Jeffrey S. Hersh. These pages really show the potential of this process. We couldn't resist running the whole set. For those of you interested in the technical, the letters were all run on congregational letterhead while the worksheets were enhanced with photocopied images of historical pieces and maps.

A Set of Family Homework Experiences: Jeffrey S. Hersh

Dear Parents,

It was a pleasure meeting you a few weeks ago at Parent Open House and seeing you again this week at Family Education. I hope you were able to learn more about the exciting program your children have been participating in this fall. At the Open House, I encouraged you to discuss each week's activity with your child to help reinforce the lesson. In turn, you suggested learning more about the lesson, including possible questions you can ask to stimulate conversation.

This Sunday, November 13th, we will be visiting the Ark. Located in West Rogers Park, the Ark provides short-term social, medical and legal services to disadvantaged Jews of all ages. Here are some discussion questions for the Ark:

- What type of services does the Ark provide?

- Where does the Ark receive its funding from?

- What Jewish values are provided by the Ark's services?

- What are examples of Righteousness (*tzedakah*) and Acts of Loving Kindness (*g'milut hasadim*) and how do they differ?

On Sunday, November 20, we will be visiting Keshet. This is an organization of Jewish Families with mental and/or physical impairments. Its activities include monthly parent meetings, support and referral services, family holiday celebrations, Keshet Sunday school and day school and day/overnight camps. Here are some discussion questions for Keshet:

- What types of services does Keshet provide?

- Where does Keshet receive its funding from?

- What gives Keshet its Jewish character?

- The English translation of Keshet is "rainbow." Why is this name appropriate for this organization?

Beginning December 4, we will begin a new curriculum titled "Out of the Ghetto, Into the Suburbs." I will tell you more about this curriculum and provide questions for discussion as we approach this date.

This past week, Judy Weiss, Lisa Goldstein and I spoke about the curriculum for next semester. Lisa will be mailing a letter to you soon detailing the choices available to your child for next semester. I think the students will find the opportunities very exciting. It has been helpful for me to meet you over the last few weeks. Again, if you have any questions, please do not hesitate to call.

B'Shalom,

Jeffrey S. Hersh

PLEASE FILL IN: JOG YOUR PARENTS MEMORIES!

Please complete this form to the best of your ability and bring it to this week's class.

1. my name is _____
   date of birth _____
   place of birth (area/city/country) _____
   occupation _____

2. parent's* name _____ *choose father or mother
   date of birth _____
   place of birth (area/city/country) _____
   indicate each move the person has made from place to place and if possible, the time and reason for moving _____
   _____

   occupation _____

3. grandparent's name _____
   date of birth _____
   place of birth (area/city/country) _____
   indicate each move the person has made from place to place and if possible, the time and reason for moving _____
   _____

   occupation _____

4. my great-grandparent's name _____
   date of birth _____
   place of birth (area/city/country) _____
   indicate each move the person has made from place to place and if possible, the time and reason for moving _____
   _____

   occupation _____

****WHICH GENERATION FIRST CAME TO CHICAGO AND WHY? _____
_____
_____
_____

Dear Parents:

This letter reviews the final two weeks (December 18 and January 15) of the "Out of the Ghetto, Into the Suburbs" curriculum. I encourage you to continue discussing your family history and immigration story during winter break. The students have been excited to share what they have learned from conversations with you and their grandparents.

In this Sunday's class, the students will interview individuals from their grandparents' generation. Three members of Congregation Solel's *Gevura* group have volunteered to be interviewed. I have attached a list of possible interview questions for the students to review prior to Sunday's class. After class, I encourage you to ask the students about how these individuals came to America, where and how they lived, and the role of Judaism in their lives. Also this Sunday, we will finish mapping each family's immigration history and discuss the trends that appear.

On January 15, the students will examine how the Holocaust dominated the expression of Jewish identity in America in the post-World-War-II era. The class will also explore the effects of the Six Day War on American Jewry. Both of these lessons are filled with historical facts and symbolic images. I suggest you discuss with the students why each of these events is so closely related to the American Jewish identity. If time permits, the class will view clips from some of today's most popular television shows and discuss their portrayal of Jewish characters and issues.

For your information, this past Sunday the students watched a brief portion of the original *Jazz Singer* movie produced in 1927. I then showed clips of the 1980 version starring Neil Diamond. The story represents an older generation of Jews fighting to hold on to religious tradition in America versus a generation that wants to move ahead, especially economically, and is willing to assimilate, sometimes completely, in order to achieve its goals. Because the class watched only three scenes of the 1980 version, I suggested to the students that they view (with you) the movie in its entirety.

B' Shalom,

Jeffrey S. Hersh

QUESTIONS FOR THE INTERVIEW OF THE GRANDPARENTS' GENERATION

Background

Where were you born? How large was your family? Who were you named after? What language was spoken at home? Where was home? What were the conditions like? What were relations like between Jews and non–Jews at school? What were your parent's occupations? Who was your childhood hero? And why? How did you become involved in your primary vocation? Was this your original goal? Did you avoid any field due to a climate of anti-Semitism?

Jewish Background

What is your earliest Jewish memory? What level of Jewish education did you have at home? How much were your parents involved in your education? Did your parents keep a kosher home? What was the role of the synagogue in communal life? How often did you attend services? Did the synagogue look different than it does today?

Personal Reflections on the Holocaust and the Creation of the State of Israel

How much were you aware of the rise of Hitler, Nazism, and the Holocaust? How did you find out about it? What did people do in response to it? What did American Jews do in response to it? Do you remember when a) Israel declared independence? b) fought the Six Day War? What were you doing? How did it make you feel? What did you do in response to it? Did you ever think about going to live there? Why/Why not? How much of a role has it played in your life?

[Joel's Comment]: Warning: Good as these materials are, the following contains a land mine. It assumes that all grandparents are Jewish. That is the kind of assumption that blows up in a teacher's face. How you get around it is tricky—edgy—and not simple.

[Carolyn Moore Mooso's Comment]: Isn't this the in-class interview questions for the Temple Members of the kids' grandparents' generation? They are referred to in the previous letter in the second paragraph. Can't we safely assume even that these three senior temple members, selected by the teacher, are Jewish? I take this as a clever way of having all students hear from some Jewish representatives of their grandparents' generation *without* an assumption that the kids' own grandparents are Jewish. The form they filled out about their own parent's and grandparent's journey to Chicago makes no such assumption. I think this is not at all a guide for kids' interviewing their own grandparents. I believe that it is just information for the parents to help kids prepare to interview these Temple elders and to ask afterward about what was learned in those interviews.

Joel's comment is important but it criticizes these materials for an error this teacher didn't make! It would be worthwhile to get feedback on any such communication to try to be certain parents *don't* mistake these questions as meant for the kids' own grandparents.

Rather than "homework," this is summer work. As far as we know, Rabbi Cherie Koller-Fox at Harvard Hillel Children's School created this notion which is carried out here by Robin Eisenberg, Temple Beth El, Boca Raton, Florida.

PUT SOME MITZVAH MAGIC INTO YOUR SUMMER

We would like every family to put some magic into your summer through the performance of mitzvot. Certificates will be given to every family who completes four of these mitzvot. Please have all documentation to Robin Eisenberg by September 1st to get a certificate at the September Family Service. The magic, of course, will be the closeness your family feels by doing Jewish activities together.

1. Add at least one Jewish book to either an adult's or a child's collection. Read it and write a brief report.

2. Subscribe to a Jewish magazine. Discuss an article as a family. Write one thing each family member learned.

3. Learn to play a piece of Jewish music or create a piece of Jewish art. Music should be taped. Art work should be brought to the school office to be displayed.

4. Attend a Shabbat evening service with your family. Write one thing you learned from the Rabbi's sermon.

5. Make and use a Jewish ritual object such as a mezuzah, havdalah candle, menorah, hallah cover. Take a photograph of a member of your family with the object in use.

6. Rotate the responsibilities of Shabbat mitzvot (candles, Kiddush, *motzi*) among family members. Have each person write which mitzvot they enjoy doing the most and why.

7. Donate five hours of your time as a family, as volunteers, to the synagogue or in the community. Hand in what you did and how this impacted you.

8. Clean out closets and drawers and donate the old clothing to the needy. Hand in how you chose who should get clothes.

> **[Cherie Koller-Fox's Comment]:** The summer work we do is our Weekly Reader reading program between third and fourth grades. The children receive a letter each week of the summer. It even follows them when they travel. It gives them fun games and stories to read in Hebrew—we call it a Weekly Reader. We find it really helps retention of Hebrew in that first critical year after they have learned to read. They get a sticker each week to add to their progress chart and a party at the beginning of the fall!

Esther Netter is another one of the Whizin crew. She is Assistant Executive Director of the Jewish Community Centers Association of Greater Los Angeles. She is founding Director and guiding force behind My Jewish Discovery Place Children's Museum, an interactive children's/family Jewish Museum. More importantly, Esther plans and makes great stuff. Here are a couple of designs for take home kits her Museum has created, but that any school would be proud as punch to have produced.

JEWISH ACTIVITY KITS

Jewish Activity Kits (JAK) in a Box are activities with objects in colorful plastic boxes readily available to musuem visitors. Each kit includes directions for the game, a list of what is inside the box, and a description of how to check the answers, where applicable. At present, 16 different JAKS are available.

JAK use objects to teach.

What does it mean to use real objects and provide actual experiences with objects? Museum educators define "objects" as "tools to motivate learning and address the developmental needs of children. Objects may not necessarily have intrinsic value...and can include constructed activity pieces and exhibit components." These interactive, object-based activity kits demonstrate how we learn by doing and encourage participants to look at objects through the eyes of a child.

JAKs are developed for different target groups and for different topics. Some of the characteristics of a JAK are:

Self-facilitating	Self-directed
Hands-on/active	Self-paced
User friendly-adult and child friendly	Convenient
Self-connecting (if necessary)	Fun
Real (put in a real shofar instead of a plastic one)	
Use as many senses as possible	Consumables/non-consumables
Variety	Jewish text/quote

One JAK is called "Things That Remind Us" and includes:

Tzitzit	Post its
Pocket Calendar	Buzzer
String	Phone message pad

It includes questions about the objects and then teaches about the concept of tzitzit. This JAK can also be used to begin a family tallit-making project.

Behrman House *Primer Partners*

Recently, Behrman House has been experimenting with family homework. They have been gracious enough to let us share a sample of their **Primer Partners, A Family Education Program for Hebrwe and Heritage** *packet in this volume.*

FOR THE PARENT

WORD GAME

Call out numbers and ask your child to read the Hebrew words.

Begin by calling numbers in order (1-30). Your child reads the corresponding word on the WORD GAME BOARD. Then call the numbers in columns going up (20-19-18-17-etc); and going across (1-11-21-2-12-22-etc.) Finally, call out the numbers in random order.

אָמֵן 21 — AH-MAYN	אַבְרָהָם 11 — AHV-RAH-HAHM	מִשְׁפָּחָה 1 — MEESH-PAH-CHAH
מִצְוָה 22 — MEETS-VAH	פָּנִים 12 — PAH-NEEM	מוֹדֶה 2 — MOH-DEH
מַלְכֵּנוּ 23 — MAHL-KAY-NOO	אֱמֶת 13 — EH-MEHT	עָלֵינוּ 3 — AH-LAY-NOO
הַלְלוּיָהּ 24 — HAH-L-LOO-YAH	אֲנַחְנוּ 14 — AH-NAHCH-NOO	יְרוּשָׁלַיִם 4 — Y'ROO-SHAH-LAH-YEEM
מָקוֹם 25 — MAH-KOHM	הַתִּקְוָה 15 — HAH-TEEK-VAH	אָדוֹן 5 — AH-DOHN
אֲנִי 26 — AH-NEE	וְעֵד 16 — VAH-EHD	לְהַדְלִיק 6 — L'HAHD-LEEK
בְּרֵאשִׁית 27 — B-RAY-SHEET	אֱלֹהַי 17 — EH-LOH-HAY	אַהֲבָה 7 — AH-HAH-VAH
דָּוִד 28 — DAH-VEED	בְּרִית 18 — B'REET	וְאָהַבְתָּ 8 — V'AH-HAHV-TAH
צְדָקָה 29 — TS'DAH-KAH	לִקְבֹּעַ 19 — LEEK-BOH-AH	כְּמוֹשִׁיעֵנוּ 9 — K'MOH-SHEE-AY-NOO
תּוֹרָה 30 — TOH-RAH	שָׁמַיִם 20 — SHAH-MAH-YEEM	אַתָּה 10 — AH-TAH

Chapter 6
SHARED PROBLEM SOLVING

Read: Classroom Management—Thinking Family

The "fantasy" actualized in this chapter is the vision that when problems arise in the classroom, parents and teachers work together to solve them. This chapter owes much to Jim Fay. We will gloss and annotate his ideas here, but his books and tapes, which really articulate them fully, are strongly recommended. (See the bibliography.)

Two Basic Principles:

- **Jim Fay teaches: We need to think of "behavior problems" as opportunities.** When we get to work with kids and families on these issues we are (1) teaching real life lessons—and not just the theoretical, (2) making the most intimate contact we will make as teachers. *Joel and Ron add:* (3) Odds are good that it is your most difficult students who grow up to be future Jewish teachers.

- **We believe: It is a big mistake to expect parents to "fix" their child's behavior or performance in the classroom.** If they could do that—we woudn't be having a problem. It would have been done already—because no parent likes to be embarrassed by their children's failures. Instead of a "confrontation" where each side tries to make the other party "responsible," we need to transform these get togethers into "team-meetings" where parents and teachers work together to solve a problem.

The best way to make these notions clear is with a story.

Getting a Drink for Throwing Brett Out of Class

[*Joel's Story*] : Brett was a year younger than all the other twelve-year-olds who began my seventh grade, and a young eleven-year-old at that. Either he only owned one set of clothes, or he owned lots of sets of the same clothes, because he came dressed in the same outfit three days a week for a year. (Three days a week was all I saw him.) His mouth was always filled with an entire container of purple bubble tape and its noxious odor flowed from him. (Note: food was allowed in my classroom as long as the kids kept it from interrupting my lessons.) Brett was not a bad kid. He had two problems, both connected to youth. (1) He had no notion of how to learn or study—including no desire to do so. And (2) his behavior was out of control—because, like a young unhousebroken puppy, he was all impulse, no self-control. The bottom line was that he was a real pain in the classroom, but never meant to do wrong. He just got lost in his play. You got annoyed a lot at him—you just couldn't hate him. The problem was, he was one of those kids for whom you wanted armchair desks with seatbelts.

It was about two weeks into the school year. Brett had been in trouble every session. Brett had failed—big time—two Hebrew quizzes and there seemed to be no intention to study or improve, so I pulled the business card stunt. ("Here is my card, don't come back to class till one of your parents calls me at my office.") Of course, no big surprise, Brett showed up for class the next day without the call. He thought he had fooled me. He figured I would forget or let it go. I fooled him. I was prepared. He went to the principal's office—who was waiting for him—and called his folks. He fooled us. He managed not to connect. (Later we learned he dialed the "wrong" number—home rather than work—on purpose.) We held our ground and he didn't come to class that day. The principal warned him that he didn't want her to make the first call. His father, Ian, called me that next morning. He said, "Brett told us the whole story and we've taken his television set away until he does better." I did, "But, but, but…" and then let it go. It was a scary moment. It was too much help. I worried—did I want this kid's life ruined (and have him hate his Jewish future) just because he failed two vocabulary quizzes on the *Avot*?

The "no TV set punishment" that Ian put in place, motivated both Brett and me. We met twice after school that week. Together we crammed for his next quiz. He aced it. I wrote a postcard. Ian called in response. The TV set was back. A week later I was at a Temple potluck dinner. Brett walks up (in a sports jacket and tie—slicked back hair) and says, "I would like to introduce you to my father." With manners I had to practice at Mr. Bradford's dance classes, he said, "Joel Grishaver, I would like you to meet my father, Ian….." Ian then responded, "Can I buy you a drink?" (actually, a glass of wine from the cash bar).

Here were the end results of this encounter:

- Brett's behavior was never great, but both he and I worked on it with a sense of cooperation rather than confrontation.

- Brett's academics floated above the "passing" line all year.

- Brett's parents loaned their home and their time for "family activities" for the class. While they were a "marginal" family in terms of congregational involvement, and not part of the social clique of the core families in the class, they became a cornerstone in the class's family education program. Here is true irony: While not being centrally committed to either an active ritual life, or significant participation in the social life of the congregation, Brett's parents were very serious about education and Jewish education. While no one would have "targeted" this family as a place to seek support (because they weren't particularly shul-going or connected), they proved to be foundational to my efforts. We would have never met or trusted each other enough to discover this, unless Brett's behavior had created the need for our cooperation.

- Brett's tzedakah project, support for a shelter for battered women (a story in itself) was probably the most powerful hands-on visit of the year.

- Brett's family still (five years later) has me over for dinner once or twice a year.

- Brett still calls me a couple of times a year and we get together.

> **[Cherie Koller-Fox's Comment]:** I was a "bad" kid at Hebrew school myself—and I've heard a lot of educators, rabbis and cantors say the same. I loved being there because it felt more like home than like school. The kids were like cousins and I remember how much fun it was to laugh and play there and get some relief from the tension of regular school. Now of course, kids like me end up in my office and part of me wonders if they'll be rabbis themselves someday. I believe in a clear and consistent discipline policy, but I don't want my school to feel the same as their secular school and I don't want the standard for behavior to be the same. I try to pace our learning differently, knowing that it is after school or on Sundays. I want them to feel at home but not cross the lines of safety or disrespect.

Problems as Opportunities (Affordable Consequences)

Jim Fay teaches: "We want kids to make mistakes, and we want them to make mistakes when **the consequences are affordable.**" He says, "The poor kids who behave only get to learn the curriculum, the kids who misbehave get some customized and more intensive learning opportunities." This is not a book on classroom management, but this attitude is a great foundation to the way we can work with parents. He has a little book called *Tickets to Success* which really teaches this lesson.

[Joel's Story]: A simple example: Recently, I taught a second Tourette's syndrome child. (Not the Ethan of the second chapter.) This one, whom we will call Robert, I never could have picked out as having "special needs." He is a fourteen-year-old *Mensa* member. He showed us his card one day when I hit him with "Which part of 'NO' didn't you understand?" He had a sharp come back for everything—usually honestly funny. There is a hyperactive edge to everything he does—sort of manic—(that is observational, not clinical). The only real giveaway is that his language is somewhat more sexually charged than is usual. But, unlike Ethan, his language, while sometimes questionable and often provocative, is almost never hurtful. One takes offense from the content but not the affect, usually, but there are moments when both are out of control. Again, I need to emphasize that this is a good kid who wants to be "at" school—not just always "in" school.

Anyway, Robert and I had been 'round the "acceptable for class" thing a lot. He got thrown out sometimes. Got himself under control often. And sometimes was the catalyst that really made the class work. What was clear were two things. First, that I really liked Robert and would work with him towards his success. Second, that even given the first, the boundaries of my class would not be violated. Middle of the year, he comes to me to talk through a problem. A "joke" he had pulled at public school had gotten him suspended and the target of an erotic caricature he had drawn was threatening to sue him for sexual harassment. I listened, empathized, and affirmed his better nature. There was nothing else I could do. It was a close call. It was the only time that I ever saw the shield of bravado totally broken (usually we did the meek head hang followed by the "Am I forgiven yet?" smile). For the first time, perhaps ever, Robert had to face the truth that the part of him that was out of control might actually destroy the potential of the bright, caring person who was the rest of him. A year of interventions which were non-confrontational gave me *enough money in the bank* to have this conversation.

When the end of the year came, rather than the regular take-home final, I gave him a copy of the Hofetz Hayyim's book on hurtful language and traded a regular essay for a book report. Someone else would have seen the choice as mean-spirited or too cute. Truth is, it hit the spot. Robert wrote the report without a nod or sly smile. He never admitted a direct connect between his issues and the book, but did comment "I learned something important." My sense is that the problem is far from over. While he has always been working "on it" or "with it," now that work has a much clearer direction and reality. A relatively happy ending for a story which is not a fairy tale.

So here is what I know:

- The key to working with Robert was not anger—but a real sense that we were working on this issue together.

- Robert's parents did meet with the school administration early in the year because of problems he was having in other classrooms. It was in those meetings that the school became aware of his problems, his medication, and his treatment program. I was not part of that process, because the core problem was not in my room. (That is another way high school is different.)

- It would have been better if just Hebrew School trouble had been enough to shake Robert into enough self-doubt to "get real" about the issues. It didn't. Often, it isn't. That is a truth that the 12-step people call 'hitting the bottom." Problems only get fixed (1) when they are easy, and (2) when there is no other choice. This is the idea of *affordable consequences*; we want kids to get in trouble and then have to fix it on their own when the *price* for the *trouble* and for the *fix* is still minor. *Thank God we got to work on it before it hit "the permanent records," let alone the courts.*

- In a less dramatic way Jim Fay tells a story of a Colorado kindergarten teacher who offers kids a chance to take coats to recess in September. She models the behavior and takes her own coat, even though it looks like it would be warm out. When they get outside and some of the kids are a little bit cold, she leaves the door locked until the end of recess. This teaches them (when the cold isn't more than uncomfortable) never to underdress. While this, at first blush, may be cruel, waiting at a bus stop in the mountains without enough clothing in February can be life threatening. A shiver in September is better than frostbite later. Done, to quote Fay, "with empathy," it drives home a life-saving lesson with affordable consequences.

- The sense that we wanted to work with Robert (not to control Robert) gave both him and his parents the security to work with us. Another Jim Fay truth is: **You only gain control by sharing control.**

As Jewish teachers, we should look forward to (not shun or resent) the chance to help kids grow, recognize their responsibilities, and get themselves under control. Kids' behavior isn't just an interruption in our Torah lessons—rather it is an opportunity to model the attitudes and behaviors we profess. Our literature is big on the *Yetzer ha-Rah*, the evil impulse. It should be no surprise that, like the rest of us, our students and even their parents need help getting their best values to control their other urges. That's human, and that is a core part of Jewish education.

Helicopters, Drill Sergeants, and Consultants

Jim Fay has a book called *Helicopters, Drill Sergeants, and Consultants: Parenting Styles and the Messages They Send.* The book's premise is simple. **Helicopter parents** (who hover and protect) rob children of the opportunities to learn how to be responsible. **Drill Sergeants** who tell kids what they should have done, eat away at self-esteem and disable the ability to act independently. **Consultants** who know that they are responsible to support their children while allowing them to solve their own problems, raise kids who actually grow up to be responsible adults. The same can be said for teachers in their relationships with kids, and the same can be said for teachers in their relationships with families. We want to be consultants—and as Jewish teachers, Torah should be at the core of our consultations.

Here are some model consultations:

- I sense Brett doesn't know what it means to study for a vocabulary quiz in a foreign language. I don't think he has any strategy for memorizing a list of things that doesn't come easily to him. How do you think we can help him to be successful? *Then:* Do you want to hear a few of my ideas? *This is the consultant part.*

- Julie is really good in class. But, because she's missed 5 out of 12 sessions this year, she seems lost. (Yes, I know she is on a gymnastics team!) How do we work things out to insure her success in Hebrew school? (I'll share what I'd like you to try—if you share what you'd like me to do.) (Then I'll let you evaluate the practicality of my suggestion if I can do the same for your suggestions.)

- Robert gets carried away in class. He sometimes loses control. I know I can't always control him and still teach my class. I know you can't control him by long distance, either. What do you think we can do to help him rein in his own behavior? Has anybody else come up with a successful formula? (I'll share my best guesses, if you do the same.)

- Meredith comes to class and spends the time talking to her friends. That disrupts my lesson and I can't teach over her. I don't think I've succeeded in convincing her that this behavior is unacceptable. I'm looking for a way to solve this without creating a big issue or escalating this to a crisis. I have some ideas about how we can handle this, but first I want to know if someone else has already found a better way of doing it . Can we work on it? If you want, I will share some things that have worked for me in other cases.

Do Not Make Parents Responsible for their Kids' Behavior

Remember "Mama Bear." (We met her in chapter 2.) She is the raging monster who storms into school in defense of her young. When we acknowledge that a child is having a problem, we often invite Mama Bear to burst forth. (One wonders how many parents jump into a phone booth on the way to school to change into their Mama Bear persona?)

We've already learned that:

- "Mama Bear" is probably in the emotional state rather than the thinking state.
- "Shame" may be at the root of his/her "emotional state."
- We can't reason with people who are in the "emotional state."
- Only his/her own words get our "Mama Bear" out of the emotional state.
- When we prove that (1) we will listen, (2) we care, (3) we understand, and (4) we will share in the problem and in the solution, *we get money in the bank*, and therefore can begin the actual work.

This all boils down to a couple of simple truths about working with parents. These suggestions come from teachers and principals who have participated in our workshops:

1. We have to expect "anger," "shame," and "reticence" at the beginning of this process. Unless we already have a relationship, **we have to be prepared to start there, to start with listening.**

2. **Start with the expectation that this is a problem you and the parents will work on together.** Ask for advice or input rather than just stating a situation and leaving the expectation that the parents—alone—can fix it. Ask about parallel experiences in secular school.

3. **Take a deep breath before responding to criticism about your classroom.** That is part of the territory. When you are "fixing" a situation, all potential elements of the problem have to be considered. Ask, "What do you think will improve the situation?"

4. **The more detail you can recall—the better.** This is not to "prove" that you are "right" and the "parent-child team" is wrong, but rather to give you and the parents the data to work on the problem. Odds are, what is happening in your classroom is also happening to this child in other classrooms. You may help diagnose a real problem. **Note:** *Often a child's problems,*

especially with Hebrew language, are clues to help understand learning difficulties which have gone undiagnosed or not yet been adequately accepted.

5. Sharon Halper teaches: "Don't depend on recall. Keep a diary of problematic situations in order to describe incidents clearly. This may also let you see the pattern more clearly."

6. The **first part** of any meeting should involve **sharing data about and defining the problem.** The **second part** involves **looking towards solutions**. While it is possible that the parents already know best, odds are what you are facing is not just a Hebrew school problem, and they don't know how to fix it, either. That means, you'll need a plan. Jim Fay suggests **coming in with a number of suggestions** (that share control). However, he also advises suggesting the bad ideas first, because they are usually rejected on principle.

7. And finally, Fay also teaches, **don't rush the solutions.** Teachers are often too smart; they see problems quickly. They see answers quickly, often too quickly. Solutions do us no good until Mama Bear has been retired and parents are back in the "thinking state."

8. On the other hand, what is happening to one child in your classroom, may be happening to many children. **Parents may also be able to help you diagnose a real problem.** Remembering (admitting) that you make mistakes too, is also an important part of this process. Modeling *t'shuvah*—self awareness and the willingness to change—is another important Jewish teaching.

The bottom line of this chapter is this: Classroom issues most often drive a wedge between parent and teacher. This is ironic and unfortunate because they actually provide the greatest opportunity for connection and significant learning. Therefore: **Begin every "intervention" with a family (1) prepared to get past the emotional tensions in order to (2) collaborate on a shared solution.**

SOME MANAGEMENT PAPERWORK

Here is a parallel pair of parent involvement in management pieces from the Susan Fish second grade team at the Jewish Day School in Seattle. The first is a beginning of the year contract. The second is the "intervention" piece.

Jewish Day School, Seattle

CONTRACT/BRIT between Sara Kupor, Vered Almosnino, and Susan Fish and

_____

"The Four Promises"

Each day I will:

1. Respect people and property
2. Be where I am supposed to be
3. Use appropriate language
4. Work hard at learning

If I am unable to keep a promise:

1. The first time, I will get a reminder from my teacher to help me remember my promise.
2. The second time, I will get a warning from my teacher.
3. The third time, it means it was very hard for me to keep my promise. I will be asked to think about my behavior(s) and to complete a "Think Paper" to help me. This paper will go home so we can talk about what happened. My parents will be asked to read and sign the "Think Paper" and return it to school the next morning.

Student's Signature _____

Morah Susan_____ Morah Sara _____ Morah Vered _____

Parent(s) Signature(s) _____

Date _____

THINK PAPER

WHAT AM I DOING?

WHY AM I DOING IT?

WHO IS IT HELPING?

WHO IS IT HURTING OR DISTURBING?

WHAT AM I GOING TO DO ABOUT IT?

WHEN AM I GOING TO START?

WHOM CAN I TALK TO FOR HELP?

Name _____

Date _____

Teacher's Signature _____

Parent's Signature _____

"The Four Promises"

1. Respect people and property
2. Be where I am supposed to be
3. Use appropriate language
4. Work hard at learning

[Deena Bloomstone's Comment]: The negativism associated with classroom management in Religious School classes has long concerned me. How to minimize the negative and underscore the positive is a great challenge for many of us. We tend to pounce immediately on the negative, highlighting it with our reactions. We often lose sight of appropriate positive responses, rarely recognizing it in the public manner that we recognize the negative. Rabbi Howard Bogot, past Director of the UAHC Department of Education, used to refer to the Temple, the school, as a Kedusha Kingdom. How is one supposed to behave in a Kedusha Kingdom? In order to create a Jewish environment and a group behavior conducive to the holy place we find ourselves in, we developed the Kedusha Kingdom Brit of Ethics. The Brit describes in Hebrew terms, the positive type of behavior desired in the school and the Temple. It joins parents, students and teachers in a discussion of positive Jewish behavioral values and ideally commits them as a team to ensure appropriate behavior.

At the beginning of each year, we send home a copy of the Kedusha Kingdom - Classroom Brit of Ethics. Families are asked to discuss the Brit, what it signifies, how students and teachers will behave towards one another. It also contains a statement of response should the Brit be broken. That's reality. Just as God delineated the consequences for good and bad choices of behavior to the Israelites, so too do students, parents and teachers know in advance what action is to be taken should the Brit be compromised. A larger copy of the Brit is posted in the classroom and reviewed by the class during the first few weeks of school. Some teachers have elected to have the Brit signed by themselves, the student and the parent.

The Brit lends itself to all types of lessons. It provides a Jewish framework for appropriate behavior and a Jewish language to use in regards to behavior. Its success has shown itself to be dependent on everyone and the way in which it is abided by.

KEDUSHAH KINGDOM—CLASSROOM BRIT OF ETHICS

We are in a *Kedushah* Kingdom, a sacred Jewish environment. While we are in our *Kedushah* Kingdom, we will act *b'Tzelem Elohim*, with *Kavod*, *Derekh Eretz*, and *Hish-tat-foot*. This *Brit*, contract, signifies our willingness to conduct ourselves accordingly in class.

We are all *b'Tzelem Elohim*, created in God's image. Because we are all *b'Tzelem Elohim*, we will act and behave well with each other. We will behave just as we believe God behaves with us.

We will behave with *Kavod*, respect for ourselves and each other. We will listen to others and respect their opinions even if we don't agree. Out of our *Kavod* for each other, whatever we say, stays with us. *Kavod* is a two-way relationship. *Kavod* is given when we earn it.

We will act towards each other with *Derekh Eretz*, manners. All of us deserve to be treated properly. We will speak to each other politely, we will not touch or hurt each other, and we will treat each other with care and concern.

Hish-tat-foot, participation, is part of our *Brit*. A partnership between students, teachers and parents exists within our classroom. Everyone is encouraged to participate and share. No one has the right to interfere with the teaching and learning that goes on in our *Kedushah* Kingdom. The teacher will be prepared and will act fairly in all situations.

Should a problem occur in our *Kedushah* Kingdom, there will be one warning given. If the problem occurs again, the teacher will speak with the parents and the student involved. If the problem persists, a conference between parent, teacher, student and Education Director will take place. If after all this a willingness to abide by the classroom *Brit* has not been achieved, the Religious School Committee will be consulted and the student will not be readmitted to the class.

We understand the concepts of *Kedushah* Kingdom, *Brit*, *b'Tzelem Elohim*, *Derekh Eretz* and *Hish-tat-foot*. We will abide by our classroom *Brit*.

Neither of the two pieces which follow (one set from Nachama Skolnik Moskowitz and one reflective document by David Barany) fully realize the ideal of cooperative discipline. They also have an edge of "Cover Your Tush" thinking. In that sense, they mirror the real work that many of us experience. The ideals of this chapter, which the authors believe are realistic possibilities, need to be balanced with the "institutional realities" many of us face.

Minneapolis Jewish Day School Disciplinary Program

Nachama Skolnik Moskowitz, Minneapolis Jewish Day School, Minneapolis, MN, sent us this parent manual and parent letter which outlines their behavior-crisis process. While some of this process is clearly designed for the school's (appropriate) self-protection, the end result is still a combination of "honoring" parental involvement while not mandating that parents "fix" behavior.

[NACHAMA SKOLNIK MOSKOWITZ'S COMMENT]: Our goal was partnership. I am no longer with MJDS and their process may have changed.

This is what they write of the management procedures which went home in the student handbook.

MDJS RULES

MDJS students are expected to become responsible for their own behavior and are given opportunities for decision-making and self-management commensurate with age and maturity. Our rules are simple and reasonable and are discussed with students in each classroom. There are four guiding principles which form the basis of the behavior we expect in our school community. They are listed as follows:

1. Everyone has the right to his/her own space;
2. Everyone has the right to a safe environment;
3. Everyone will respect himself/herself, others and property; and
4. Everyone will actively participate in his/her own learning.

Teachers have established all school philosophy and procedures for helping children behave appropriately at school. In-class infractions are usually handled by the classroom teacher. Parents will be notified if there's a continuing problem, or if a child receives 3 in-class consequences in a four-week period.

Infractions which occur in the common areas of the school (lunch, recess, halls) or are more grievous classroom incidents are handled through our after-lunch time-out system. "Time Out" is shorthand for "Time Out To Think." Students sent to Time Out are given a structured way to process the problem: what they did, to whom they were disrespectful, what they would do differently the next time, and a way to record amends.

If a child receives a Time Out, parents are sent a note from one of the faculty explaining in adult terms what has happened, as well as a copy of the child's Time Out to Think sheet. A child sent to the Time Out room 3 times in a four-week period is considered to be having a continuing problem. In that case, a conference is called with the parents, teacher, child and principal to set an acceptable behavior plan.

When problems continue, as identified either through the classroom system or Time Out, it is especially important that school and home work together. When 2 or 3 interventions have been tried without success, a conference will be called to set goals and strategies to help the child meet those goals. At this point, outside referrals are also a potential intervention, as a team approach is more effective. If an outside professional consults with either the family or school, s/he becomes part of the behavior plan process.

If, after multiple meetings and adjustments of the child's learning and behavior plan/support system, the school feels it cannot provide an optimal learning environment for the child, the school will withhold the child's contract for readmission in the following school year.

This letter is sent home along with behavior notices.

Dear Parents,

Enclosed you will find a *Behavior Notice* issued to your child today. If the incident happened in the morning, you should also find a copy of our *Time To Think* sheet in your child's backpack; this sheet provides an opportunity for your child to think through other ways the problem might have been handled and to consider the issue of amends. If the incident happened at or after lunch, the *Time to Think* sheet should come home in tomorrow's backpack. If you don't receive the sheet in a timely manner, it's possible that your child did not fulfill his or her obligation to go to the Time Out Room to work on the sheet.

Please use the information the teacher wrote on the *Behavior Notice* and your child wrote on the *Time to Think* sheet to discuss the incident. You need to sign the *Time to Think* sheet and return it to school in the backpack the very next day; a child who does not bring the sheet back must return to the Time Out Room after lunch to fill out another one.

If you have questions beyond what is written on the sheets, please call our office and leave a message for the teacher who issued the Time Out Behavior Notice to call you back.

Receiving a *Behavior Notice* is one of the most serious consequences MJDS has for an infraction of the rules. If a child receives 3 notices in a 4-week period, a conference is called with the parents to discuss the continuing problems.

Thanks for your support!

Nachama

This is the call for the conference which is mentioned above.

It has recently been brought to my attention that _____ has been in the Time Out Room at least three times within the last several weeks. Here's a schedule of what happened:

Date	Sent by	Reason

Date	Sent by	Reason

Date	Sent by	Reason

Date	Sent by	Reason

As I'm sure you know, the Time Out room is one of the most serious consequences we have in our school. A child who is sent to the Time Out room three times or more in a four-week period is having quite a difficult time following the rules at school.

_____ coordinating teacher, _____, will be in touch with you to set up a meeting to work together to help develop a behavior plan for _____; she'll coordinate your schedules, hers and mine. Our personal concern is making sure that home and school are working together to help _____ demonstrate a knowledge of, and respect for, the overarching rules which help our school be a physically and emotionally safe place to be.

L'shalom,

Nachama Moskowitz, Principal

cc: TEACHER

[Nachama Skolnik Moskowitz's Comment]: This wasn't done for self-protection. We did want our parents to know the philoosphy and procedure for incidents. First and foremost responsibility was placed on the child for his/her behavior. What happened in the classroom (e.g. Robert and Brett type stories) isn't really discussed here. Our Time to Think program was a form of t'shuvah process. Children were asked to write about the incident. What happened? To whom was I disrespectful? What would I do differently the next time? The teacher who staffs the Time Out room at lunch made sure the children processed this well and made amends. This was the core of our policy.

However, for the few children who had recurring issues, parents were called to work with us in partnership to set a behavior plan—we wanted parental input and insights. Most of our conferences for this were simply set up by a teacher or the parent. I think in my last year, with a school population of 150, five "3 times" letters were generated from our office and some for the same child. Yes, besides the "processing," we saw the "Time to Think Sheets" accompanying letters and the "3 times" letters as a kind of documentation—including parental receipt of information. We didn't want parents to feel surprised at receiving a verbal or written notice of a recurring problem with no prior knowledge of a situation that wasn't resolving itself. I write all this because reading the documentation out of context makes me feel MJDS was a heavy-handed, inaccessable CY Tush type of school. It really wasn't.

[Joel's Comment]: We chose to include the pieces from MJDS because they represent a wonderful balancing of the "ideal" of parent involvement and the realistic need to "document" your actions in this day and age. I believe the work requires no apology. I chose to include Nachama's entire statement because it teaches us an important lesson about the gap between paper trails and relationships. Here, all of her thinking about the creation of a process is made manifest. That is a gift.

David Barany's Classroom Management Strategy

David Barany is the educational director at B'nai Joshua Beth Elohim (BJBE) in Glenview, Il. This is a supplemental school. These are his notes on his cooperative management strategy.

Teaching is an Art: Teaching is an art, in the sense that no single method is ideal for every practitioner. The methods one employs to keep the students focused and on-task are left to my teachers' discretion. If they wish guidance in this area, I tell them to consult with their Principal or with me.

Documentation: If a child is being a pain, document examples using an *Incident Report Form* and confer with the Principal about how to proceed.

Sending Students to the Educator's Office:

*Grounds: If a student is keeping others from learning, or is disrespectful to a teacher, that person should be sent to my office (with an assignment to keep them current with the class).

*Philosophy: We want our students to make positive choices about how to interact. This system recognizes that youngsters need to fail, need to experience the consequences of failure, and need to have the opportunity to learn from their mistakes and change their behavior. Respect for them as problem solvers is the (sometimes unspoken) message that after one visit, we do not call parents. Recognition that they are not yet adults, not yet completely responsible, is the rationale behind setting up contracts and contacting parents at the second contact. Respect for our teachers is the reason why we involve parents if behavior does not change.

*Procedure: I will see a child three times in a given year under these circumstances. [Extenuating circumstances, (family trauma, change in medication dosage, etc.), temper the system on rare occasions.]

Visit #1:

- I explain my system of three visits.
- I escort the child back to class.
- I need to hear from you if the child's behavior conformed to class standards for the remainder of the period.
- I make a record of the visit.

Visit #2

- A second visit indicates to me the child is having difficulty dealing with the classroom as a learning community.

- The child and I write a contract to which s/he will adhere. The contract is based on their own words about what is appropriate behavior in a classroom. Words like "respect," "listen to...," "wait my turn," "hands to myself," "do the work as best I can," are the most common frames for writing expectations.

- Occasionally, contracts include checking in with the teacher before class begins and setting up a way for dealing with minor incidents.

- The child signs the contract as a promise to work towards the stated goals.

- I record the student's second visit. (As the year progresses, I like to show students how many names are on the "1 visit" list, how relatively few names are on the "2 visit/contract" list, and that there are no names on the "3 visit" list.) This shows the students that the system works, and that we are serious about consequences.

- There was one student who required his parents in the classroom to ensure his cooperation. Five visits were enough, and we were able to manage through to the end of the year. I did not write his name in the "3 visit" list; that would have been a *busha*. But I did tell some of the students that there was one student who had gotten that far. This again to demonstrate "truth or consequences."

- Parents get a photocopy of the document and a cover letter from me explaining the specifics of the situation and the plan for the remainder of the year.

- The teacher and I keep copies of the contract, and the student keeps the original.

- The student is informed that if s/he makes it through the year without requiring a third visit, then they will have fulfilled the terms of the contract and could tear it up.

This proved to be a remarkable motivation this past year.

Notes: This system empowers teachers by giving them a system with concrete consequences in which to work. For example: "Brad, I know you have already been to Mr. Barany once. You need to leave Matt's pogs alone or you will be going to work out a contract." One drawback is that teachers who are aware of students having contracts may protect them from consequences rather than letting them incur the follow-through of the system. (Unfortunately, teachers punish themselves most with this response.)

Visit #3

- A third visit shows me that the child cannot make the commitment necessary to participate in a class structure without intervention. I schedule a conference with teacher and parents to determine what is the next step.

- Options include: parent sitting in the back of the room to ensure their child's behavior is appropriate, child working on their own in the curriculum, temporary private tutoring funded by the parents.

*Appendix: I have not yet suspended a child from school. I firmly believe that every child who comes to us is deserving of a Jewish education.

> **[Cherie Koller-Fox's Comment]:** Miriam Newman of Newton worked with a Derekh Eretz committee at Schechter to create a discipline policy based on Jewish values. I agree with Miriam that discipline issues are an important opportunity to teach our children our values. I teach them that we are community to each other and that ups the ante on how we treat each other.
>
> Hebrew school doesn't happen often enough to have a discipline structure of its own. I've found it works better to use what the kids are used to in their school or at home. For example, if you are having problems with a child at Hebrew school, you might guess this might not be the only situation where this type of behavior is an issue. If the child's secular school has given them a chart of smiley faces that each teacher fills in at the end of each class, we continue that system at Hebrew school. If the parent takes away television time if they don't get enough smiley faces at school, we ask that this be extended to their behavior at Hebrew school. We learn what is done at school by speaking to the parents, and both the parent and the child seem to appreciate the continuity of approach.

Chapter 7
FAMILY EDUCATION DAYS

So far we have talked about communicating with the home, sending things to that home, expecting some things to come back from that home, and then collaborating with parents on difficult situations. Next, comes the part which is both the most fun and the most scary: bringing parents into the classroom. In chapter 8 we will present some family class models and theory to aid in your planning and curriculum writing. In chapter 9 we will deal with the "management issues" which arise when both parents and students are in the room at the same time. Then, in chapter 10 we will explore the possibility of expanding such intergenerational experiences from special events to regular learning modalities.

A Letter From a First Year Principal:

Joel got this paragraph as part of a long e-mail letter from a first year principal who was inheriting a new school. In many ways, this chapter is a response to his letter.

My predecessor set the days of school and no school, and major holiday programs, all that's left to do is open school, parent teacher conferences, report card dates and dates for confirmation class trips. Last year we had three parent functions—open school (visit and faculty explains curriculum), back to school (parents sit in on class), and parent teacher conferences. Three opportunities to disrupt the orderly (!) learning process. How does this sound—one "parents day" call it anything but—

A. Parents come to class with kids

B. Teachers take 5-6 minutes to explain curriculum

C. Teacher does "typical class" but only about an hour's worth

D. Last hour parents and kids have juice/coffee and bagels while individual parent conferences take place.

Have a sign-up sheet before class. At a different school, during a different life, we did something similar to this and it seemed to work. Personally, I think parent-teacher conferences are a waste. If the kid is doing well, then it is a mutual admiration session. Teacher: "Your child is so wonderful." Parent, "Yosi just loves to come to your class." OR if there is a problem, it should not wait for a formal conference to be brought up.

Once upon a time, schools did individual parent conferences and back-to-School nights. It seemed the professional thing to do. Today, an event called "Family Education Day(s)" has tended to replace them. It is an attempt to fuse "family learning" with school contact with parents. This chapter (and the following two) are attempts to talk about how to maximize the opportunity they offer.

But as a set induction to this chapter, here is the answer Joel sent back.

- Family Education Days are better than conferences and "Back to School" things.

- I recommend (eventually) 4 to 5 a year per-class.

- These events should ideally include (1) some family learning experiences, (2) some parental involvement in the "regular" curriculum, (3) parent-teacher "focus groups," where both sides share feedback, goals, and visions—doing some cooperative evaluation and some cooperative planning.

- The goal should be both to strengthen family Jewish learning and build relationships between teachers and parents. Conferences should be reserved for "need only" situations. There are plenty of other ways to communicate everything else.

Bringing parents into school should be first viewed and then actualized as opportunities to extend and deepen, not disrupt learning.

> **[Esther Netter's Comment]:** There is a wonderful story that might have a place in the family education section. This is a parable of a father who went on a journey with his little son. This was their manner of going: Whenever they came to a place that was narrow, or difficult to traverse, such as a river, or a mountain, or a hill, the father lifted his son to his shoulder and strode through that difficult place with him. Once they came to a walled city and the day had ebbed to evening. The gates were shut, and there were only narrow windows in the side of the wall. The father said to his son: "You know, my son, up to now I have spared you much difficulty when I lifted you on my shoulder and took you in my arms. But now—you can see it with your own eyes—there is no way to get into this city, and it is not given into our hands to go through the gate, unless you, my son, climb through the holes and the windows of the wall, and open the gate for me." Sometimes children provide the way to reach and teach the family.

Relax

Listen, we know this chapter seems scary to many teachers. The idea of having parents in your room scares a lot of us.

- **The biggest fear is the clipboard.** We live with the fantasy (and occasional reality) that parents will walk into our room, clipboard in hand, score our class (occasionally holding up the scores, where our routine will be consistently under-rated by the Russian judges) and then provide the data to whichever committee is in charge, which will use the data to fire us.

- **The next biggest fear is making a mistake.** Kids often share the nightmare of being naked in a classroom, having to stand up and recite without knowing a single answer. The parallel teacher nightmare is teaching a lesson (on a subject which we have barely mastered) and having the students systematically refute and disassemble everything we have taught. Parents' presence exacerbates this fear. It is our version of being caught naked.

- **Also on the list of fears is chaos.** Walking into a classroom of parents and kids together often feels like trying to work with lions and tigers in the same cage. (In case circuses aren't your thing, that is something only a few people in the world do well. That is, just enough to prove that it can be done at all.)

The purpose of this chapter and the following two are (1) to assure you these fears are worse than their bites, and to show that (2) there are easy ways to avoid their ever actualizing, and (3) there are some wonderful benefits to these kinds of events. So let's break it down.

The Nature of Family Education Events

The Patterns

Family Education Days tend to have one of four rhythms—all tend to resemble visitors' days at camp:

- **Model Seders and Performances** where parents become audiences for their kids activities. It is the universal belief of the experts in the family education field that these events are not family education. They will, however, acknowledge that such events have their place in the school calendar. (They merely aren't as effective as events which are interactive.)

- **One-Shot Events (Multi-classroom)** which Harlene Appelman has labeled "extravaganzas." These, usually run by a family education coordinator or the educator, bring large numbers of parents and kids together (often for holiday events). The events are usually good for the families involved, and provide opportunities for teachers to meet and network with parents, but they do not fulfill the promise, either.

• **Classroom Events** which are usually run by the classroom teacher (with/without outside support) and bring parents into the process of the classroom. Sometimes teachers plan unique and special events specifically designed to involve parents; sometimes they merely adapt a normal "lesson" to include parents.

• **A Series of Classroom Events** creates a very different experience. When such gatherings happen four or five times a year, a different kind of feeling and relationship develops. While these start out planned by the teacher, parents often become part of the planning process.

These kinds of occasional involvements point the way towards "family schools" where parents become an on-going presence in the learning process.

• A **Family Class/School** is a process by which parents don't just sporadically "visit" classrooms, but actually become (on some kind of schedule) regular participants in the classroom's learning process. (Chapter 10 focuses on this kind of whole-family learning.)

This list of possible events should not be viewed as a menu, but as a hierarchy. While all of them have their purposes, they should lead us in a direction.

A Hierarchy of Goods

This book is written out of our common experience which suggests the following hierarchy of truths. An event involving parents and students learning is a good thing.

• Events which create actual interaction between parents and students are significantly better than events which merely have both age groups participating (or even just attending).

• Joel believes that it is better if this is not an "all-school" event, but a program which takes specific classes into consideration. But Joan Kaye disagrees and adds, "except where the school is very small or where all-school events can allow the whole family to be together." Sharon Halper adds: "I disagree, too, we want to mix ages sometimes. One's goals should determine the audience."

• We all agree family events which create a system of relationships, an ongoing process, are better than one-shot or impersonal events.

- It is even better if the classroom teacher, and not just an outside programmer, rabbi, or educator, is the active facilitator of this process. We want family education to result in relationships which affect both the home and the classroom.

- It is still better if the learning which takes place on this day is an extension of the ongoing curriculum of the classroom.

- It is best if each of these events is part of a series of such programs which take place over the course of a year, programs whose goals include:

  - developing positive relationships between teacher and parent

  - directly involving the parents in the classroom curriculum

  - providing ways for the curriculum to transcend the classroom and enter the home.

The goal here is to move up the progression away from a "visitor's day," where parents witness evidence of their child's experience, and towards moments where families do significant learning together.

Not Your Model Seder

[Joel's Story] : **Mrs. Macintosh and the Fireman's Hat.** It is more than thirty-five years ago, but I can still feel the pain. It is a foundational *shame* moment in my life.

My first-grade (public school) teacher was named Mrs. Macintosh (as she used to say, "Like the apple"). By community standards, she was a legend. The first day of school every kid got an apple—of course it was a Macintosh—to help us remember her name. The high point in the year was Valentine's week, where the room was transformed into a post office where each student in all four first-grade classes decorated a shoebox (lots of doilies and red construction paper), transforming it into a mailbox. Meanwhile, in a series of math and English lessons, plus with a lot of rubber stamps, Mrs. M's room was transformed into a perfect interdisciplinary social studies experience. She was a "Disney" teacher for her time.

Somewhere in the middle of the year, we did a mothers-come-to-school thing. It was the kind which started with "A" papers up on the bulletin boards and ended with punch and little cupcakes. In between, were a series of perfectly staged and rehearsed performances. The single moment which is vivid among the blurs in my memory was thE finale, for which each of us had cut a fireman's hat out of red construction paper. The "magic" was that it was a flat piece of paper which was "engineered" to become a hat when we picked it up and put it on. We were supposed to leave it flat on the desk, and pick it up and put it on at the last moment. It was supposed to be a first-grade Busby Berkeley moment at the culmination of who-remembers-what kind of pageant. All I remember is that I blew it. Over and over I picked up the hat and put it on. Each time I did, my mother's face wilted with shame. I didn't understand it that day. Later she explained it to me. Her shame became my shame. Today that hat, her face, and deep nausea still haunts me. It will not go away (just ask my therapist).

Mrs. M was state-of-the-art for 1957. But her "family" event had all the makings of a model seder. My shame was not her intent, not even her fault, but it was inevitable in the mismatch between who I was and what the event mandated. (By the way, I know the shame I have long lived with was not caused by, but rather crystallized in, that moment.) Still, our state-of-the-art is different. This chapter is all about creating very different family experiences in your classroom.

We know that:

- the way you invite parents
- the way you greet and welcome parents
- the way you interact with parents in your room
- the kinds of interactions you enable among the various-aged students in your rooms
- the kind of follow-up you do

all make a difference. So, let's work our way through the menu.

[Ron's Story]: **Seders, Plays and Videotape.** I've been to dozens of Model Seders in my life. Most of them are based on the number-one motivational tool Jewish educators use to get parents out of the car: When kids perform, parents come. (The second motivator is food.) Tell a parent that a child will be performing a part in a play or a Model Seder, you know that parent will be there, often dragging along grandparents, cameras, and camcorders.

One look at the classroom where the Model Seder is held tells me what will happen. There is usually a square table in the center of the room around which the kids sit. It is set up with all the objects of the Seder ceremony—grape juice, matzah, haroset, parsley, salt water, and a Seder plate. The kids hold in their hands a copy of the script, or often, just a copy of the few sentences that make up their "part." The teachers sit or stand near the kids, orchestrating the performance like conductors.

Where are the parents? They are sitting in the back of the room or around the circumference of the table. What are they doing? Kibbitzing with each other—until, of course, it is time for their "Devorah" or "Shlomo" to perform. Then, on come the red lights of the camcorders, out flip the flashes of the Pentax, all to record for posterity this "Kodak" (dare I say "Kodesh") moment! Once the targeted child has completed the performance, back the parents go to kibbitzing.

Where is the Jewish learning? Where is the interaction between parent and child? What has transpired in the "model" Seder that will inform what the parents might do in their own Seder at home? Unfortunately, the answer is usually: "Nothing."

The Jewish early childhood educators have a better idea. Their model Seders usually seat the parents next to the children at the table. They often ask the parents to read a part of the Haggadah story, to partake in the ritual foods, right along with the kids. Really good teachers send home the text of the children's Seder, along with the songs the kids have learned, so that maybe, just maybe, the parents will get the idea to include them in their own Seder at home.

Performance is not education. Jewish family education is not a spectator sport.

If You Invite Them (Right) They Will Come

[Joel's Story]: **The Story of Dick Cooper and the Shabbaton.** When I was a Rabbinic student, I was assigned to work a "Shabbaton" program at a local synagogue. The deal was that kids camped out at a home for Friday night. Saturday morning they walked to shul and then back for lunch. After lunch, the parents arrived for an adult study session. Then parents and kids had a combined study session. Then dinner. Then Havdalah. Then home.

I went to my first meeting and outlined my involvement in the program (which had already been running for a few years). I made my whole presentation, then this guy who was running the meeting (a VP of the congregation) leans into my face and asks, "What do we get to do?" I mumbled some quick rhetoric about support and policy and funding. Then Dick Cooper leaned into my face again and said, "I didn't say 'What do we 'have' to do?' I asked, 'What do we 'get' to do?' We want some of the fun!" After retreating to the bathroom to regroup my thoughts, I came back and we created together the concept of house-parents. We evolved a model where two or three couples worked on each Shabbaton as part of the staff, the only rule being that they couldn't do it on a Shabbaton when their own kids were attending. House-parents called other families and coordinated their children's attendance. House-parents did food and that stuff. House-parents also led discussions and were part of the program.

There were two results. (1) As a compulsory program, Shabbaton had about a 60% attendance rate. (Not bad!) When the house-parents went on-line, and replaced mailings with personal ("We will not take 'No' for an answer!") contact, that rate went up to over 90%. Sometimes lay people can accomplish things not even a professional can master. That is the same lesson learned in (2). The first weekend this guy by the name of Marv helped to put the kids to bed. He went from group to group of kids. Everywhere he went the kids were fast asleep. Later, when I asked him how he did it, he said, "Easy, I am an anesthesiologist." Sometimes lay people can accomplish things that not even a professional can master.

It is always good to do "slick publicity," but these two lessons should also be learned:

- Personal contact does better than anything you can put in the mail.

- Extant relationships are the right way to make personal contacts.

Such events should be built on the foundation of the positive communication which both initiated this year and which have been sustained through the year (so far). (See chapters 2 and 3.)

Chairs, Coffee (Tea) and Handshakes

The second part of "having parents" into your room is the regular stuff you need to do anytime you have company. You need to prepare to make them comfortable. This basically boils down to chairs, coffee, and handshakes.

Chairs come with two considerations. First, they need to be adult-sized. Just think about how much fun it is for any adult to sit in kid-sized furniture. Now think about how many forms are between you, the custodian, and the chairs you need. Odds are you don't even know, yet. This is the first part of being a good host. It will not be appreciated, but if you don't do it—watch out.

Second, you need to work out the seating philosophy in advance. If you do not do so, your room will default to Model Seder set up-automatically, and much of what you want to accomplish will be lost. Chairs convey the kind of relationship you want with parents—and the kinds of relationships you want parents to build during this session.

Now let's talk about **Coffee**. In the original draft of this book, I said, **"A good rule of thumb: Always have coffee available and always make sure you send something home which**

will review and extend the day." Handouts are very good; books are even better. That was a good truth. However, a better one was learned in the notes that I got back from reviewers.

> **[Susan Shevitz's Comment]:** "Tea, too, please."

> **[Sharon Halper's Comment]:** "'De-caf' as well as 'regular'—but often food and coffee get in the way."

The lesson is clear, whenever you give a party you need to attend to your own style, and individual needs of your guests. Whenever I have parents in, I like to "imprint" on the model of the brotherhood breakfasts I knew as a kid. Other teachers have other internal images. Food and coffee is often, but not always, a good idea. What we really want is comfort!

Handshakes are both literal and symbolic. Ron has already talked about being at the door to welcome students: important with kids, very important with adults. (Although, in the lesson learned from Dick Cooper, appointed "lay" greeters are also valuable.)

Should the room be arranged or unarranged? Yes, the room should either be "arranged" or "unarranged." An arranged room is a stage ready to perform on. An unarranged room is an opportunity to build participation, cooperation, and ownership. (Either should happen on purpose.) Both can be handshakes.

Is waiting for a lesson to begin, good or bad? Yes, it is good or bad—depending on whether waiting will build isolation or a sense of group. A good handshake takes planning.

Name tags are good, too (sometimes). They provide all kinds of opportunities.

There are all kinds of handshakes—all kinds of greetings.

> **[Vicky Kelman's Comment]:** I would say name tags are a must. [1] It is hard to relate to someone if you don't know or can't remember his/her name and [2] there are few things more embarrassing or distracting than trying to remember names you think you're supposed to know.

> **[Cherie Koller-Fox's Comment]:** I prefer to think of parents as partners not guests. We have an open invitation for them to come in at any time and sit in a class—they don't have to make an appointment. It's an open-door policy and they are always welcome—really.

The Actual Experience

In her book *Family Room, Linking Families into a Jewish Learning Community*, our colleague and friend, Vicky Kelman, provides this list of elements. *(It should be noted that Family Room meets monthly and this kind of sense of community can't be built in a day)*:

- Study a Jewish Text (or other body of Jewish content)
- Conversation within the family, between families, among peers (about the Jewish learning and about being a family)
- Creative expressions in a variety of media
- A "take home"
- A "bring in"
- Fun
- Breaking bread together
- Time to shmooze and play

> **[Joel's Comment]:** It is usually good to get **20 to 30 minutes alone with parents** in a "focus group" context. I usually share my expectations and evaluations of what has/will go on, and provide parents with an opportunity to do the same.

While not every family experience will contain all of these, it is a good starting list of the elements which ought to be considered.

Let's break out and underline a couple of these elements: **[1] Learning about Judaism. [2] Learning about being a Family/Community. [3] Social Time.**

[1] Learning about Judaism. Good family education events include all three of these elements. Everyone should learn/re-learn/expand a piece of Jewish knowledge/understanding. Parents as well as kids should feel they are getting something new. *Kids as well as parents—it works both ways.*

[2] Learning about being a Family/Community. When you put adults and kids, parents and children together, you widen the horizons of a lesson. Suddenly, there are a lot more perspectives. Good family/intergenerational programming takes advantage of this diversity by allowing it to blossom. You want to set up processes (often small groups) where opinions and insights can be shared across generations and between family members. In the process, the meaning of family and community is almost always deepened.

[3] Social Time. We want people to make friends and form communities. That is one of our major goals. This is a process which takes time and space (and often food as a catalyst). We need to both encourage and allow for this.

Programming Ideas:

Here are some of the good kinds of program ideas which can take place at a family education event:

- eating together. (Preparing the food is also a great possibility.)
- a performance created and staged that day, with parents and kids working together.
- crafts projects done together.
- texts studied together (or in small groups and then together).
- a series of stations that families visit (usually completing something at each station).
- regular classroom learning in which parents (i) co-participate as learners or (ii) serve as facilitators. We have a lot of stories about the power of an ordinary day with parent involvement.

It is good if these things can happen, too:

- Parents have a chance to study together on an adult level.
- Parents have a chance to meet as a group with teacher or other facilitator to (i) voice their needs and evaluation, and (ii) network concerns about the difficulty of raising a Jewish child.
- Parents and children also have time to "play" together. Family recess is a good thing (if it fits in the schedule).

Groupings. There will be enough people in your room that you want to take advantage of the adults and do lots of things in small groups. Here is the secret. Children ages 3-8, always work by family. Children ages 14-18, never work by family. But for the interzone, children ages 8-14 take your best guess as to the natures of the families and the groups. These rules apply except for the time when they don't apply. The nature and content of the interaction often dictate counter-intuitive groupings.

Younger kids often only feel safe within the family. By 9, or so, families have often developed patterns of not listening fully to their children (and vice versa). Working with a different set of parents/children often gives new perspective and breaks down the "transference" which has been built up over certain issues. That is especially true of teenagers. However, when you want to work on "family themes" or develop family histories, rituals, etc.—by-family groupings are more logical. Over the course of time, many groups and sub-groupings should be utilized. Remember, change the grouping, change the experience!

> **[Nachama Skolnik Moskowitz's Comment]:** My mother would ask: "Why not group 14-18 year olds with their own parents." She thinks (and I agree) that you need to engender these connections whenever possible. Also, I hate "nevers"—I've had to "eat" many of my nevers.

Make sure things are safe for parents. Never put them in a position were they will look stupid or foolish (except by their choice) in front of their kids. That means never demand Jewish knowledge or skills you aren't positive every one of them has. Also, remember, parents are pros at helping with their children's homework on a "learn as they go through it basis." That is a skill they do have.

Remember: Odds are not all of your parents:

- are Jewish by birth
- have intact (or Norman Rockwell) families
- speak/read Hebrew
- are "fluent" in Jewish rituals
- are comfortable with being in your room.

You need to help them succeed.

The Bennies

[Joel's Story]: A few years ago I taught a seventh grade with five family sessions built into the year. Here are three outcomes which were totally unexpected—not built into the experience.

- Barbara Zeidman turned to me and said, "What day do you want me to come in and make potato latkes with the class?" (I never thought to ask.)

- Jason's mother said (in a parents' meeting) that she wished we could have a baseball game or something, because all the families were spending so much energy fighting with their kids right now (because that is what happens with 12-year-olds) that they didn't get to play with them very much. We converted one of our five family events into a little study followed by a parents versus kids softball game and picnic. Great moment.

- Erika's mother and I wound up cleaning up a room together when everyone else went down to services. We had this amazing talk about how hard it was to teach and to parent these kids. I don't remember the content (or even her first name), but I remember the support both of us felt. It was one of those days which made teaching worthwhile.

Post-It Notes:

- Take-home stuff for families (as we have said before) is a good idea.

- A parent probably taught you the value of thank you notes. After a family event, make like a Bar/Bat Mitzvah kid. Say, "Thank you and see you again" on the way out (and a mailed follow-up is always good).

- Make sure you communicate "We missed you" (with a make-up kit) to families who couldn't be there. We'll tell you a great story about this process in the next chapter.

- And because we haven't said it previously, end of the year letters are important things, too.

[Ron's Story] : **Susie's Goody Bags.** My creative wife, Susie, a Jewish early childhood educator, thinks of most Jewish holidays as theme parties. So, when our children were young, Susie would always create a "goody bag" filled with wonderful things for our friends' children to take home from one of our holiday celebrations. For example, one Passover, the theme of our Seder was "frogs." We had "froggy" centerpieces, napkin holders, and salt and paper shakers. The "goody bag" had froggy stickers, a story about the plagues, the words to the "froggy" song ("One day when Pharaoh awoke in his bed, there were frogs on his head and frogs in his bed…"), some Pesahdik candy, and an Afikomen present.

The same idea of "take-home goody bags" has developed in good family education programs. I think of it as a reaction to the popular idea of "Shabbat in a Box," a box filled with the ritual objects for celebrating Shabbat that schools circulate among families. My problem with "Shabbat in a Box" has never been the box; the problem is that it circulates! So, what is a family to do next week when they want to celebrate Shabbat? The "goody bag" or "take home" kit consists of ritual objects, texts, and other materials a family can use to celebrate a holiday or observe a lifecycle event at home, and it is theirs to keep.

Here's an example. I once received a phone call from a layperson who was the chairwoman for the Shabbat family dinner I was to lead as part of a Scholar-in-Residence appearance at a synagogue.

She asked how I wanted the room set up (I have a whole sheet of instructions just for this—write me if you need it) and what could they do to make the evening special. I said: "Learn from Susie and let's make the Shabbat dinner into a real celebration." So, I suggested flowers and centerpieces on the tables, beautiful invitations, decorated name tags for each member of the family, and a goody bag to take home. When I got to the synagogue that Friday night, I was thrilled with what I saw. The room was fully decorated, the tables were beautifully arranged, and, at the back of the room was a long table with the Shabbat goody bags for each family and individual in attendance. The goody bag itself was a very attractive laminated blue and white gift bag with a Jewish star motif, the kind you would find in a Jewish gift store. Each bag had a label on it that said: "Compliments of the B'nai Chayim Family Education Committee—Shabbat Shalom" and room for the name of each family/person. Inside the goody bag were the following objects: two white candles, a pair of aluminum candle holders, a copy of *The Art of Jewish Living: The Shabbat Seder benscher*, a make-your-own challah cover kit, a read-aloud story about Shabbat angels, a tiny bottle of Kedem grape juice, an audiocassette of the tunes for the blessings of the Shabbat dinner, and a packaged piece of halvah! The committee finished off these phenomenal bags with colored tissue paper and attached a helium ballon to each handle. I can't even begin to describe how excited the families were to receive these bags at the end of the evening. After experiencing a learning Shabbat Seder in which I taught the major blessings and ritual acts, these families could now take home a kit that enabled them to create their own Shabbat Seder the following week. Instead of being told to leave the kippot at the back of the shul or to put away the prayer-books, they were given a present from the synagogue and school. I wondered when had been the last time that had happened in an institution that always seems to ask people to give of themselves and their resources. Our friend and teacher, Vicky Kelman calls this "portable scaffolding," providing the support and materials for building a temporary structure to assist the building of a permanent Jewish identity in the family. The goody bag is one answer to a basic question for family education programming: "What goes home?"

> **[Cherie Koller-Fox's Comment]:** I try to always send home something from every family event. I send home a yahrzeit candle for Yom HaShoah, a tape with the songs for Passover or Purim, a book with blessings, stories, study pieces for Shabbat, and recipes, samples, ritual objects. I want them to have this stuff at home—I always include this gift in my thinking about the cost of the event.

Beyond the Model Seder II

Because Model Seders are the paradigms we are trying to shatter, let's look at a number of alternatives to the extant process of families whose names begin with a-d providing the grape juice and then sitting in the audience (waiting for the paper fireman hats to make their appearance).

The Carol Starin Plan (1st Grade) Teams of parents play various games and visit various stations with groups of kids before the seder. Then, they sit together with their kids participating in a cooperative learning seder. And she adds, make sure that every family has an age-appropriate haggadah to take home from the event.

The Rabbi Cherie Koller-Fox Plan (Whole Families) An order of the Seder Board Game in which the parts of the seder (Kadesh, U-rehatz) are randomly placed at stations around the room. Families go to each listening, reading, tasting what is there. Then they sit down as a family to decide what they think the order of the seder is. They work with each of the fifteen parts of the seder on what is a self-correcting puzzle that fits together if they are correct.

Alternatively: A Passover Fair with demonstrations of Passover cake-making, gefilte fish making, wine tasting, matzah and macaroon tasting. There was a display of Haggadot, videos and computer programs about the holiday, and a board for people to share multiple copies they made of their favorite recipes. In rooms to the side, there was a *bedikat hametz* game, making haroset, workshops on holiday songs, Sephardic traditions, craft projects, etc.

> **[Cherie Koller-Fox's Comment]:** I remember Model Seders very well. Our table loved to fill our "Elijah's cup" with gross stuff—hard-boiled egg, wine, parsley, napkin scraps, macaroon crumbs—you get the picture. I think Passover events should be preparatory in nature. What can we learn to enrich our seder experience at home? It could be as simple as a new song to sing or a new understanding of a text. It could be a play to perform for guests or a prop to add to the fun of Had Gadya. It could be a seder plate or a special cup. But it shouldn't take away from the seder itself by creating a shadow of a seder without grandparents, guests, and favorite foods.

Joel Grishaver and Don Rossoff's Seder Board Game (Whole Families) Intergenerational teams work their way through a board game by brainstorming answers to questions which all read "list as many...." and then performing (at breakneck speeds) parts of the seder ritual. Families learn about and practice parts of the seder via play.

The Epilogue:

The central message of this chapter has been that "family education days" are nothing to fear—rather they are major opportunities to both network and influence the families with whom you are always interacting.

Remember, even if we do nothing about it, the home is always at the other end of the carpool, exercising immense influence on the work we do. (Have you ever clicked your heels together and said, "There's no place like Hebrew School?")

We have intentionally resisted reducing family education events to a paint-by-number set. Here however, is a review of the basics:

- Family Education Events should be built out of courted and developed relationships.
- They should be run like a good dinner party with nice invitations and careful planning.
- The first parts of the event are in the set-up and the greeting.
- Often Family Education Events bring together new groups, so introductions and meeting opportunities are necessary.
- The actual program usually consists of a combination of discrete activities which add up to a total experience (see below).
- Good family education days should include a number of diverse groupings and learning experiences. We want participants to have both a family and an intergenerational community experience.
- It is a unique opportunity for networking when a teacher can get time with his/her parents, alone.
- Each of these family events should be used to set up the next event and the next communication between school and home. (Like a cocktail party, much of the work is done tete-a-tete rather than through public presentations.)
- The after-event follow-up can be as important as the event.

We have not presumed to know your context. The age, size, curriculum, history, and demography of you and your class (let alone their families) all influence proper planning. Therefore, any cookie-cutter program would fail to meet your needs. In that sense, as in most (if not all) good teaching, you have to adapt these basic patterns, techniques, and attitudes to fit your setting. To enable that process, a portfolio of family events follows this chapter.

Nine More Things from Ron

Now to end this chapter, here are nine more basic principles from Ron. They sum up all of the specifics mentioned above.

[1] Tell Your Own Story/Let Them Tell Theirs: I continue building this connection by sharing a story or two about my own experience with Jewish living. If I am teaching Shabbat, I will tell my by-now-oft-quoted story of how I wanted our baby daughter Havi to have a white dress to wear on her first Shabbat with us and ended up buying a christening outfit. If Passover is the subject, I will talk about my Zaydie Louis-the-grocery-man's Haggadah—Maxwell House, of course—and the rather abbreviated Seder I remember as a kid back in Omaha. If it is the December Dilemmas, I will admit to my nervousness the first time our son Michael asked if we could put up "those pretty lights" on our house. If it is my newest book, *A Time to Mourn, A Time to Comfort*, I will share my own bereavement experiences as a way to enable the audience to identify with me.

Then, I ask them to tell their stories. Inevitably, the stories are similar as are their messages—"I'm searching," I'm frustrated," "My kids know more than I do..." I want them to see that they are not alone and I want them to know that I am there to listen and respond to their needs and concerns. This is the essence of comforting a mourner—and it is the essence of good teaching.

[2] Use Humor: My stories are almost always humorous, often downright hysterical. I use humor not just as a way to "grab" an audience at the beginning of a class or lecture; I use it to make people feel comfortable. One of the most difficult things for laypeople to overcome is their fear of Judaism. Many people I see are intimidated by Jewish practice. Why? Because as smart as they are, as competent as they are in most things secular, put them in a Jewish environment and they turn to mush. They have little fluency, if any, in Hebrew language, their experience with ritual is spotty, and their knowledge of Judaism is Sunday School level, at best. Yet, they are at that lecture or workshop because they are motivated to learn. They are courageous enough to admit "I don't know"; the ones who aren't there have said "I don't care." So, as their teacher, I want to welcome them—with warmth, with humor, with a personal connection—because once they are relaxed, I can begin to teach.

[3] There's No Such Thing as a Silly Question: Early on in any class I teach, I send a message loud and clear that any question, every question, is a great question. I cannot count the number of times I have heard people preface their queries with "I know this is a stupid question…." And they're the ones brave enough to ask. Think of all the students who never raise a hand!

I learned this lesson when an adult student once asked me which Shabbat candle is lit first. I began to chuckle, because, of course, it doesn't matter. Big mistake. The student, by then embarrassed, told me she had been to a workshop on *Hanukkah* where the teacher had made a big deal about setting up the candles on the *hanukkiyah* to the left and lighting them to the right. It was a great question! From that day forward, I have never laughed at any question about Jewish practice. In fact, I invite any and all questions, no matter how insignificant they may think it is. This creates a climate of comfort in the class and gives the student permission to learn.

[4] Create Easy Access Opportunities: A problem many lay people have in approaching Jewish studies is the feeling that the material is simply overwhelming. There is such a long history, so many observances, so much Hebrew. It often feels insurmountable. One of the techniques I utilize in the *Art of Jewish Living* series, I learned from books like the *Metzudah siddur* and *machzor* and the old Camp Ramah siddurim. I break down the text I'm teaching into small phrases, number them, and position them linearly on the page in three columns; Hebrew on the right, transliteration on the left, and translation in the center. This allows those who can read phonetic Hebrew to read right-to-left in the right column, while those who cannot read Hebrew read left-to-right in the left column, and we all meet in the center. I want them to say the words, to understand the words, and to learn to chant the words. it is an approach that is called "direct instruction." It is an approach that offers "easy access' to all learners.

> **[Esther Netter's Comment] :** This is a BIG issue and could fill a chapter, a book, a set of books.

[5] Model Behaviors: It has always amazed me how much time is spent teaching "about" Judaism and not how to "do" Judaism. My audience has not, by and large, grown up with Jewish ritual practice in their homes. And, if they did, they hardly know why they do what they do when they "do Jewish."

So, I spend a lot of time actually modeling the ritual behaviors I'm teaching. I light the candles, I break the matzah, and I spin the dreidel. When I teach the chant of a *berakhah*, I sing the loudest. I constantly provide a model for the learner to follow.

A rabbi once told me it was "beneath" him to teach this way. He wanted to teach spirituality to his people. Well, guess what? It's no accident that the center of "spirituality" is "ritual." I suppose there are other ways to find God, but for me, and most of the students I work with, ritual behavior is the fundamental path to spirituality.

> **[Nachama Skolnik Moskowitz's Comment]:** Also, give families access to resources for use at home. When you lose the photocopies, brakhah lists, etc—where do you turn for candle-lighting information? (i.e. a basic Jewish how-to libarary.)

[6] Don't be Afraid of the "F" Word: Here's another heresy: Jewish living can be fun. I teach people that it's OK to laugh at a Seder. I teach families to do "the wave" during a boisterous singing of "Shalom Aleichem." I teach people how my brilliant wife, Susie, turns holiday celebrations into "theme" parties (her avocado "froggy" Passover centerpiece has graced lots of Seder tables)!

There is a joy in Judaism that we must teach to our people. Not only is having fun during most Jewish holidays a good motivational "hook," it happens to be true to the tradition. I don't want my students to think of Judaism as a series of "no's." Clearly, there are plenty of prohibitions, and I certainly teach them. But, I prefer to begin with the "yeses," the permission to enjoy being Jewish.

[7] Take Baby Steps: One of my favorite "lessons" is about the meaning of the word "halakhah." I explain that the literal meaning is "to go," or "to walk," and, where do we walk? Along a path. Jewish law offers a path, a way, each of us is somewhere along that path, some further along than others. But, no matter where I am or where you are at this moment, we can progress to the next point.

This is my version of the "Rosenzweig" story, the "Do you keep kosher, Dr. Rosenzweig? Not yet…" gambit. One of the most powerful ways I empower those who want to learn how to live Jewishly is to accept them "where they're at" when they come to me and then encourage them to take baby steps along that path.

"But, aren't I hypocritical to have Shabbat dinner with my family and then go to work on Saturday?" "I can keep kosher for Passover because it's only for eight days, but I can't manage it during the year." I want to ban the word "hypocrite" from any discussion of Jewish living. It's used as an excuse, an obstacle, a "put-down." It can easily be used to justify the elitism of those who are already way down the path, or to mix the analogies, up the mountain. Well, it's about time for those who are on high to come down and meet the people. For God's sake, even Moshe did that!

We would be much better served to encourage people to add one more step to their ritual, to try one new thing at their Seder—to understand that, unless you are a true "ba'al/at t'shuvah," adopting a full Jewish "lifestyle" takes years of practice. Let's enable our people to "ease on down the road" one step at a time.

[8] Be Enthusiastic: We have this "Course Evaluation" form that our students at the University of Judaism fill out at the end of the semester. There are some forty statements about us professors that they get to rank on a scale of 1 to 5, 5 being best. They are mostly the typical things you find on surveys like this: "knows the subject," "comes prepared to class…." The one I've always liked is: "Enthusiastic about the subject."

If there is one quality that is absolutely fundamental to my approach to teaching it is enthusiasm. I truly love what I do. I truly love Judaism. And I want my students to know it. So, I approach teaching or lecturing with all the enthusiasm I can muster. I suppose the best indicator of this is how spent I am at the end of a class or a talk. It takes enormous energy to teach for an hour or two or three. But, it's worth everything. Because enthusiasm is catching. It rubs off. If I'm excited about what I'm teaching, the students often get excited, too. And when they get excited, when they learn what Jewish living can do for them, their kids, their families—the baby steps get bigger, the crawl turns to a jog, and the learning flows.

[9] Jews Are Made One at a Time. One of the nicest compliments I ever received was from the president of a synagogue, a rather wealthy man who owned a group of car dealerships, after a Friday night Scholar-in-Residence lecture. It had been a particularly responsive crowd and the talk really sizzled. He approached me at the Oneg Shabbat and said: "That was great. Gee, you could make a million. Have you ever thought of being a salesman?" I replied: "I *am* a salesman."

If you think about it, there are a lot of characteristics salespeople and teachers share: good communication skills, knowledge of product, enthusiasm for the product, marketing ability and knowing when to close.

I'll close with my last point: Jewish education is a retail business. We make Jews one at a time. It takes a lot of work to reach and teach someone to be Jewish. It begins with the personal connection and proceeds from there. And even then, it is only a beginning. Once on the path, it takes a supportive community to keep someone with us. But, in the end, when a student tells you she took your idea and had the best Seder her family ever had, or he tells you he decided to celebrate Shabbat every week, or she tells you she gathered up enough courage to make the shiva call and it went fine, it feels like more than a million. It is one of the most rewarding feelings any human being can ever have.

[An Epilogue from Linda Kirsch]: You were right. Rather than complaining or worrying that no one would show up for a family program, I am putting the program in the hands of some parents. They will do the fine tuning and the inviting. I already have one Middle School parent working with me and she suggested a couple of others, so I think we'll end up getting a good turnout. Had I done it, alone, it probably would have had only nominal attendance.

[Esther Netter's Comment]: Whenever you get parents in, start thinking of what the next step can be. How can we get them back? How can they become more involved? Maybe help plan the next family education day? Here is the handout I use in my workshop.

Checklist for event itself:
- Sign in—name, address, phone, names of children, ages—Can your name be circulated?
- Program Evaluation sheet/card—to be completed at program
- Take home materials
- Automatic entitlement
- Camera
- Art (to be displayed)
- Name tags (for all participants)
- Sign-out book—space for comments—"One thing I learned today is...?"

Other:
- Checklist for week/month after event:
- Mailings—Suggested activities
  —Articles
  —Program info
  —Just a hello
  —Kids' activities
- Telephone contact
- Ask for planners for next event
- Article in newsletter

Other:
- Checklist for long-term/ongoing follow up:
- Develop a lay committee (use teens/children if appropriate)
- Begin newsletter
- Long range—calendar programs
- Holiday communications
- Connect families with other parts of institution
- Outreach/Inreach
- Pair families together

Other:
- And now what more can I do?

A PORTFOLIO OF PROGRAMS

Temple Beth El, San Antonio

Deena Bloomstone is the Educational Director of Temple Beth El in San Antonio. She is a consummate educator who brilliantly runs the gauntlet of being an educator in a city with a very small Jewish community and limited resources. She is also an important member of the Torah Aura Family, having served as editor of the Torah Aura Bulletin Board and as a contributor to a number of our materials. She shares two items from her portfolio within this collection.

[Deena Bloomstone's Comment]: One of our concerns here is that parents have a variety of "Religious School Baggage" they carry with them. Part of the process of establishing a meaningful long-term relationship with families is to deal with that baggage. We've developed part of a series of orientation programs around life-cycle events, Consecration and Bar/Bat Mitzvah, which deal with some of this baggage. The twist to our program is that we have a family life educator from Jewish Family Service come and process with the parents. In her sessions with parents, the family life educator has dealt with issues of past experiences (negative and positive), the personal significance of sending one's children to Religious School, watching children grow older and realizing your own growth, developing connections with other families.

The use of an outside counselor/facilitator to discuss such issues has been a great success and has taken over the majority of the program. Parents enjoy the interaction and personal discussion that takes place. Through guided questioning parents share memories about their own religious education, good and bad, Jewish and non-Jewish. They find that they are not alone in their worries or desires for their children. Each orientation is different, emphasizing different aspects of the life cycle and its parallel tie to Jewish education.

The Consecration Orientation which is conducted for new members whose children have entered our Religious School for the first time, is a particularly rewarding experience. In a two and one half hour session, parents spend a significant portion of their time processing. Since most of those parents participating have young children who will be consecrated on Simchat Torah, they then engage in an experiential exercise with their children in which they complete together a consecration questionnaire. (Enclosed)

The Bar/Bat Mitzvah orientation is a three-session program. The first session is held in January, when families receive the Bar/Bat Mitzvah dates. This orientation is devoted to family processing. The parents meet with the Family Life Educator and the students meet with the Education Director. Towards the end of the session, parents and children come together, share their worries and concerns and complete a Bar/Bat Mitzvah Brit in which they commit to experiencing the

Bar/Bat Mitzvah year in some Jewish fashion or form. Part of this Brit includes a statement in which both parents and child understand that children who become Bar/Bat Mitzvah at Temple Beth-El, will continue on in their Jewish education through Confirmation. What is so rewarding is that virtually all students see their Jewish educational commitment through. To help families bring Jewish opportunities home, we give the families the JET pack for Bar/Bat Mitzvah and we monitor their use in the other two orientation sessions held at other times of the year.

We also conduct an orientation program for Confirmation, but we have not yet included a personal processing component. Given the success of the other two programs with the family life educator, I would consider developing just such a program with this age group. The focus here would be on the teen/parent relationship, giving room, letting go, and the challenge to recognize in a rebellious period of life and that Judaism has something to offer a young adult.

To My Child

I am so happy that you are beginning Religious School because _____

_____

My special Religious School memory while growing up is _____

_____

I wish I could go to Religious School now so that I could learn more about _____

_____

What I like most about your going to Religious School class_____

_____

I believe it is important for you to attend Religious School because _____

_____

Message to your child _____

_____

Signed _____

Consecration Questionnaire

Name: _____

Hebrew Name: _____

Reason for Name: _____

Address: _____

_____

Place of Birth: _____

Mother's Name: _____ Father's Name: _____

Hebrew Name: _____ Hebrew Name: _____

Reason for Name: _____ Reason for Name: _____

Grandparents: _____ Grandparents: _____

On the Occasion of my Birth, there was: ꟼ A Brit   ꟼ A Naming   ꟼ Other

Place _____

My Siblings are: _____

Pets: Type _____ Name _____

My Favorite Jewish Holiday: _____

My Favorite Jewish Food: _____

My Favorite Jewish Home Ritual: _____

My House has a *Mezuzah.*   ꟼ Yes   ꟼ No

My Room has a *Mezuzah.*   ꟼ Yes   ꟼ No

My Parents wanted me to be consecrated because: _____

Now that I'm beginning my formal Jewish education, our family will increase its Jewish activity in the following ways: _____

In honor of my consecration, I would like my family to contribute to *Tzedakah* in the following way:

My Favorite Sport or Hobby: _____

My Special Talents are: _____

When I grow up, I want to: _____

Bar/Bat Mitzvah Brit

As I_____, prepare to become a Bar/Bat Mitzvah in 1997, I promise to learn about the importance of responsibility.

For my Jewish Education I promise to _____

For my family, I promise to _____

For my Temple, I promise to _____

As, _____, our/my child, prepares to become a Bar/Bat Mitzvah in 1997, we/I,_____, promise to be there for him/her, helping him/her as s/he grows into his Jewish responsibilities. For his/her Jewish education, we promise to _____

For his/her development into Jewish responsibility, we promise to _____

For his involvement in Temple activities, we promise to _____.

We mutually agree that_____ will continue his/her Jewish education through Confirmation.

Signed on this day of _____,

We commit to the Jewish development of_____.

Signed: Parent_____ Child_____ Parent_____

The Community Hebrew School of Greater Philadelphia

Rabbi Phil Warmflash developed this inventory for a parent education program at Community Hebrew School of Greater Philadelphia where he is the educational director. Part I is the inventory. Part II is the Family Action (Refrigerator) Contract. This is a minor family activity which a lot of Phil's families reported to be very valuable.

Jewish Practices Inventory

Check any of the items below which you have done in the past year. Remember, you decide for yourself what constitutes a "regular basis" or a "Shabbat dinner."

q   Learning something Jewish on a regular basis.

q   Light Shabbat Candles.

q   Support a Jewish Charity.

q   Give charity regularly and decide as a family where the money should go.

q   Volunteer time to help others.

q   Have a Shabbat dinner regularly.

q   Read a Jewish book.

q   Attend a Passover Seder.

q   Observe major Jewish holidays.

q   Visit grandparents, extended family members.

q   Go to a synagogue.

q   Problem solve as a family.

q   Other _____

Part II: Compare your responses with others in your family.

Part III: As a family, choose 1-3 items which you will do during the next year. Write those items and list them on the Family Action Contract on the following page. Review the list in 3 months and see how you are doing.

Family Action Contract

During the next school year (1993-1994), corresponding to the Jewish Year 5754, our family has decided that we will undertake the following Jewish activities:

_____

_____

_____

_____

We sign below to indicate that each member of our family will help in fulfilling this goal.

_____

_____

_____

_____

Date: _____

When you have completed this contract, put it on your refrigerator.

The "Family Matters"

Susan Fish et al, The Jewish Day School, Seattle

Susan Fish is a teacher at the Seattle Jewish Day School. She is everything you could want a teacher to be. Creative, reflective, energetic, etc. A few of her programs were relayed to us by the director of the local Central Agency for Jewish Education. We then included some of her things and sent her a copy of the manuscript for her input. What came back was a wonderfully prepared booklet of other family programs she had done, set up so they could be shared with other teachers. We've excerpted from the booklet and other resources to form a Susan Fish portfolio for this book. Included with the packet was a business card: Susan Fish, Educator. Here is a teacher with pride and professionalism. That says a lot.

"PARSHA AND PASTRY," "THE POWER OF LIGHT,"
Searching for Noah, a man who was right.
Matzah and springtime, questions and more,
Retelling stories—PESACH '94.
"A CELEBRATION OF BOOKS" — authors and art, Torah, Jerusalem—
all from the heart.
A PARENT EVENING with Diane as host,
We want our parents to have the most!
Families and children—the part and the whole,
How special—the Day School can add to their soul.
Education that's Jewish family, and FUN,
An ongoing process to make us all one.
With tools to build spirit for learning and growing,
We plant and we harvest the sharing and knowing.
We bring special gifts and we take some home, too,
To enrich the dear family with learning that's new.
We layer, empower, cre-a-tively,
And experience life—Jewishly!
In 2nd grade we build the relation,
Jewish Family Life Education!

Susan Fish

GREAT BEGINNINGS: This program grew out of a major change in the JDS Curriculum Night format. As a school, we decided to make this informative evening more hands-on and interactive in order for families to hear and experience some of the information focused on during Curriculum Night. Teachers and staff, Parent Association, and Development worked together to provide families with the best vehicles for relating this wealth of knowledge. In 2nd grade, we wanted our families to sample the flavor of their child's learning, so we created learning stations in our classrooms that reflected teaching and learning in all subject areas. Our goal was to provide information, experience, and fun and at the same time recognize the importance of our integrated, developmentally appropriate curriculum. The stations focused on the current week's curriculum—Parashat Bereshit—Great Beginnings. This also included Rosh ha-Shanah, introductory lessons in math, integrated activities related to SUCCESS In Reading and Writing—*A Holistic Language Art Philosophy*, and some of the beginning activities and lessons in Hebrew, Torah, and Tefillah. Parents are welcomed into the classrooms for one hour, followed by short presentations from Development and Parent Association, and then a formal curricular overview was given in each class. Refreshments were served during the open house portion of the evening. While experiencing the curricular activities, parents were able to ask questions, take notes, and enjoy the learning!

The stations include the following, [1]**Warm-up** (introduction to the experience), [2] **Math** - *Ten Black Dots* by Donal Crews, [3] **Art** - make a creation picture based on a poem about one of the days of creation, [4] **Research** - locate pictures and/or words in magazines related to the days of creation ("God's Work"), [5] **Reading** - a Creation poem, [6] **Word Study** - locating words related to "God's Work" from "Beresheet" in *My Weekly Sidrah* by Joel Grishaver, [6] **Hebrew** vocabulary game related to "God's Work" [7] 613 **Torah** Avenue songs about Parsha "Beresheet."

SUKKOT: "Sukkot" was a whole-school one-shot program developed for JDS families. Learning took place through the use of stations which included model sukkot building (Cookie sookies), art and crafts involving decorations for the sukkah (paper chains and playdough lulavim and etrogim), brachot, explanations of the symbols of the holiday, and singing in the sukkah.

The afternoon culminated with storytelling, singing, and honeycakes and apple juice for a snack. Families took with them information on sukkah building, Sukkot brachot, and many art projects and ideas to use in their own sukkot. The event lasted for 2 hours on a Sunday afternoon during Sukkot. The main objectives were education including a variety of entry level points appropriate to day school families, fun, and family interaction within one's own family and among the school community.

NOAH AND THE GREAT ZOO EXTRAVAGANZA: "Noah and the Great Zoo Extravaganza" celebrates the first three parshiot and allows for a window on the integrated 2nd grade curriculum while setting the stage for building community for 2nd graders and their families. It is also a way to bring together tzedakah for the classroom community and for the Seattle community. This family experience took place on a Sunday afternoon at Woodland Park Zoo. It was open to 2nd grade families, including siblings, grandparents, etc. The class had been studying parshiot *"Beresheet,"* *"Noah,"* and *"Lekh-Lekha."* We had learned about caring for animals, mitzvot related to animals, Hebrew vocabulary, stories, songs, and games, how to build caring communities with animals, animal research, word study, writing, and reading about animals. A visit from the King County Humane Society, complete with guests (a very special golden retriever) allowed us to donate our tzedakah for the months of September and October through our class Pet Food Drive. We also donated two "Caring For Animals" quilts to the King County Humane Society to thank them for their informative visit.

The afternoon began with a gathering of families where they met other 2nd grade families, picked up their "research" packets and maps and began their tour and discoveries at the zoo. After an hour, the families returned and read parshiot midrashim stories, snacked, sang animal songs to the accompaniment of Cantor Kurland's accordion, and danced the "Goat Dance" under the able choreography of Sara Kupor. Families were then free to continue their zoo explorations, socialize with other families, or to depart.

THE POWER OF LIGHT: This program has been implemented in a variety of day school settings—a 2nd grade family program, a program for senior citizen guests, (Council House) and a joint 2nd grade program with the Seattle Jewish Primary School. The tzedakah component was the same for each group—light up someone else's life by bringing a food item for the Kosher Food Bank. The focus of each program was built around eight different stations all related to light. The integration of science, math, Judaica, Hebrew, language arts, and art was apparent at all times. There were four stations set up in two classrooms and the children and their guests moved from station to station. Parent helpers were always employed in all settings and parent help was needed beforehand for prep work for the art project and sofganiyot pick up, cut up, and serving. The program lasted for about 2 hours, beginning with all group *Hanukiot* lighting and brachot and ending with a beautiful slide show entitled "The Power of Light." The show featured each child in the class doing something related to the power of light—Shabbat, Torah, learning, Hanukah, etc. The accompanying music featured "Don't let the Light Go Out," "Light One Candle," and "*Yad B'Yad*." There was not a dry eye in the house!

The stations included: [1] "Cooking Light" (cooking), [2] "A Light in the Window" (art), [3] "Candle Count" (math), [4] "Light Research" (language arts), [5] "Light Reading" (reading), [6] "Have Light Will Travel" (science), [7] "Lotto Lights" (Hebrew), [8] "Candle Questions" (Judaica).

PARSHA AND PASTRY: "Parsha and Pastry" was a morning program built around the weekly Torah portion, *parashat ha-shavuah, "Va-yakhel."* It was a program designed for 2nd graders and their families (no siblings) in order to provide a window on an integrated curriculum, to celebrate and study art and artists, and to experience and learn Torah "hands-on." The program lasted about 2 hours and included interactive learning stations, large group stories, exhibits, a Judaica museum, and refreshments! Two classrooms were used for the program; one housed the exhibits, food, and gathering place, the other was set up with 4 learning stations and a sharing area. Debbie Friedman's "And You Shall Be A Blessing" tape played throughout the rooms and provided ambiance and spirituality. Students and families interacted together at the centers and then shared experiences and projects with the whole group. Pastries and a story pulled everyone together at the end of the morning. "Gifts" were brought to the *Mishkan* for modern tzedakah such as toys, books, and games. Families were able to take with them two stories and questions related to the parsha that they could use as springboards for Shabbat discussions that coming week.

Stations to visit and participate at included: [1] "Special Gifts We Give to God" (art), [2] "Special Gifts God Gives to Us" (creative writing), [3] Famous local artists (biographies and art examples), [4] SUCCESS curriculum materials—journals, related literature, charts, [5] Family Education articles, [6] Pastries, [7] Judaica "museum" (*mishkan*)

PESAH '94: This program was created out of the challenge of teaching an interactive family Passover program without it being a model seder. We decided to focus on specific elements of the Seder and to emphasize the message of "retelling our stories." The Haggadah was the main impetus for our stations that were repeated in our two classrooms. The children and their families were divided into their regular groups and covered four different learning stations. The program began with a warm-up which asked families to pair up and retell a Passover family event they remembered. After families had time to do this, we then went into an explanation of stations. In 1990, we did a program for families and their 2nd graders entitled, "Exodus." This music and slide show retells the story of the going out of Egypt to the Promised Land. Lovely spring flowers graced the food table as refreshments of fruit and macaroons were served as families socialized.

The stations included the following: [1] "Play With the Plagues"—Hebrew vocabulary matching games, [2] "Four More Questions"—Four more questions to ask at the Seder, [3] "The Three Symbols of Passover"—Artistic collage related to "freedom", [4] "Dayaynoo—We Are Grateful For What God Has Given To The World." - Research using magazines to locate words and/or pictures related to the song.

2ND GRADE PARENT EVENING: The "2nd Grade Parent Evening" was an example of a parallel family learning experience. The children participated in various activities, exercises, role-plays, and problem-solving blueprints in the classroom with Diane Zipperman, the school counselor. Parents were introduced to the concepts of "Blueprints For Problem-Solving" at spring conferences. A survey agenda was distributed at this time for parents to brainstorm topics of interest for a parent get-together. After tallying responses, it appeared most people were interested in issues of child rearing, self-esteem and child development guidelines. Diane structured the meeting/conversation to include and integrate these topics. Handouts were available and meaningful information disseminated. Many of the activities in which the children had been involved in at school were presented and parents were also able to participate in similar situations. Coffee and cookies were available at the beginning of the evening allowing for schmoozing, introductions, and general tone-setting. Many parents agreed that they would love to see this continue for each class at JDS and they had a great time!

AUTHORS' CELEBRATION: The integration of the celebration of books—Torah, siddur, and personal publications—with our study of Jerusalem make this family program a wonderful end of the year event. Two classrooms are used to depict the

Old and New cities of Jerusalem. The Old City houses the Kotel, Bet Knesset, Dome of the Rock, the walled city, the gates of the Old City, and the *shuk* (market). The New City hosts the Israeli Museum and Cafe Jerusalem on Ben Yehuda Street. In the Old City, children and parents join together for the *shaharit* service in front of the Wailing Wall. To the sound of the guitar, the morning service is chanted in culmination of a full year of *t'fillah* study in *Kitah Bet*. The class is then divided into the two groups—one group performs a Hebrew play in the streets of the Old City, while the other group boards an Egged tour bus to travel to the New City. There, children and guests sit at checkered-cloth tables to read their publications, snack on an Israeli nut and raisin mix, and enjoy faux lattes and cookies. Classical music adds ambiance to the coffeehouse atmosphere as barristas, authors, and parents experience incredible books! (The groups switched and repeated the performances after about 25 min.)

JOURNEY TO JERUSALEM: This program was similar in nature and classroom set-up to "Authors' Celebration" as it takes place in the Old and New City of Jerusalem; however, the family group focus is the extended JDS senior community and the JDS 2nd grade family community. The "journey" includes four family interactive stations mirrored in each room. Each station involves the student as the "teacher" and facilitator for his/her senior guest. Our relationship with Council House penpals brought us to our fourth interaction with these people. Each child was responsible for a guest and a student tour group. Each group traveled from place to place, participating, teaching, and interacting with the guest and the materials. The morning began, once again, with an abbreviated *shaharit* service where both students and guests participated in a story-telling by Safranit Margo who represented the Torah portion of our service. We then moved to the stations. At the end of our time together, we met in "Cafe Jerusalem" for coffee, tea, juice, and cookies. We ended the morning with a story and songs about "building Jerusalem." 2nd grade parents were invited to attend and also helped to set up, clean up, transport the seniors, make arrangements through phone calls, and acted as general aides at the centers.

The stations included the following: [1] "Jerusalem Travelogue"—Hebrew matching game about places in Jerusalem, [2] "Jerusalem Artists"—Quilt responses to sights and sounds experienced in the "Old City" and the "New City", [3] "Cooperative Cooking"—making kibbutz breakfast salad, [4] "Noteworthy Notes"—writing messages and prayers for the Kotel, [5] A visit to the *shuk* (marketplace).

HAVDALAH: This program was designed in much the same vein as "Journey To Jerusalem." The target families were our extended Council House "grandparents," and also included 2nd grade parents as guests, helpers, and support people. Shabbat is a major curricular focus in 2nd grade in Jewish studies with support from General studies. Three Shabbatonim occur from January through March with groups of 10 children participating each time. Havdalah is celebrated with parents after Shabbat has ended and families come to pick up their children. The havdalah experience for the program with Council House is an extension and enrichment of the experiences related to separating Shabbat from the rest of the coming week. It also provides an opportunity for the children to once again "teach" their Council House guest about Havdalah and to participate in different activities related to the celebration. Guests and children were asked to bring Havdalah sets from home and/or artifacts to create Havdalah sets (any candlestick, wineglass, spice box). Guests were welcomed into the classroom and the havdalah service was shared. We then broke into our two groups, _Hesed_ and _Rahamim_, with our guests and participated in stations in each classroom.

The stations include the following: [1] "Candle Creations"—Making Havdalah candles, [2] "Spice and Sniff"—Guess the different spices while blindfolded, [3] "Wineglass Wonders"—Decorating wine glasses, [4] "Havdalah Highlights"—after hearing a story together, [5] "Stars"—A math place value game, [6] The end of the morning was spent coming together for Havdalah songs. We shared refreshments with our guests and had another opportunity to be hosts and hostesses.

Susan Fish, Jewish Day School of Metroplitan Seattle, Bellevue, WA
The "Family Matters" Jewish Family Education Programs

Jacksonville Jewish Center

Here is a program from the Jacksonville Jewish Center. It was a "community extravaganza" (not class-room activity). But, it models a kind of potential for family events. Think about scaling this down for your classroom.

Noah's Ark

This program was geared to the kindergarten, first and second grades. The lesson began in the classroom with a review of the story based on the Bible. The children were then shown a film by Hanna/Barbera entitled "Noah's Ark," followed by a discussion period about the message of the story. Our lesson culminated on Sunday, November 8th, with a boat trip to the Jacksonville Zoo.

A water taxi was reserved for the journey down the St. Johns River. The children and their families met Rabbi Dov Kentof, Educational Director (who was dressed as Noah) and our Sunday School staff at the dock. As we floated down the river, the story of Noah was again told by "Noah" himself with emphasis on today's environ-mental problems and the destruction being caused by humans who are abusing nature and ignoring the effects of their actions.

Upon arrival at the Zoo, the children and their families left the boat and spent two hours visiting all the animals—the highlight, of course, being the petting zoo where the children were actually able to experience the animals "hands-on."

Before returning to the boat, we stopped and enjoyed a picnic lunch on the Zoo grounds.

As we traveled back up the river, we discussed the big task Noah and his family undertook and the children told us what they had learned from this Bible story. The parents and children involved in this activity really appreciated the live experience of the day.

Fern Amper

In response to your collecting material for a new book with Ron Wolfson, I enclose this program for families of sixth-graders. The format of the diagram where one value is placed on each holder of a Hanukiyah comes from Sharon Halper. Other than that, the program is mine. I like it because it teaches families to extrapolate and prioritize Jewish values from the holidays. It also reminds the teacher that older students need a more sophisticated approach to teaching holidays then we ordinarily give them. Fern Amper, JES Family Education Consultant, Teaneck, NJ.

MENORAH OF HANNUKAH VALUES

Purpose:

- To engage older students and their parents in a deeper understanding of the Hannukah story.

- To encourage efforts to extract valuable lessons relevant to modern life from the Hannukah Story.

- To teach students to prioritize ethical principles.

- To begin a process which we hope will continue at home, whereby older students and their families discuss Jewish ethics and values.

Program: Give each family group a one-page story of Hannukah, a practice sheet of a Menorah of Hannukah Values (see below) and a pencil. Open the session by reading the story. Then give each family the task of extracting ethical statements or lessons from it. Write each ethical statement, in order of importance, on each blank candle. It is not necessary to fill all eight candles. The entire group then reconvenes, shares their ideas and notes, and agrees on a total of eight values. The values are written on large "candles" which have velcro on the back. They correspond to a poster-size enlargement of the menorah, which has velcro on each candle. The final task of the whole group is to put each value candle in order of importance. At the end of the program, the poster-size Menorah of Hannukah Values serves as an attractive bulletin board display, an illustration of the lessons of Hannukah, and a reminder of parental involvement in the class.

Temple Akiba, Culver City

Submitted by Eileen Ettinger, Educator, Temple Akiba, Culver City, CA. While this program was done at a family retreat, nothing about it is inappropriate for the classroom.

THEME: Sephardic Jewry
Culminating Activity: The Jews of Rhodes

The culminating activity of the Temple Akiba Family Retreat was made up of approximately 70 people: 14 children of intermediate school age and 56 adults. The main objective was for the participants to role-play the Jewish customs that were practices on the Island of Rhodes.

The nucleus of the activity was The Bureau of Jewish Education's Sephardic Trunk, "Children of the Expulsion: Jews from Spain to the Ottoman Empire." Most of the information was culled from the book, *I Remember Rhodes*, by Rebecca Amato Levy. To augment the activity, I borrowed middle eastern costumes from the HUC Skirball Museum. They were made up of long coats, hats, scarves and dresses, etc.

In preparation for the activity, I met with the children at three different times to prepare them to be my assistants in the activity. They had the opportunity to explore the trunk and discuss the customs. They also prepared a skit which they performed before the whole group as a demonstration. Each group ultimately had two children to help them with the activity.

The participants were broken up into seven clusters, with each one sitting in a circle. Each cluster had a different subject. The subjects were taken from an object or theme in the trunk. The different subjects were: The Wedding—wedding dress and groom's outfit; Brit and Fadas—doll; Shabbat—Kiddush cup (candlesticks and candles were added); Home Remedies—taken from book; folk tales; leaving Rhodes—taken from book; Letters.

After breakfast each participant was given a "ticket" to the activity. The color of the ticket determined which circle each person was to go to. Paper bags were in the middle of each circle with corresponding colors attached to them. Each bag contained an object, a written description of the customs using the object and a general description of Jewish life in Rhodes. On the outside of each bag was taped the general directions sheet for the activity.

As the people entered the room they went to their corresponding circles. The general directions were read together. Each group was given 1/2 hour to make up their skits. They were told that the skit should last approximately 3-5 minutes. The costumes were on a table in the front of the room for them to use as they pleased.

The two main goals were for the groups to entertain themselves and the audience, and educate everyone about their customs. They went far beyond what I imagined they would do. The wedding customs and brit were depicted; the folk-tales were acted out; the home remedies were hilariously demonstrated, etc. They all used the costumes which helped expand the enjoyment of the activity and the depiction of the customs. The trunk and the costumes complemented each other beautifully.

This activity is an example of taking an existing program and expanding upon it. It is also an example of a Los Angeles educator using two major educational institutions as resources to create a program—The Los Angeles Bureau of Jewish Education and the Hebrew Union College Skirball Museum.

Jane Golub, Tifereth Jacob, Manhattan Beach

Jane is a big fan of bringing families in to do regular classroom studies. She believes that parents like to see what their children do when they are in Hebrew School. Here is a sample Family Day:

Bet Class Family Education Day

I have been teaching Hebrew schools with family education days for awhile. I have always taught a normal lesson, except for one year where the school had a long history of running special family programs. Parents are always interested in seeing what their students do at Hebrew school. A regular set of lessons shows them the content and dynamic of class. Parents know at the end of the day what I do with their students.

WELCOME: I have name tags, coffee, tea, juice and a danish available to begin class.

TORAH TIME: *Being Torah*—Chapter 7: Leaving Home
Being Torah, page 63-64, *Student Commentary*, pages 28-29

I always make sure there are enough copies for parents and students. The students will have their books, but parents always appreciate having their own copies.

1. **Introduction:** Share items people would bring if they had to leave home forever. Introduce the story of Abram following God's command to go to Canaan.

2. **Read** and review the story and the clues.

3. **Move on** to the *Student Commentary*. Share Comments.

4. **Break** students and parents apart. Both will write their own guide to being a blessing and then share them.

HEBREW TIME: *Ot la-Ba'Ot* is what I have been teaching lately. Not only do parents support their children's reading efforts, but often I get students volunteering their parents to read. I also play some kind of Hebrew game.

OTHER TIME: Most schools have art, music, etc., time or services. There is no break for parents.

Chapter 8
PLANNING FOR MULTI-GENERATION CLASSROOM ACTIVITIES

Village Torah

If you want to understand why we argue so strongly for family and intergenerational learning, listen to this story!

[Joel's Story]: **Lauren, Josh, & Jessica.** It was an intergenerational family Torah class, about fifteen people, portions of about 6 families. In each case, for a different reason, a child or a parent was not there. We had grandparents, but they were not related to anyone in the group. It was a lovely little community. On the third week, we were doing a thing called Family Bet Din. It was an exercise where, in groups of three, people had to serve as judges of difficult legal cases (mainly about family law). Bet Din (which means "House of Judgment") is the name for the foundational court of three rabbis used to resolve most disputes in Jewish law. Lauren (11), Josh (70), and Jessica (9) were a group. The second case involved a twelve-year-old who chose almost certain death for a higher quality of a short life, over longer and more painful medical treatment. He and his mother had agreed to cease treatments—the doctors had filed suit to insist upon medical intervention. The groups were working alone. I was lurking. Lauren said, "My grandmother is in a nursing home. She is on dialysis. Sometimes I think that the machine is sucking the life out of her, not putting it back in." Then after a pause she said, "And we only have time to visit her once every three or four weeks."

Josh, with great wisdom responded, "The last time I was in the hospital, they kept on giving me choices about what they were going to do. But, I was so sick, and I was on so much medicine, that I didn't know what they were offering me. The good news, I'm still here." They both smiled.

ANALYSIS: The real conversation went, "I am scared for my grandmother. I am guilty, too." The answer went, "It is scary, but there is hope—and, I know you care for her a lot." It was a grandchild grandparent moment, which probably could not take place between real relatives. Our teacher, Vicky Kelman, likes to quote an African folk saying which goes, "It takes a whole village to raise a child." This story explains it clearly.

That evening, we shared things in families and between families. We studied pieces of Torah and Talmud which comment on the Jewish values dealing with life and death. Adults learned what they could have in a good adult class. Kids got more than they normally would have in a Hebrew School class. (There were a number of SAT words.) But, everyone got something more—the "village" piece. That is what we are going to try to describe in this chapter.

Our Method—Our Madness

Family Education (all this stuff we are talking about here) started as a vision and then became a practice—long before there was a field, long before there was a theory. The academic side of this emerging field is just beginning to catch up. The field, as yet, has no official "language" and its jargon is borrowed from all over. Therefore, rather than dealing with it as a science, we need to treat it as an art. (We are still working on the science.)

No one can tell you the "right" elements of a good family experience. All we can do is show you a few good examples and talk about some common elements.

Ice-Breakers/Set Inductions

Because most family education experiences are one-shot or one of only a few shots, often the first activity in such programs is what the "group process people" called an **ice-breaker**. These are activities where people learn each other's names and somewhat "meet" each other, usually by sharing something they have in common. When the educators are also exerting influence, these **ice breakers** also double as a **set induction**, the "motivational" activity which "introduces" the **set** of elements or ideas which will be utilized through the lesson.

In other words, usually we (1) allow people to meet each other and begin to form a group, and then (2) begin to create a topic or theme that will be actualized in the program. It is often really stylish (though not always better) to do these two things through a single activity.

Learning Experiences

Most family programs tend to be built out of a combination of **small groups** and **whole community meetings.** There are two or three common (but not exclusive) patterns.

1. **The Carousel:** (Also known as Stations). Here "stations" or "learning centers" are set up and families rotate between them. Each station contains resources and activities (plus usually a

resource person or good directions) so that families know what to do. Families work their way around these stations—building up a "gestalt" of on-topic experiences. Usually, "town meetings" precede and follow The Carousel in order to introduce the activity (**set induction**) and then provide **closure.**

2. **The Paper Bag Dramatics Model:** A paradigm that includes art, music, writing, dancing, problem solving—any creative group task. The model is very simple—groups are given resources, a task, and time for a creative process. At the end of the time, groups share (perform) their creative output for each other. Again, town meetings for "**introductions**" and "**closure**" usually bracket these experiences.

3. **The Hevruta Model:** A _Hevruta_ is an organic Jewish study mode which is found in Yeshivot. Classically, a teacher presents an opening lesson (lecture) which is an overview to a task, then students (usually in pairs) go off and "study" that text, preparing for an interactive lesson. After _Hevruta_ time, the class comes back together and in a question-and-answer session ("_Paper Chase_" kind of dialogue) using probing questions, the teacher works with the class to deepen the understanding of the text. This basic pattern (often in much less confrontational form) is often adaptable to intergenerational learning.

4. **The Regular Class:** Parents and kids (in some combination) sit in an "ordinary class" doing seatwork, group work, and participating in guided discussion together.

1. **The Arts & Crafts Model:** After some kind of set induction, individuals work on projects (usually involving white glue at some point). The secret here is that the "working time" allows for a lot of "sidebar" conversations among the artists and craftspersons. Usually the vicarious conversation is as valuable as the actual crafts experience.

Food, Social Time, Closure, and some Take-Home Piece.

Food is a comfort point. It also provides a non-structured interacting time.

Social Time is important because the making of "same-aged" and "intergenerational" friends (in other words, the building of community) needs to be one of our goals.

There are a lot of **Closure Needs.** Not only does the "lesson" need the "bow tied" to complete the package (and make sure the lesson is manifest), but groups need permission to leave. Closure is as much an ending ritual which allows the experience to be over, as it is a review of the elements which have been learned.

Take Home: Goody Bags are an important part of the Family Education process. Our goal is always to create experiences which transcend the classroom (synagogue) and move into the home. Therefore, we always want to give families the resources to extend the experience. Sometimes, the "take" are additional pieces of paper (texts, guides, how to pages, read-aloud stories), etc. Sometimes they are complete objects which now can be used at home: (*hallah* covers, *Hanukkiyot*, etc.) Sometimes, they are "homework assignments" which create family process.

Finally, Family Education Days are also chances for **Parent-Teacher** gatherings.

> **[SHARON HALPER'S COMMENT]:** I don't think so! Too many agendas spoil the whatever.

> **[JOEL'S RESPONSE]:** Sharon's truth doesn't play in my experience (which doesn't mean it isn't true for her). But, from a lesson I learned long ago from Cookie Gross, Temple Sholom, Chicago, part of each family education day I do (for a specific grade) is designed to give parents and teachers a chance to meet and share agendas. It has always worked for me.

What follows is a collection of examples. If this book was more high-tech, and if we had the footage, we would have had you click on the square and "run" the film of each of these programs. Instead, you'll have to read the descriptions and let your imagination do the rest. (And all of us know that teachers' imaginations are pretty good!)

FAMILY PROGRAM MODELS

Vicky Kelman's Family Room

Vicky Kelman is a master family educator who has created Windows *and* Together *for the Melton Research Center, run family camps for Camp Ramah, and has written about these experiences in* Jewish Family Retreats: A Handbook *(Melton Research Center and Whizin Institute).* This is the opening program from her latest book Family Room *(Whizin Institute).* Vicky is presently the director of the Jewish Family Education Project at the San Francisco BJE.

[VICKY KELMAN NOTES]: I think this program only works as the first of **many**.

MIFGASH* I: Getting to Know You

*Mifgash is a Hebrew word for a gathering. Carol Starin thought you needed to know that.

Check In: Have a name tag setup where everyone can either make a name tag or find a pre-made one that can be decorated. This is not a big decision, but there are reasons for each. Make-your-own: It provides something to do while people are arriving, people often like to make their own, you may not know nicknames (i.e., does Steven want everyone to call him Steven or Steve?). Have-them-made-already: It helps people feel prepared for, all the names can be large and legible to all. The large white square ones with peel-off backing are just right. Put out a few thick markers and/or some stickers for decoration.

It's also helpful to roll out some shelf paper and put out some crayons so there is "something to do" while everyone is arriving. You could also have stickers and paper, colored pipe cleaners, etc.—not enough to be really interesting (i.e., not "a project"), but sufficient to keep those kids who need it busy while families are arriving, bringing their food into the kitchen, "shmoozing," and so on.

Warm-ups: This set of activities is the first step in building community—learning each other's names, getting to know something about each other, and interacting in a nonthreatening, playful way. Even if you have a group in which some or many of the participants know each other, do not skip this step!!!

Name tags and warm-up game: (at least one of which should be a name game), should be a part of at least the first three mifgashim. (I have found that fathers, in particular, have a hard time learning everyone's names. I'm not sure why, but you can hypothesize.)

Name Games: Make a selection based on the ages of the children in your group. If your group includes many young children (kindergarten and below), they may not feel comfortable with the circle game format. They may be reluctant to say their names aloud in front of everyone. If the first round doesn't take, go on to "face pass" or "pass the squeeze"; do a whole family list name(s) game and save other games for later on in the mifgash or a future mifgash.

Names: Sit in a circle and have everyone say his or her name in turn.

I am/I like: Go around again and have people say their names and something they like that starts with the same letter of the alphabet as their name (*My name is Mollie and I like multiplication*.). It facilitates this to have a "family huddle" first in which family members can help each other decide what to say.

Adjectives: Do a third round in which people say names with adjectives (*I'm joyful Josh*). Add the family huddle here, too.

Name toss: *Easier version*: You say your **own** name and then throw the ball to someone else (this version does not involve remembering anyone else's name—less pressure). Play both, first the easier version, then the more difficult version.

Harder version: Call someone's name and toss a ball or koosh to him/her.

Rhythm name game: Ask people to count how many syllables or beats in their names. (For example: Sarah = Sa rah, two beats; Jonathan = Jo na than, three).

Easy version: Say your name with a clap for each syllable. Each person says his/her own name and everyone repeats.

Harder version: Players take a minute to come up with an arm movement that goes with the beats in their names. Each person says his/her name with the arm movement and the whole group repeats name and movement in unison.

Hardest version: Name and motion are presented and repeated by group. Next player says his/her name and motion. The whole group repeats and then repeats player one's name and motion. Player three presents, the group repeats, then repeats player two's name and motion, then player one's and so on till everyone has made a presentation.

More circle fun—Face pass: The first person to be "it" makes a funny face, turns to his/her right, and looks directly into the face of the next person (as in a mirror). The second person duplicates the first person's face, turns slowly, showing the face to the group, changes the face or his/her own funny face, turns to the right, and passes the new face on to the next person to the right. Continue on around the circle.

Pass the squeeze: Everyone holds hands, gets quiet, and concentrates, waiting to feel a squeeze on either hand, which is then passed on. (The leader starts the squeeze in either direction by squeezing one of the two hands he/she is holding.) Start a slow pace. It can then go faster, and it can even go in both directions at once. Do three to five rounds. This game can be played sitting or standing. If played standing, it can be a good transition to a standing or moving game.

Family by family getting-to-know-you activities—Meet a family who...: This game always works. If your circle games (above) don't seem to take off, switch to this one to get everyone up and moving. This also doesn't require anyone to be "in the spotlight." Family members hold hands or link arms with each other and follow these instructions (all of which involve finding another family with something in common and introducing themselves). The five below are suggestions; vary them as you wish. Five rounds are usually enough, but you can keep it going if the group is with it.

Think of your phone number. Think of the last digit in your phone number. Find another family that has the same last digit as you do. Introduce your families to each other.

- Find a family that has the same number of members as yours. Meet them.
- Find a family with a different number of members as yours. Meet them.
- Find a family in which a parent is wearing the same color shirt as a parent in your family. Introduce yourselves.
- Find a family in which one of the children has a birthday in the same month (or season) as one of the children in your family. Introduce yourselves.

Family cheer: Families have three to five minutes to huddle and develop a family cheer using no words except their last name(s), handclapping, and motion. Each family presents its own cheer, and everyone else cheers for them when they're finished.

Family album: Families have three to five minutes to prepare a silent "snapshot" (sometimes called a "tableau") of their family doing something they like to do together, something typical of their family, or a recent family special event. Each family takes a turn presenting its "tableau" with a one-sentence explanatory oral "caption."

STUDY

This study session is about community. This topic was selected because it reflects the stage of the group at this point—they are embarking on becoming a community. The study session has three parts. Part 1 is a little simulation of building community, using small children's building blocks. Part 2 involves small groups of families reading and discussing various stories/texts that introduce ideas of community. There is a wide selection of texts to choose from depending on the age of the children participating. Part 3 is a whole group wrap-up of the small group discussions.

Part 1: Building blocks of community

Each person gets a small block (from a child's building block set) and writes his/her name on it (parents help younger children). Ask participants to see what they can do with their one block. (Have people demonstrate what, if anything, they can do with their one block.)

Ask each family to make a creation with its members' individual blocks. Allow a few minutes for families to build together; have some time to view each family's collaboration.

Then ask all the participants to repossess their own blocks and build a creation with the entire group.

Take a few minutes to "process" this little experiment with everyone:

- What's the difference between doing something with one block, a few blocks, and lots of blocks?

- What can we learn from this about community?

- If we took one block out, what would happen?

- What does that tell us about each person's role in the community?

Take a photograph of everyone with the community block creation.

Part 2: Stories

This is time to read and talk about a text that stresses community. Pair families for this part of the mifgash based on the ages of their kids, and give each pair of families a text that seems suited for them.

The texts for this study session are:

- Swimmy*—You'll need a copy of the book and copies of the question sheet; this is an ideal story for families that include three- to four-year-olds.
- Pirke Avot 2:5—The handout has the verse and the discussion questions.
- "Lost in the Forest," a Hasidic story. The story is a metaphor and will work best with kids who are third grade and up.
- Ecclesiastes 4:9-12—The handout includes the quotation for study and discussion questions. Also needed: paper, pencil, and three pieces of yarn, ribbon, or string.

You might have all the families work with the same text, or each pair of families with a different text, or any combination of texts and families.

Some other choices for texts if the above selections aren't quite right:

- Martin Buber once wrote: "When a person is singing and cannot carry the tune, and someone else comes along who can carry the tune and joins the first person and sings along, the first person will be able to keep the tune, too. That is the secret of the bond between spirits."**
- "Right or Wrong," from *Jacob the Baker*.***
- If groups include more upper elementary or junior high age participants, use the Marge Piercy poem, "The Low Road."****

Part 3: Community wrap-up of study

Call the group together. Pull the study session experience together for them by saying something like:

> Today is our first meeting. We're going to meet many times during this year, and we hope we will become a community. Just now, we all studied—and we all studied something that was written to teach us something about community. Let's hear what each group learned about community.

Have a representative from each group (choose a parent or an older child) tell everyone else what his/her group learned.

Some other questions for whole group discussion:

Can anyone think of a way to use this idea tomorrow or the next day?

How is what we read similar to what we did with our blocks before?

HaMotzi, Supper, and Birkat Ha-Mazon

Closing Circle: An Appreciation Circle

Have each family take a few minutes to huddle and decide together what they liked or appreciated about this first mifgash. Then go around the circle and have each family tell their thanks and appreciations to the group.

Take Home: To Do

Each family is given a square of cloth (10 to 12 inches square is a good size) to take home and decorate in such a way that it tells important things about their family that they'd like other families to know. After the next mifgash, all the squares will be attached to make a tablecloth for the group's dinners at future sessions.

Suggest that they can use: markers, puffy paints, fabric or felt applique (cut and glued on), crayons, etc. Tell them to leave a two-inch border all around, so the squares can later be attached to each other by overlapping (it's helpful to give out the squares with the margins already sketched in).

Used with the permission of the Whizin Institute for Jewish Family Living

*Leo Leonni, Swimmy (New York: Dragonfly Books—Alfred A. Knopf, 1963).

**Martin Buber, Ten Rungs: Hasidic Sayings (New York: Schocken Books, 1947), p. 85.

*** Noah ben Shea, Jacob the Baker (New York: Ballantine Books, 1989), p. 26.

****Marilyn Sewall, ed, Cries of the Spirit (Boston: Beacon Press, 1991), p. 170-171.

Joel Lurie Grishaver's Sampler

Here are the sketches of three diverse programs from Joel's files:

Joel's Seventh Grade: First Family Education Day:

Pre-Game: Bagels and cream cheese, coffee, tea, and hot chocolate were available in the hall. Room was set up in "the roundtable" conference style. Everyone had adult-sized chairs. We did no introductions or name tags. Everyone in this class knew each other. This class had been together for four or five years without a new member. They had done lots of family education days together. It is a small synagogue.

Earliest Jewish Memories. There were fourteen students in the class. Eleven were at this session. We had about twenty-six or twenty-seven people in the room. Every present child had an adult. I had done my homework. There was no real warm-up. I did some welcomes and began the first activity. I had a gym bag with "things" in it. I pulled them out one at a time, and passed them around the circle. Each person got to/had to share their earliest or strongest memory associated with them. That day we did (1) a Mickey Mouse snow globe. (I wanted to start in family, not Jewish.) (2) A Consecration Torah. (Enter the Jewish.) (3) A menorah. (4) A picture of Hitler. (5) A (miniature) Israel flag. (I intentionally chose pretty universal, ubiquitous, non-threatening objects—even to the Jews by Choice. We had five or six out of the eleven couples. No intermarried couples.) This activity put parents and seventh-graders on equal footings and had everyone amazed in a balance of shared and unique experiences. Very warm. Very Fuzzy. Good intergenerational, but very soft content. It was designed to set a tone, build community, not do content.

The Parent Meetings: The kids then went to services and recess. I had about 25 minutes with the parents. We did three things. (1) I did the "back to school night" thing of reviewing the class curriculum and procedure. (2) I then asked them to share their expectations and goals for the year. (3) I then involved them in planning the rest of the family events. Some pieces were delegated. Interestingly, the baseball game idea evolved at this meeting. NOTE: The second such meeting I studied a *T'shuvah* (Responsum) about Jewish education with the parents—and did some adult learning.

The Second Hour was intentionally a regular class with adults, not a family directed class. I was still looking for control in the room, and I wanted the good learning. Using a map from the *Bible People Ditto Pak*, they read a passage in Judges, a passage in Joshua, and compared the areas that were described as conquered and unconquered. This led into (1) political geography, and (2) questions about the Bible as history verses the Bible as ideology. Basically, parents helped their own kids complete the seat work, but held back for the most part in the class discussion.

Closure: We reviewed the day. Went over the family tzedakah project obligations. Talked about the "allocations" meeting which would happen next time. Then closed with people's statements about "My favorite part of today was…"

It was GTHBA.

Joel's Family Torah Class: Second Session:

In the summer of 1994, Joel taught an experimental "Family Torah Class" at the University of Judaism, Department of Continuing Education. It was attended by anywhere from 7 or 20 people. No whole family came regularly. Rather, portions of families made up a wonderful intergenerational class. It met from 7:30 to 9:00 on a weekday night. Joel had expected to cancel the class at the first session, but 7 people showed up. Enough that he was committed to do the work to form the second session, which, in many ways, was the first real class. We had begun the week before, but needed to rebegin. Week two we had twelve people.

Preclass: Joel gathered and talked to people. We filled out name tags and hung out.

Set Induction: We read a paragraph from the Larry Kushner book, **God Was in this Place & I, i Did not Know.** It says that "everyone has their own Torah that they teach." We read the passage out loud, and went around the circle allowing everyone to explain what it meant to them. This did three things. (1) It set a tone that Torah came from the class, not just the books. (2) It equalized adults and kids as everyone listened equally to each. The "everyone" rule meant equality. (3) The "I want to add to…" "I want to build on…" tone set a standard for the class as well.

Set Induction II: In intergenerational non-family pairs, people shared one piece of their "family Torah." Family Torah = some piece of wisdom, some rule or advice, which is often repeated as a family mantra. My mother's statement (which I always use as an example) is: "Go home with the one who brung you!" The best I ever got was in Charlotte, SC. "Don't whiz on the electric fence." Each person wrote down their partner's family Torah and then presented it to the class.

James:	"No thinka too much"—from father
Joshua:	"Live life to the FULLEST—because life is good"—*From the Torah of Marcus*
Lauren:	"If you don't have something nice to say—don't say anything at all."
Judy:	"It is as easy to marry a rich man as a poor man."—*Sylvia and George Samson*
Bobbi:	"What's for dinner?"—*Avi's Torah*
Avi:	"What's the homework situation?"—*Bobbi's Torah*
Cody:	"Crowd the plate."—*Dad/baseball coach*
Joel:	"Go home with the one who brung you."—*Dorothy Lurie Grishaver*
Barbara:	"You get out what you put into it."—*Bob Steinhardt*

Transition: Whole Group Activity: Next we went around the room and everyone picked one statement. These were then posted on the walls using "*Stick'em*." (Often, I do this activity, but have everyone run around the room with a marker, making "Rashi" on the comments.) In this case, sitting in a circle we had a conversation where each person picked one they wanted to comment on or explain. Here are some highlights from that conversation.

Cody (12):	*No thinka too much*—because when you think too much you don't act on your instincts, and a lot of times it makes you insecure about your decisions.—and it's not good to live life and not care about you.
Barbara (adult):	*You get out what you put into it.* It sort of says to go through life not passively—don't react—be pro-active.
Loren (10):	*Crowd the plate*—I think it means—you should eat.
(Joel)	I thought it meant always having a connection at home.
Barbara (Adult):	*Go home with the one who brung you*—know who you are; don't go too far from your roots—remember where you came from.
Josh (13):	*If you don't have something nice*—Can I disagree? That is a nursery school truth. You want to question. You want to stand up for what you believe.

Joel (Teacher):	Perfect—I don't know that you are right—but it is perfect—it is right for you—and that's what you need to be!
Judy (Adult):	*What's for dinner?* The nurturing between people.
Bobbi (Adult):	My son and I have two speeds: Where are we going for a quick dinner? Or, what kind of dinner can we make? Then there is the third where he wants me to make him an elaborate dinner with salad and courses and dessert.
James:	*Go home*—Don't be so quick to desert the thing in life which has carried you so far.
Joel:	*It's just as easy to marry a rich....* and it is damn hard to stay married to either (laughter). Married and easy don't go together, and besides—who is really rich?
Josh (70):	We left out the purple one: *Live life to the fullest.* You shouldn't take it literally. You don't have to go out and do completely everything. You should have the experience of doing everything (you do).
Judy:	And there is the second part that life is good. You don't need to go through life being fearful, being worried that someone is going to jump out at me if I happen to cross in this direction.

Text Study: We read as readers' theater (from a text script I had prepared), chapter one of Genesis. Note: This is from a forthcoming book, *Make a Midrash Out of Me*, where the real biblical text is set up for readers' theater. This text is fun, because it has the chorus that everyone joins in on.

The Break: Five minutes for bathrooms and stretching (also for informal conversation).

Arts & Crafts: We did torn-paper midrash (for details, see Jo Milgrom's book, *Handmade Midrash*, JPS). It was construction paper, glue sticks, and informal conversation. Everyone sat on the floor, or as part of the cluster in the arm chair desks. Here is a note from my teacher's log:

> During the tearing and making, I forced small talk which bridged into a longer conversation with Joshua (13). He asked about the primordial light—if the light was general light, or just light for the land. He struggled with wording: Is this earthly light, or the concept of light? Often when he runs out of words he stops. When he can't

fully express it—he won't play. Then I pointed out the fourth day thing—Avi was the one who guessed the days—Scott when he didn't know it—didn't guess.

Later in the day we got a long monologue on meaning of light and all that; we also got into a truth-versus history thing. The idea of truth as abstract, not historical, was predictably hard for him.

Just before the end, Cody asked to do it over. I let him. Meanwhile, Lauren was nowhere near finished, either. In contradistinction, Joshua was done almost instantly.

Then we went around and shared the art work and our understandings of it.

Straight Teaching: In the last five minutes, I taught the Cassuto creation pattern and everybody did interpretations. (Cassuto shows that days 1 and 4, 2 and 5, 3 and 6 are connected, and that what is started on the first three days is completed or fulfilled in the next three days.) Then the class did some interpretation. (Again, here are my final journal notes:)

Barbara didn't like the fact that it was good on days without life. Everyone came to the same conclusion about day two and the missing good—just division. Then we came back to light. I did the *or zaruah* thing and Joshua had a minor epiphany—he saw the light—that light could be a symbol.

Class drifted out—without a great climax or a real cool-down. We were overtime.

This week felt different. It was more playful. Less introspective. I think it was just as good. I don't know how the class felt. Both temporally and personally, I've been afraid to ask for evaluation.

P.S.—Before class, Bobbi told the story of Avi not wanting to come last week—then liking it—then thinking of renaming the class *Torah Comedy.*

Oneg Shanah: A Large Group Family Game

Don Rossoff and Joel Lurie Grishaver wrote this game as the culmination to the first ever Mini-CAJE which was held in Los Angeles in 1977 (or maybe it was '78). In those days, they were known as the "Havdalah Brothers." Today, the separation is unfortunately greater. The game, imprinted on Joel's design for the Prayerbook Board Game, works this way.

Bunches of people, families, or mixed family parts are clustered into teams. Teams can be anywhere from 6 to 20 people. Each team makes up a name, a cheer, and colors a paper plate as a giant game board marker—anything to help the group "form."

On the floor is a giant game board—one square per Jewish holiday. Each game square (usually a sheet of poster board) has an attached manila envelope. In the envelope are bunches of copies of the following sheets (sorted by holiday).

Rosh Ha-Shanah

Rosh Ha-Shanah is the Jewish New Year. On Rosh Ha-Shanah we hear the Shofar call. There are four Shofar calls:

Tekiah: 1 long blast.

Shevarim: 3 short blasts.

Teru'ah: 9 very quick blasts.

Tekiah Gedolah: 1 very, very long blast.

Practice making each of these sounds. When you are ready, hand this slip of paper to a judge. He or she will ask you to perform the sounds in this order.

*Tekiah * Shevarim* Teru'ah * Tekiah*

*Tekiah * Shevarim * Tekiah*

*Tekiah * Teru'ah * Tekiah Gedolah*

Warning: Practice well. If you make too many mistakes, the judge will send you back.

Yom Kippur

Yom Kippur is the Day of Atonement. It is the day when we say "I am sorry." It is the day when we devote all our thoughts to making ourselves into the best possible people we can be.

Have every person on your team list three things a person should stop doing if she/he wants to become the best possible person she/he can be. These should be "sins" we are trying to stop doing.

Also learn and sing the words and melody to Avinu Malkeinu.

Avinu Malkeinu Chaneinu Va-aneinu, Ki ein Banu Ma'asim

Asei Imanu Tzedakah Va-Chesed V'hoshi-einu.

Sukkot

Sukkot is the festival of booths. It recalls times when Jews had to live in sukkot. We lived in sukkot during the forty years we lived in the wilderness. We lived in sukkot when we harvested our fields. And, we lived in sukkot when we went on a pilgrimage to the Temple in Jerusalem.

Your team needs to do two things:
[1] Write an original Sukkot song, and
[2] Perform it as a Human Body Sculpture of a sukkah
When you are ready, find a judge.

Simhat Torah

Simhat Torah is the holiday when we have a Torah party. It celebrates the time when we read the last story in the Torah and then go back again to the first story.

Again, your team needs to do two things for the judge.
[1] Stand in a line and have each team member list a story you will find in the Torah. You must go through your line twice. If you can go through your line three times, you can skip part two.
[2] Write and present, with motions, a Torah Cheer.

Hanukkah

Hanukkah is the holiday which recalls how the Maccabees won their fight for freedom. Every night for eight nights, we light the Hanukkah lights. On the first night we light the *shamash* and one candle. We say three blessings. On the second night, we light the *shamash* and two candles. We say only two blessings. On the third night, it is the *shamash*, three candles and two blessings—and so on.

Do a candle lighting ballet. First, the *shamash* and one candle and sing three blessings. Then the *shamash* and two candles, and sing the two blessings, and so on up to eight when everyone must sing both blessings.

Both nights: *Barukh atah Adonai eloheinu melekh ha-olam asher kidshanu b'mitzvotav v'tzivanu l'hadlik ner shel Hanukkah.*

Barukh atah Adonai eloheinu melekh ha-olam she-asah nissim La'avoteinu ba-yamin ha-hem ba'z'man ha-zeh.

First night only: *Barukh atah Adonai eloheinu melekh ha-olam, she-hecheyanu, v'kiyimanu v'higiyanu la-z'man ha-zeh.*

Purim

Purim is the holiday which tells the story of Queen Esther. On Purim, we make up plays (which we call spiels) all about her story. Write and present a Purim spiel. It must have these scenes:

[1] King Ahashuarus has a party to which his wife Vashti won't come. The King gets angry and asks for a new queen.

[2] Out of all the women in Shushan, Esther is picked to be Queen.

[3] Mordechai, her uncle, saves the King's life. Mordechai hears men plot to kill the King, then warns the King.

[4] Haman, a wicked man, becomes the King's chief assistant. He asks everyone to bow down to him. Mordechai won't, Haman is angry.

[5] Haman plots to kill all the Jews.

[6] Mordechai tells Esther that she must ask the King to save her people. She is afraid to tell the King that she is Jewish, but she agrees to do it.

[7] Esther goes to the King and asks him and Haman to come to a party.

[8] At the party, Esther tells the King that Haman wants to kill her and her people. The King orders his guards to kill Haman and makes Mordechai his new chief advisor.

Passover

Passover is the holiday when we remember that once we were slaves in Egypt and God took us out and brought us to freedom. We have a Seder and retell this story. We use a Seder plate to help us tell the story.

On the plate we have:

Z'roah: A roasted shank bone.

Betzah: An egg.

Maror: The bitter herbs.

Charoset: A special mixture of wine, nuts, and fruit.

Karpas: A fresh vegetable (parsley).

On the table, we also have wine, salt water, and three *matzot.*

Make a human Seder table. Have each object on the table recite a poem about what they do or teach at the Seder.

Counting of the Omer

There are seven weeks between Passover and Shavuot. Jews count every one of the 49 days.

Have your whole team count from 1 to 10 in Hebrew.

Tu b'Shevat

Tu b'Shevat is the Jewish New Year's Day for trees. It is a day we celebrate and plant trees.

Have your team sing three songs which include the word tree.

Yom ha-Atzmaut

Yom ha-Atzmaut is the day we celebrate the creation of the State of Israel. Israel is the Jewish homeland.

Have each member of your team list three things which can be found in Israel, and then dance a Horah out the door on one side of the room, around the balcony, then in the door on the other side.

Shavuot

Shavuot is a harvest holiday. It is when Jewish farmers brought their first fruits to the Temple as a gift. These were called Bikurim.

Have everyone on your team pantomime bringing a basket of fruit (or vegetables) to the judge. Every person must bring a different kind of fruit (or vegetable).

Shabbat

Shabbat is the day of Rest. We celebrate everything God created in six days and that God rested on the seventh day.

Sing three Shabbat songs, say the blessings over the candles, wine, and challah, and then rest for thirty seconds.

Around the room are a number of judges. Best is about one judge for every two and a half teams. Each team is asked to pick a starting holiday and to write their team name on that holiday. When the starting shout goes off, each team works their way around the year at the quickest possible pace. Teams are invited to "scream" for judges when necessary. The nicest part of the process is that except for waiting for an available judge, each team moves at its own pace. We have tried the game with a judge per team, but that proved to be too easy, not chaotic enough, and less fun.

In process, a good time is had by hall, a general review of the Jewish annual cycle takes place, and some non-measurable learning happens for each participants. This game is usually played with families. It has been used effectively on a classroom scale, and with more than 500 participants.

[Sharon Halper's Comment]: There is something new I am doing this year. I call it GRAND FAMILY ED.

TARGET AUDIENCE: Our grandparent members who look at our new models and wish they could have done these programs with their children. They also feel that the congregation doesn't serve them the way it does "families."

ASSUMPTIONS: No knowledge on the part of kids, no practice in their homes. Ergo, don't send them home with challah covers or spice boxes and risk friction with grandparents//parents.

FIRST PROGRAM: Sukkot (Columbus Day—no school anyway—no issues with parents—cool planning, eh?) pizza lunch in the sukkah—a little lulav and etrog with the rabbi.

PROJECT: Bookmaking (no, not that kind) 2 versions of text: for 4-5 year olds, 5+ year-old text on leftside of page teaches about holiday/history. Right side: creative expression of text—using stickers, glue-ins, rubber stamps, etc. Every kid has a book—this one made with a grandparent which doesn't demand a ritual practice of parents.... everyone is happy!

Chapter 9
MANAGING PARENTS AND STUDENTS AT THE SAME TIME

Already, we have acknowledged the potential fears involved in bringing parents into the classroom. While we have suggested that these fears tend to lie more in imagination than reality, this chapter is devoted to practical solutions (in those cases where such fears do come to fruition).

To begin, two stories:

[Joel's Story]: **Ben and John Skip Class.** Following our first Family Education event in my seventh grade, I asked Marilyn Ortner to call the two missing families and share with them the wonderful time we had at the first event—making sure that they would be there next time. (It was the lesson learned from Dick Cooper.) When she called the Hargis household and spoke to Susan (mother), she said, "You are mistaken—Ben (son) and John (father) left together to go to this program." We laughed a lot over that, wonderfully ambivalent about father and son skipping Sunday School together.

[Joel's Other Story]: **Handfuls of Sugar Help Nothing.** On the second Family Education day, I had the kids working in one group and the adults working in another. (Each group was listing things parents should do for kids and that kids should do for parents.) Bagels, cream-cheese, coffee cake, coffee, and stuff like that were out in the hall on a rolling cart—available to anyone. It started with Erika, spread to Brett, then to Kent and the others. One by one, the kids were sneaking out into the hall and "stealing" handfuls of sugar. They'd come into class and swallow the stuff by throwing their heads back and shoving it in. I kept waiting for the parents to intervene. They were either distracted or ignoring the problem or waiting for me to fix it. I "evil-eyed" a couple of them into stopping. It worked on most. I whispered to Erika to "Cool it." That worked, too, but Brett and a couple of the others were still into sugar fixing. I didn't want to embarrass either him or his parents. I think they felt the same way about me. (Still, I was shocked that kids were "acting out" in front of their parents.) I solved the problem in four steps: (1) shortening the group working time and moving quickly towards the all-class part of the experience, (2) making the sugar disappear, (3) cornering Ben in private over his behavior, and (4) having a "please don't eat the daisies when we have company" conversation with my class over sugar eating.

Here is what I now know (that I didn't know five years ago). Dealing with sugar eating is much less of a big deal than I felt it was. "Please don't eat the sugar," would have been enough. Today, I am a much more confident teacher than I was then. Confidence makes a big difference. (So find your confidence. I can't tell you where it is. All I can tell you is that it is somewhere—and you have to find it.) Today, I know the parents of the kids I teach much better than I did then. Not being scared of them has also helped my confidence. The final note is, the patience and the positive response of that first set of seventh-grade families made it much easier for me to go even further.

A final reflective irony: Fifteen years earlier, I had been a youth director in a huge congregation. I did all kinds of family stuff and regularly "lived" in the homes of the kids with whom I worked. We did family retreats and family ulpans. We did all kinds of family stuff. I have a long history in working very successfully with families. Yet, each time in my life that I return to the classroom, I find a certain tightness that comes from fear of parents. I know better, but I still have to find my "confidence place" when I work with parents. I have to remember that they, too, are scared (but want to be my friend as well). I have to remember that they aren't just parents, but people, too.

The Big Concerns and The Right Responses

[Nachama Skolnik Moskowitz's Comment]: This was a big issue at the MJDS. Teachers discussed it a lot. The issue boils down to this: In a family and/or parent-child program, who's responsible for "child management?" We found parents often abdicated this responsibility figuring they were in school space. Teachers figure that since parents are, well, parents, it's their responsibility to manage their children. What teachers felt was a problem (kids running in the hall during the evening—eg. a science fair type night) was not one to the parents...who were too busy socializing to watch after kids...

What if a child misbehaves?

Simple. S/he probably won't if the parents are in the room, but if they do—first give the parents a chance to handle it, and only if they don't, handle it just as you would with no parents present (minimal force used fairly).

So let's review the basics we already know:

Pre-Emptive Strikes

- Well planned events have many fewer problems. (Think Mrs. Macintosh.)

- Kids whose behavior is clearly out of control won't always get better. They will need the same support they usually do.

- In general, a classroom of parents is like having the principal or the rabbis sit in on a class.

Non-Intrusive Interventions

- The "evil eye."

- Moving into the offending student's space.

- A public (to everyone in the room) restatement of the rule or the desired action. (Include the word "please.")

- The shoulder touch or hair tousle.

- The whispered request.

Minimally Intrusive

- A gentle statement which goes, "Jon, I need you to......"

- A chair move. Done discreetly.

A Truth: If it goes beyond these measures, it is a real problem. (You are not the problem unless the whole class rebels—then I would re-think the lesson.) If the parents do not step in gently, use minimal necessary force, minimal possible embarrassment, and get it over fast.

The Bigger Worry: That the parents' response will be worse than the kid's behavior. Go gently. The best bet is to let it go, and then use it as an opening for a conversation with parents later. You can open the conversation with, "It's interesting that both of us seem to run into the same kind of behavior from Matilda...." (Why don't we put our heads together...)

The Big Lesson: Think of any major incidents as opportunities to work individually with families and get to know them better. Make such events (if they are real) part of your follow up. Remember, the parents will be as embarrassed as you are. Warning: You have to get past Mama Bear to get to these issues. That is the first step in this adventure!

What if a parent misbehaves?

Also simple. They almost never do, but if one does, and if the other parents don't step in (which they almost always do), follow the same basic steps you do with kids (working up the non-intrusive ladder without being condescending).

Here are the two big parent behavior problems and their solutions:

Problem 1: Parents sit in the back, don't participate, and start talking. Solutions: (1) Rethink your activities. (2) Literally "re-group," redistributing the family and age balance. (3) Ask (in a general way) for cooperation. My usual language is, "To make this work, I need everyone to...."

Problem 2: Parents are over-involved (drowning out the kids). Usually they take the same kinds of prompts that kids do. "Wait until I call on you—everyone needs a turn," etc., addressed to the whole group, not an individual. Remember, parents are people too.

We'd like to tell you the story of how to cope with a really explosive parent experience, but none of us have ever encountered one. Our experience has been that parents are often inappropriate when they face teachers one-on-one, or sometimes in front of kids. Parents always seem to be (in our experience) well behaved in front of other parents. We just don't think you have to worry.

What if I make a mistake?

Relax, you will. Just as in your regular teaching, all mistakes are fixable. Likewise, just as with kids, "I don't know" is a perfectly good answer, when it is the truth. "I'll find out, and let you know," is an even better one. It is okay to get things wrong—if you do other things right.

S.A.T. Words

[Joel's Story]: Last summer I taught an intergenerational Torah class. It ran from 7 to 70. It averaged about 12 to 15 participants. The first night, Scott (10) used some big and impressive word. I said, "Wooo—S.A.T-word, very impressive." He didn't understand, so I told this story:

When I was in 5th grade, my Sunday school teacher was Mr. Temple. Perfect name! On the third or fourth week of school he wrote "anthropomorphism" and when we looked like he was crazy, he told us: "It means something which is not human being described in terms which only fit humans— remember it, it is a good S.A.T. word." We still thought he was crazy. Then he explained that (1) he was a high school English teacher and (2) high school kids took these big exams called S.A.T.s in order to get in college, and (3) we had to take out our notebooks and make a list of S.A.T. words—because he was giving us a head start.

"S.A.T. word" became a shtick in that class, and I have regularly re-inserted the shtick (artificial insemination) into other intergenerational classes I teach. It does a bunch of things:

- Slows the language down so everyone in the room can follow.
- Makes the adults (and older kids) re-explain themselves more clearly.
- Makes the younger kids feel really adult.
- Emphasizes Jewish learning as real learning.
- Provides a laughing opportunity.

A Final Word

Teachers do have a lot of fears about working with families. Most of them just don't happen.

If you are (1) well planned, (2) have done a meeting and welcoming process of on-going communication, (3) relax and operate with sensitivity and confidence—you are going to get big rewards, not nightmares.

The other truth, leaving out all the good things you are doing for families by providing them with interactive learning experiences: **Your life will be much easier working with parents you now know.**

Chapter 10
HEALING CARPOOL TUNNEL SYNDROME

"Carpool Tunnel Syndrome" is a pun coined by our friend and teacher, Rabbi Jeff Salkin. It is perfect. Just as sore wrists are the byproduct of the technology of computers, carpools have tended to be the ache built into the suburbanization of Jewish learning.

But, carpooling is a mitzvah. (See below.) While the Torah (and particularly the Talmud) has taught that parents should be their own children's Torah teachers, that was meant to be more symbolic than actual. (The rabbis, who hadn't yet done enough therapy to know the word "transference" did understand the concept.) The real notion of Torah life was that the home was a place which lived Torah, spoke Torah, used Torah, and even taught Torah—but that the hard core (the "have-to-memorize-*binyan-hit-pa-eyl*" part of Torah) was always better done by a "professional teacher." Paying the teacher and getting the kid there were parts of the mitzvah, too. Enjoy the following.

CONCERNING THE LEARNING OF CHILDREN

Zevi Hirsh Kaidanower
Lithsania, Germany, 17th-18th Century, From *Kav Ha-Yashar*

Our masters, blessed be their memory, said that the world endures only for the sake of the breath out of the mouths of children who go to school. From this, you see that great is the reward of those who teach children. And in every place where children are learning from a wise man, in that place dwells the Divine Presence. There is a passage in the Zohar, in the portion "*Lekh Lekha*": When Rabbi Simeon ben Yoḥai came and wanted to see the boys in school, he said: "I am going to gain sight of the Divine Presence." But the fact that this is emphasized, and it says, "When he came and wanted to see the boys in school," is because this was the custom among men of saintliness. When they were free from work, they went to the teachers to gain sight of the Divine Presence. And that is why a man must be careful, for whoever enters the house of a teacher will find there "the mother"—that is, the Divine Presence"—sitting upon the young"; the wings of the Presence are spread over the little lambs. But the breath from the mouth of a child can split the vault of heaven and the firmament. And so the teacher should take to heart that the Divine Presence dwells beside him, and perform his work faithfully, and without falseness, for it is a work of heaven. And he shall see to it that the room in which the children learn is clean, unspotted with any kind of soiling, and make real the words, "Therefore shall thy camp be holy," for it is the camp of the Divine Presence.

And when the time has come for the child to go to school, so he may study with a teacher, the father should rise early in the morning and take the child, so that he himself may bring it to the house of the teacher. Whether the father be an old man or a great man, an elder or a master, he must not be ashamed to take his son to school this first time, but rather give praise and thanks to the Holy One, blessed be he, for according him the grace to accord his son grace by placing him "under the wings of the Divine Presence." And on this errand, the mother or the father has the duty of shielding the child with a mantle, so that nothing unclean in the world can lay eyes upon it. And when the father has brought the child to school, he should place it in the teacher's lap, according to the Scriptures: "Carry them in thy bosom, as a nursing father carrieth the sucking child"; and "I taught Ephraim to walk, taking them by their arms."

Then a slate is brought, on which the *aleph-bet* is written, and the teacher should read aloud to the child, "*Aleph, Bet, Gimel, Dalet, He, Vav,*" and then in reverse order, "*Tav, Shin, Resh, Koph.*" Then the child is to repeat these letters after the teacher. Thereupon the teacher should read the verse, "MOSES COMMANDED US A LAW, AN INHERITANCE OF THE CONGREGATION OF JACOB," and then the first sentence from the Third Book of Moses, and the child should speak along with him, word for word. Then a little honey should be put on the slate, and the child should lick the honey from the letters. Thereupon the father should take the child again, and carry it home, and in such a wise that the child may see nothing unclean. And it is right that on this day both father and mother fast and pray to God in heaven that the child may prosper in the Torah and the fear of God, and in good works all his days and his years. But in the evening, when the fast is over, they should prepare a meal for the poor and do charity according to their means. Then verily, the father's heart may have firm faith that the fear of God will rest upon his child. These instructions will suffice.

But great will be the merit of those women who are denied children, if the husband rears an orphan in his home and if both strive to guide it along the straight path, as if it were their own child. And if it is within his power to take into his house those who are learning the Torah, and to provide for them, that thus his house may be full of Torah, then, indeed, hail to him and to this destiny! We find the like of this in the case of Rashi, blessed be his memory, who when he emigrated from France, was a guest in the house of a rich elder. This rich elder besought him to stay in his house and there to study the Torah. And because the rich man besought him, and begged him, Rashi, blessed be his memory, composed a book and named it for the rich elder. In doing this, however, Rashi, blessed be his memory, intended also to exalt and honor others who practice charity. And so, happy the man who selects a fair and pleasant place in his house and destines it for the learning of the Torah. For the Holy One, blessed be he, is present in the house where the Torah is being learned, and the honor of his house will be great in time to come. For when the scattered people of Israel will be gathered, the houses of learning and the houses of prayer will also be gathered in the land of Israel, and will be full of glorious beauty. Amen.

The Pro

Jewish Learning is an adult mitzvah (not a kid's mitzvah). The modern Jewish world tends to get these things backwards. We've tended to forget that "kids'" study is just the preparation for adult learning, not an end in itself. Consider this classic <u>H</u>assidic story.

A man once came to the Kotsker Rebbe and complained that his son did not want to learn Torah. (Even though it wasn't Hebrew School he was talking about—we know those Sunday morning fights.) He asked the Rebbe: "What should I do?" The Kotsker Rebbe told him: "If you force your child to study Torah, he will study Torah as long as you make him do so. And, in fact, he will grow up and make his child study Torah in his time. However, if you devote yourself to Torah study, soon you will find your child by your side, asking to study with you."

The Point

To grow Jewish life in America, we are not looking to replace all carpools, but to transcend the alienation between classroom and home which the carpool often creates.

> **[Nachama Skolnik Moskowitz's Comment]:** I don't see carpools as alienating. It's a cute statement, but I see carpools as a bridge. (1) Remember the old carpool curricula? Anyway, it's a bridge to a bridge. (2) A social worker once told me that one study showed the further a family lived from the therapist, the faster they progressed in counseling. Why? The long rides allowed for some good, uninterrupted work.

Most of this book has spoken of communications and collaboration between teachers and parents. In the last part of this work, we have dealt with limited time-frame events where parents become co-learners and co-teachers in their children's Jewish education. Now, in the last chapter, we want to look towards times and settings where that kind of learning is actively extended. That is one of the paths towards the future. In an ideal world:

- Jewish homes will universally be places of Jewish living and learning.
- Jewish adults will consistently be committed to growing their own Jewish education.
- Jewish schools, camps, youth groups, centers—will provide children with wonderful, rich dynamic Jewish educations.
- Jewish families will have rich opportunities to learn together, and in combination with other families in intergenerational "whole village" learning experiences.

All of these truths are essential. None can replace the other. This last part of the book looks at how people are actualizing the last of these in depth.

Model Programs

Together 1: A Child-Parent Kit: (Melton Research Center) The nine issues in this magazine-like kit are oriented toward children and their parents. Each kit contains a wide range of activities: games, puzzles, stories, cut-outs, recipes, craft projects, plus reading materials and bibliographies, both at the level of the children (8-9 year olds) and at the level of adults. *Together* attempts to provide positive, structured Jewish sharing time for a parent and a child. Its materials are built around the Jewish life cycle and the beauty of celebration, sharing and the importance of Jewish values. Individual families or community groups can use these materials to great advantage.

Windows: Together 2: (Melton Research Center) Following on the success of the original *Together*, we have developed *Windows: Together 2* for 11-12 year olds and their parents. Built around the four themes of Bar/Bat Mitzvah, law and ethics, theology. and community—which are explored and worked on through drama, text study, simulations, writing, and discussions—these materials have been produced as a series of four booklets, one for each participant per activity. Each one takes about two hours to complete. A Leader's Guide is also provided. Preparation and wrap-up activities are done at home by students and their parents. The main activities, on the other hand, are planned as communal events.

Jewish Family Retreats: A Handbook: (Melton Research Center) *Jewish Family Retreats* is a rich resource for all areas of Jewish education. It provides expert guidance and a wealth of know-how for synagogues, *havurot,* Jewish community centers, schools and camps interested in creating successful and inspiring retreats. Culled from Vicky Kelman's groundbreaking work in family education, the handbook includes: effective models for programming, staffing and evaluation, lesson plans, schedules, menus—and much more. This handbook was jointly published with The Whizin Institute for Jewish Family Life at the University of Judaism.

I Can Learn Torah: (Torah Aura Productions) *I Can Learn Torah* is an innovative K-2 Bible program that actively involves parents as partners in the process. The student book presents each story in age-appropriate English that remains true to the Hebrew text (for a parent or teacher to read aloud). There are opportunities at pivotal moments for students to make meaning from each story via pencil-and-paper exercises (drawing, connect the dots, writing comments, etc.). For parent and/or teacher, there are questions in the margins to help draw the students into an interactive storytelling process.

Building Jewish Life Activity Books: (Torah Aura Productions) BJL Activity Books (Blue Label) are designed for children in kindergarten, first and second grade and their parents. These are books about Jewish family rituals and about Jewish families participating in community rituals. They focus on Jewish symbols and objects and the feelings we get when we use them. In BJL Activity Books, the vocabulary is carefully limited, the concepts are simple, the hands-on activities are readily mastered, but the sense of meaning and connection is profound. BJL Activity Books have also been designed to introduce a fundamental "Jewish vocabulary," specifically designed to enable the acquisition of Hebrew. BJL Activity Books are designed to connect the classroom and the home, and in doing so, provide the best possible foundation for a successful Jewish education. Each BJL Activity Book tells the story of the holiday (or the synagogue or blessings), in simple vocabulary, focusing on the symbols for each. Every two or three pages, there is an age-appropriate exercise: matching, mazes, connect-the-dots, sequencing, etc. In the back, there is a two-page essay for parents.

Building Jewish Life Red Label Books: (Torah Aura Productions) BJL Red Label Books are ones we hope would become part of every Jewish home library. Known as "Red Label" books, these *Building Jewish Life* texts are designed for families whose children are in second, third or fourth grades. BJL Red Label books were specifically designed to take the study of Jewish celebrations and practices beyond mere knowledge of the objects and procedures to concepts and meanings, and to enable parents to become real partners, rather than just symbolic ones, in the process of educating their children to be Jewish. Each Red Label book includes a review of the story of each holiday, ritual objects and concepts, a separate read-aloud story, classroom and home activities, detailed information for parents and lesson plans.

PACE: (Originally developed by Jo Kay for Temple Emanu-El, East Meadow, New York). PACE, an acronym for Parents and Children Education, was a setting where parents and children regularly studied together in the same class and where parents also studied alone, in a parallel setting. It was both interactive and parallel learning. In the original version of PACE, kids came weekly, parents bi-weekly (once for a family class and once for an adults-only class). Families were regularly assigned to (1) make a poster, (2) write a poem or prayer, (3) read and answer questions together, (4) study a text together, etc.

PACE JAMPLER

Jo Kay is a gentle giant in family education. Most of us family educators are center-stage kind of folk (that is why our meetings are always so interesting). Jo, who is a consummate teacher and educator, is much softer—firm, but gentle. She is empowering and nurturing. While PACE was started at Temple Emanu-el of East Meadow, with Jo as the first teacher and director, Jo is now the educational director of the religious school at Rodef Shalom in New York. When we asked Jo to provide us with a "PACE Sampler," rather than drawing from her own work, she took materials from two of her teachers. That's Jo. Particularly interesting to note is the dual presentations of family and adult (parent) learning.

PACE: Parents and Children Education—
A One-Year Fourth-Grade Curriculum

Introduction

There are several unique aspects to the PACE program. First, it was totally voluntary. Families that joined the class chose to be in the program (there were other fourth-grade classes available). These parents made the commitment, at registration, to come to school with their children at least two times each month. The children studied with me approximately three times each month. During adults-only classes, the parents studied and discussed related material. During joint classes, the families encountered some experiential form of the work we had all covered. Some sessions were craft workshops; during others, we played games, went on trips, saw films, and listened to guest speakers. We were looking to create family interaction within the framework of our prayer curriculum.

Second, we never encountered any attendance problems that needed follow-up. The children seemed more eager than ever to attend school; they felt very "special." Their parents came to school with them, and sometimes, their brothers and sisters and even grandparents came along. (Our family class was always open to all family.) Perhaps that's the key here. As long as the children were so eager to attend, the parents were naturally going to be around. How could you send a child to a family class without his family? We had several instances when the parents came to adult or family classes on days when their children were absent from school because of illness; a strong indication of the commitment these parents felt to the PACE program.

Third, parents and children didn't only come to school together, they did homework assignments together, wrote prayers together, attended services together, and generally functioned as involved, committed Jewish families on a regular basis. PACE was not just a title.

Fourth, the class directed and coordinated the publication of its own newsletter, Keeping PACE. It became a vehicle intrinsic to the program. Children reported on their classes. Parents reported on what happened at the adult sessions and parents and children both reported on family classes. Copies of each issue are included in this package. This newsletter was presented to the members of the class and to their families. Although it reached non-PACE families (school board members, among others), the PACE parents felt strongly that the entire congregation should know about the wonderful things that were happening within the program. Therefore, on several occasions, parents volunteered to write articles to be published in our temple's monthly bulletin, *The Voice*, copies also attached in an appendix. The feedback our class received as a result of *The Voice* articles was amazing. The entire congregation was talking about the PACE program. The widespread acceptance and support can be seen in the increase of the program to three classes in Fall, 1979 (4th, 5th—last year's PACE class, and 7th grades). Next year, the plan is to increase to five classes—4th, 5th, 6th, 7th, and 8th).

The question now becomes, "How does one get a PACE program started?" We followed several simple procedures before embarking on our first year. First, the program had to be presented to our school board. It was going to cost some extra money for a stipend for the teacher who was to write and teach this new curriculum. Money was also needed to pay for a second teacher to meet with the children when the PACE teacher met with adults only. The board agreed to support one class the first year.

Second, space had to be allocated for the class. A regular classroom could not house 20 children and their parents, approximately 60 people in all.

Third, with the go-ahead from the school board, and the use of a double classroom, we needed to entice the parents into the program. Several orientation meetings were held with all of the parents whose children would be fourth graders in September. At these sessions, we outlined the program, explained what their (the parents') time commitment would be and provided time for questions. When registration was held, most parents had a definite idea about where they'd be going.

Finally, we had a rabbi and a principal who were committed to Jewish family education.

Jo Kay, Temple Emanuel-El, East Meadow, New York
Copyright 1979 Jo Kay and Temple Emanu-el of East Meadow, New York

[Nachama Skolnik Moskowitz' S Comment]: PACE-type programs have run into problems because parents "did it already" by the time child number 2 or 3 comes along into the grade. Family educators talk about planning with level two or tier two in mind.

[Jo Kay's Comments]: One thing that has helped us with the problem of second time parents, is to have the class taught by a different faculty member. Teachers are always encouraged to bring "themselves" to the curriculum. By doing so, each year the course takes on an entirely new perspective.

5th Grade PACE Class: Conversion Unit

Mary Lande Zamore

Family class

Materials: Biblical role model worksheets, Bet Din question sheets, pencils, file cards, declaration of faith, conversion ceremony text, have ark opened,

Discuss: Friday night service parts/attendance

1. Parent-child pairs work on biblical role model sheets.

2. Group feedback:
   Are all of these conversions?
   Do any seem strange?
   Are these different from why people convert today?

3. Bet Din Simulation:
   What is a Bet Din?
   Who sits on one?
   How many people?
   What does a bet din do in a conversion?
   What type of questions do the bet din ask?
   Is it a mean, harsh inquisition or a friendly talk?

4. Response time:
   How did it feel to answer such questions?
   Were any of the responses surprising?
   What type of extra questions were asked?

5. Declaration of faith at Ark.

WORKSHEETS

Worksheet on Ruth: (Includes the Text of Ruth 1:1-22, followed by questions:)

What is Naomi and Ruth's relationship?

What does Naomi tell Ruth and Orpah to do?

What does Ruth do?

Why do you think Ruth converts?

Do you know who is Ruth's grandson?

Worksheet on Abraham (Genesis 11:27-32, Text of Midrash, followed by questions)

Note: Abram is Abraham's original name before God changes it.

Terah, Abraham's father, did not believe in One God. He was a polytheist, believing in many gods like the sun and moon.

What does the Bible tell us about Abraham's childhood?

What do you think the Midrash is trying to do?

In what way does Abraham convert?

Worksheet on Jethro. (Text of Exodus 18: 1-12, followed by the questions)

What is Jethro's job/profession? Clue: Is he Israelite?

Does Jethro convert? Is his "speech" a surprise considering his profession?

Bet Din Worksheet

Congratulations! You have been asked to sit on a Bet Din. This is an honor only given to knowledgeable Jews! You will be (gently) questioning a potential convert. Here are some questions to ask; add your own questions, too. Take turns.

1. Did you grow up in another religion?
2. How did you feel about that religion when you were a kid?
3. What made you reject that religion?
4. Why did you pick Judaism?
5. How does your family feel about your decision?
6. What do you especially like about Judaism?
7. Is there anything you do not like about Judaism?
8. Do you believe in God?
9. What is your favorite part of Shabbat?
10. What is your favorite Jewish holiday?
11. Are you willing to become a Jew even though Jews have been persecuted (hated) throughout history?
12. What will you contribute to Judaism and the Jewish people?

Adult class—Conversion Class Questions:

History of conversions
The process of conversion
Reform policies on conversion
Role of non-Jew in the synagogue
How do we feel about converts?
How do we feel about Judaism?
History:
Eleazar ben Pedat
Josephus
Mathew 23:15
Christian Rome/Muslim rulers
Middle Ages

Process

Study
review by a Bet Din (Jewish court)
Mikveh with Adim (witnesses)
circumcision or shedding of a drop of blood (HEBREW)
public ceremony
children
Kohens—not allowed to marry converts

Reform policies — outreach

the numbers
Reform Judaism article
What programs do we want?
What guidelines for non-Jews?

PACE 6th Grade Lesson Plan

Anne Ebersman

Family Class

THE RISE OF THE NAZIS

Goals:

- to explore the political, economic and social realities of Germany in the 1920's
- to consider how these realities contributed to the rise of the Nazi party and Adolf Hitler

I. OPENING

Tell story about symphony

Have people introduce themselves — personal connection to WWII, kids -?

Why is it important to study the Holocaust?

Put reasons on the board. How many are as human beings, how many are as members of Jewish families? In their opinions, is there a difference between how this is being studied here and how it would be studied in public school? Give my opinion. Then say that today we are putting on our universalist hats to try to get inside the heads of Germans in the 1920's/30's.

II. GERMANY IN THE 1920'S

1. Tell story from my days at Hebrew school.
2. Focus question for film: what does the film present as the major factors contributing to Hitler's rise to power? (For parents: What do you think of this point of view?)
3. Show film.
4. Family time— readings about inflation
5. Process film—write factors on board

III. THE 1932 ELECTIONS

1. Split into groups: give each group the platforms of the SDP, Nazi, Communist parties
2. Assign each group an identity: who would that person have voted for and why
3. Conduct ballot
4. Show results of actual election

5.   Process results—what have we learned?

IV. Closing. One more High Holiday drash — memory/rebirth

Insertion of Nazi bios: Otto Hauptmann, Eric VonRonheim, Karl Schmidt.

Insertion of Nazi program outline, Communist party platform.

Adult Lesson

Anne Ebersman-Congregation Rodeph Shalom

Lesson One — Introduction

Objectives:

- To start getting to know each other
- To induce them to begin thinking about what studying the Holocaust means to them, especially vis-a-vis teaching their children.
- To give them a taste of the topics we will be studying together
- To provide a forum for their input on what they would like to learn and how

Activities:

1.   When they come in, have on the board the questions I asked the kids. Have them write down on index cards an answer to one or two of the questions that most engage them.

2.   Introductions—How many years in PACE, the most important thing gained/what they'd like to gain this year/if new, what attracted you to PACE/what is the one thing you wrote. Introduce myself. Show kids' answers (10-15 minutes).

3.   Corners of the room. How do these statements reflect your view of why and how to study the Holocaust? Would the answers be any different if this was public school? (20 minutes)

4.   Etymology of Holocaust/Shoah/hurban. (10 minutes)

5.   Study from Pirke Avot, first mishnah—how does this advice apply to teaching your children about the Holocaust? (20 minutes)

6.   Pagis poem—study together (10 minutes)

7. Plan for the year —Teaching children; Holocaust in Literature; Different Historical Theses; God in the Holocaust; their suggestions (10 minutes).

6. Evaluation/Summary

SAMPLE LETTER

Dear 6th Grade PACE Parent,

Happy New Year. As promised when I spoke with many of you on the phone last week, I am enclosing the 1995 PACE calendar. Per this newly revised calendar, the first parent/child class will be Wednesday, October 11th at 5 p.m. and the first adult class will be Tuesday October 24th at 7:30 p.m.

I'm very much looking forward to meeting all of you, and to learning with you. I hope to see many of you next Wednesday. In the meantime, I am enclosing an op-ed from last week's Times by Frank Rich, in case you missed it, which I thought was extremely relevant both to the High Holidays and to our course of study.

Sincerely,

Anne Ebersman

Congregation Rodeph Sholom

Here are some other, non-PACE family classes that are run in Jo Kay's School.

DANCE MIDRASH PROGRAM

This program was designed for our third-graders and their parents. The children are studying Torah (using the **Being Torah** text). They also meet monthly with dancers from the Avodah Dance Ensemble for a "creative movement" session related to their Torah study. Thus, they dance and create movements which answer questions posed by the text.

The second half of the year (children are now comfortable with the movement exercises) parents are brought into the equation. Parents, from one class (we tried whole-grade programs and they were too big to work successfully using this format) are invited to come to school to study "What is Midrash?" with one of our rabbis. They are then introduced to the concept of dance as a form of midrash. Finally, they are joined by their children, and together they create "dance midrash" related to the biblical story studied that day.

YAHAD PROGRAM

Parents and children join together, a few times during the year, for grade-wide programs based in the child's curriculum. We have YAHAD programs in grades K through 9.

Just recently, we had a YAHAD which focused on Israel as both an old and a new country. One part of the program had families reading ancient texts related to a particular area in Israel. They next read a story, about the same area, set in modern Israel. Following some discussion of both texts, and how they are connected, the children were asked to create a picture of the modern text and the parents were asked to create a "microtypography picture" of the ancient text using the actual words from the text. They next tried to blend them together.

SEVENTH GRADE FAMILY SHABBATONIM

Three times each year, 7th graders and their parents come to a Friday evening Shabbaton. What this actually means is that the family is at a Kabbalat Shabbat Service; it is followed by a Shabbat dinner and a special program which involves study, discussion and then processing. There is always some table mixer to start. Sometimes the kids stay over after the parents leave. At other times, it is only a Friday evening program for the entire family.

Family Education Programming 1990-1993

Ellen Brosbe is a family educator in Santa Rosa, California (a very small Jewish community). These are her notes about the variety of programs her community managed to run over a four-year period. Now use your imagination.

"Apples & Honey & Much More": Drive-through approach to Jewish Learning @125 people, cute activities, popular approach. Did not evaluate formally (done 3 times with different focus-religious school, nursery school, and community).

Nursery School Sukkot Get-Together: Similar format used short evaluation form that wasn't specific enough. The best evaluation proves to be most time consuming—collecting anectodal records of families. Individual phone calls to the participants. Recordkeeping of #'s and demographics.

Congregational Holiday Dinners with Programs: Parallel or mixed. We've had storytellers, round-robin activities, discussions, tzedakah projects, sing-alongs. (The usual quickie program.)

Building Jewish Memories: Open house Family Education activities at the nursery school: 1) making hallah covers with an artist (yr. 1), 2) making instruments for Jewish music month (yr. 2), and 3) making tzedakah boxes (yr. 3).

Tot Shabbat: (Someone asked me what "tot" meant in Hebrew.) Pajama Shabbat—Rabbi opts for Early Retirement. (Everyone wore pj's. Short service, *Kabbalat Shabbat* snacks).

Holiday Workshop Series to parallel holiday activities in the N.S. Yr. 1 - Holiday how-to's; Yr. 2—Sensitive issues to discuss with your child; Yr. 3 - Parents sharing resources with other parents. Packets available of resources.

In-Home Shabbat/Holiday: 4-host Sukkot with activities-family-led/hosted.

Sefer Safari: Jewish book month program to encourage nursery school use of the congregational library. Informal; child and parent or caregiver or carpool person go into small congregational library and selects books. Cute zoo theme with stickers.

Shabbat Shelanu: A monthly springtime Mommy/Daddy and Me Shabbat. One hour activities to do together with young children. Shabbat-related activities. Usually was Mommy, not Daddy and me. Only did this about 6 times. Might recreate this year. Very similar to "*Mishpahah*" "*Shabbat Hevrah*" programs.

Family Education Scholar In-Resident: Goal—to spread the word about the program and offer a quality discussion. Vicky Kelman—Using the G-word—Talking About God with your Child.

Hallahthon: How-to with parents in the nursery school (the kids start from the prepared dough made by the parents, but I hear in upscale programs they buy ready-made dough from bakeries).

Religious School Programs took place when I was teaching. I took two years off to run programs and develop a family education program. I did most of my work with the Rabbi and met periodically with the principal and staff.

Windows: 7th grade and 1 spring program for 6th grade.

Are We Surviving the Bar and Bat Mitzvah Year? Companion program to Windows. JFCS therapist Debbi Freed meets with parents separately and kids and parents together to discuss Sally Weber type issues of "battle on the bima," coming of age, transition to Jr. High plus pressures of the Bar/Bat Mitzvah.

We're Standing on the Shoulders... Relating the above issues to a ropes course. A successful experience in role reversal. Parents & kids attend a wonderful ropes course in Occidental called Four Winds. Risk taking, teamwork and cooperation—what's Jewish about it? Very expensive per family.

Parent Connection Reading Program: First Grade

The First-grade teacher also introduced the **"Adopt a Cabbage Patch Doll" Program:** The teacher loved it. Not my first choice but it got her going on Family Ed.

Kiddush Levanah and Moon Watch: Sonoma Astronomical Society. Goal—outreach to families who drive longer distances to come to our congregation. Howling at the moon as therapy.

Family Room: Tried to start Vicky's program last year in a *Havurah.* It didn't work with a veteran (cynical) group but this year, we recruited a group of families with 4th & 5th graders and it is great so far. (Kathy Chesto's program)

Intergenerational Programs:

Gefilte Fish (Sally Weber's Program): Post-B'not mitzvah, mothers and grandmothers view the video and discuss tradition.

Intergenerational Tu B'Shvat Seder: N.S. parents (moms) and Senior group.

Intergenerational Read-aloud with Seniors and preschoolers. Started by an interested parent without grandparents nearby. Very successful though our senior librarian didn't like calling seniors "Grandparents." We call this whole program, Bridging the Generations: The Grandparent Connection.

Family History Video Project: Created by B.J.E. of S.F. 6th graders interview family members about family history and videotape each other telling stories.

Collage Project—Work with Artist in Residence using similar themes and ideas of the Bar/Bat Mitzvah Parashah, coming of age or family history and do a color xerograph.

Misc. Ongoing family information on bulletin board, newsletters, and via shtick—me being "out there" talking to families and recruiting support for families.

Babies & Bagels: Support group for new parents. Cooperatively run.

Family Education Programming 1990-1993, Cong. Beth Ami, Santa Rosa
Jewish Comm Ctr Nursery School, Santa Rosa, CA